D1429372

Community Action and Race Relations

Community Action and Race Relations

A STUDY OF COMMUNITY RELATIONS COMMITTEES IN BRITAIN

MICHAEL J. HILL and
RUTH M. ISSACHAROFF

Published for the
Institute of Race Relations, London
by
OXFORD UNIVERSITY PRESS
LONDON   NEW YORK   TORONTO
1971

Oxford University Press, Ely House, London W.1

GLASGOW   NEW YORK   TORONTO   MELBOURNE   WELLINGTON
CAPE TOWN SALISBURY IBADAN NAIROBI DAR ES SALAAM LUSAKA ADDIS ABABA
BOMBAY CALCUTTA MADRAS KARACHI LAHORE DACCA
KUALA LUMPUR SINGAPORE HONG KONG TOKYO

ISBN   0   19   218196   3

Printed in Great Britain at
THE PITMAN PRESS, BATH

CONTENTS

ABBREVIATIONS

N.C.C.I.	National Committee for Commonwealth Immigrants
C.R.C.	Community Relations Commission
C.R.O.	community relations officer
E.I.F.C.	Ealing International Friendship Council
E.C.R.C.	Ealing Community Relations Council
H.C.R.C.	Hackney Community Relations Council
C.C.T.H.	Council of Citizens of Tower Hamlets
B.C.R.C.	Birmingham Community Relations Committee
W.D.I.C.	Wycombe and District Integration Committee
B.C.C.C.C.	Bradford Consultative Council for Commonwealth Citizens
H.I.L.C.	Huddersfield International Liaison Committee
S.C.C.R.	Sheffield Committee for Community Relations
S.R.A.	Southall Residents Association
B.N.P.	British National Party
I.W.A.	Indian Workers' Association
W.I.S.C.	West Indian Standing Conference

LIST OF TABLES

Preface and Acknowledgements

This book is a study of some of the committees set up with government support to improve race relations in Britain by means of voluntary activities.

In order to evaluate their work, it is necessary to raise some fundamental questions about the way community relations committees relate to social and political structures. The existence of the Community Relations Commission, and of the local committees it supports, is often pointed to as evidence that something is being done about race relations in this country. While there is some truth in this as far as a range of individual welfare issues are concerned, this is mere 'tokenism' as far as the social structure as a whole is concerned.

We have tried to show the relevance of some sociological insights for the planning of practical activities in the areas of race relations and community 'social engineering'. Two initial descriptive chapters provide a historical account of what we will call the 'community relations movement', and give relevant factual information about the areas covered by eight committees with which our study was primarily concerned. We have tried to ensure that our data are related to the relevant theoretical issues. In Chapter 3 we discuss the central theoretical issue, the problems posed by the concept of 'community', and suggest themes that are followed through the rest of the book. Chapter 7 raises some of the problems to be faced by voluntary organizations trying to formulate goals in the face of opposition and ambiguity. In Chapter 8 we look at community power theories in relation to minority interests in Britain. Chapters 9 and 10 are necessarily rather descriptive and are only partly related to our main theoretical themes. They had to be included to provide a rounded picture of the organizations we have been studying.

During the year before the study started both authors had been carrying out, independently, preliminary interviews with several community relations officers. We had independently interviewed C.R.O.s in Ealing, Tower Hamlets, Hackney, and Lambeth, and one of us had also interviewed C.R.O.s in High Wycombe, Manchester, and Slough. We were interested in extending the work into a full-scale research study as a result of our own involvement in local committees, one as the secretary of the Reading Council for Community Relations, and the other after having spent a short period observing the work of a C.R.O. in a London borough during the summer of 1967. A more thorough study was made possible by a grant from the Social Science Research Council during 1968–9.

Various research designs initially appeared possible. However our short experience of the workings of two committees made us aware that not all would be useful for our purposes. Other writers, notably Martin Rein and Robert Weiss, have pointed to the difficulties involved in evaluating community action programmes in the American war on poverty.[1] Our short experience of community relations committees made us realize that their impact in changing the conditions of life of the bulk of the population in the areas in which they were working was negligible. Any attempt to try to evaluate success or failure from an examination of the social and economic characteristics of the residents of the area 'before' and 'after' the inception of the community relations programme would prove a futile exercise. What seemed more feasible was to examine the actual machinery of the community relations committees to evaluate them on their own terms. By interviewing members of the executives of the committees we wanted to show what they thought the committees should be doing, and to what extent their existence as a committee assisted, or militated against, the clarification of goals by the C.R.O.

The research study was launched in autumn 1968. It was decided to select eight committees to investigate in depth. A number of factors determined which eight of the seventy-eight committees then in existence should be selected. Our main interest was in community relations committees already fairly well established and employing a full-time officer. In March 1968, forty-two local committees were in this position.[2] Our next

[1] Robert S. Weiss and M. Rein, 'Evaluation of Broad Aim Social Programmes', unpublished paper presented to the American Academy of Arts and Sciences Conference on the Evaluation of Social Action Programmes (2–3 May 1969).

[2] *Report of the Community Relations Commission for 1968–9* (London, H.M.S.O., 1969).

concern was to avoid duplication of work done by any other researchers. Hannan Rose had been interviewing C.R.O.s and some committee members in Bedford, Bristol, Camden, Manchester, Newham, Nottingham, Willesden, and Wolverhampton.[1] Ira Katznelson had exhaustively examined the evolution of Nottingham Commonwealth Citizens Consultative Committee in his comparison of the political machinery of the U.S.A. under the impact of migration from the South in the first three decades of the twentieth century, and the present situation in the United Kingdom.[2]

We were anxious to avoid re-interviewing the same people and to obtain a selection of committees operating in local authorities of differing size and type throughout England. We also wanted a selection of areas which offered a variety in the predominant Commonwealth immigrant ethnic groups.

The eight areas eventually selected were never considered to be a representative sample, but a deliberate attempt was made to achieve a wide spread in geographical distribution and to adhere to our three conditions. The eventual choice comprised committees in two 'inner' London boroughs, Hackney and Tower Hamlets; one 'outer' London borough, Ealing; one county borough in the Midlands, Birmingham; three county boroughs in Yorkshire, Bradford, Huddersfield, and Sheffield; and one non-county borough in the South, High Wycombe. It may be objected that this list contains no committee from the North-West, but at the time we started our work there was only one really well established committee in this region, the Manchester committee, which was ruled out because it figured in Hannan Rose's study. The variety of types of areas, and kinds of immigrant settlement, provided by our group of eight will be made more clear in Chapter 3.

In each of the eight committees we initially interviewed the C.R.O. This took the form of an unstructured discussion without the use of a questionnaire. All the C.R.O.s co-operated fully both in this initial encounter, which lasted between one and a half and two hours, and in subsequent meetings. They also provided, we understand with the approval of their committees, access to

---

[1] B.Litt. thesis, Oxford, in preparation.
[2] I. Katznelson, 'The Politics of Race in U.S.A. 1900–30 and the U.K. 1948–68' (Ph.D. thesis, Cambridge, 1969).

reports and minutes. Subsequently, interviews lasting between forty-five minutes and three and a half hours were held with 133 of the total number of 144 executive committee members. We regard this as a very good response rate, as most of the members were very busy people and we wanted to interview them on a controversial subject. A questionnaire was used, but it was loosely structured and respondents were encouraged to talk freely about topics of interest. The average interview lasted about an hour and a half. Nearly all the interviews were conducted at the homes of the committee members. Two respondents chose to fill in the questionnaire themselves (they are included in the 133 quoted above). Everyone else was interviewed personally by one or other of the authors, between October 1968 and June 1969. Where we have used the present time in this book, for example to refer to the characteristics or functions of committee members, such statements of course apply only to circumstances during this period.

Nearly all the non-respondents were inactive members of their committees. They were in this respect untypical. Three of the six white non-respondents were Conservative councillors (two of whom were sick, and all of whom played little part in the work of their committee). The other three white non-respondents were a housewife, a small businessman, and a Police Superintendent. The latter had sought the advice of his superior officer as to whether he should see us, and his Chief Superintendent wrote to us refusing permission on grounds of pressure of work. However some questions were answered by letter by the Superintendent, a member of the Birmingham committee.

There were five immigrant non-respondents. Two were in the West Indies at the time we were interviewing. One other non-respondent was a Pakistani woman who had never really played any part in the committee and had just resigned. The remaining two, a Pakistani on the Sheffield committee and a West Indian from Hackney, could not be contacted. One hundred per cent response was achieved from three committees.

In addition, a number of people were questioned about their acquaintance with the work of the committees. These included local authority officials, some of whom attend meetings as observers, and a number of immigrants in different areas who had left the committees over points of principle.

Information about the work of the committees was also

TABLE A.1
DISTRIBUTION OF EXECUTIVE COMMITTEE MEMBERS

	Interviewed	Not interviewed	Total
Birmingham	16	4	20
Bradford	10	1	11
Ealing	28	2	30
Hackney	16	2	18
Huddersfield	10	–	10
Sheffield	15	2	17
Tower Hamlets	17	–	17
Wycombe	21	–	21
Total	133	11	144

Note Observers and other non-voting members of the committees have not been included in the above figures. See Chapter 3 for a discussion of the ambiguous status of some of these people.

obtained through the minutes of their general councils, executives, and subcommittee's meetings. We were also able to attend some meetings of some of the committees. Other records of the activities of the committees were examined, including annual reports, special reports, and news-letters. Finally, in each area back numbers of local papers were examined for relevant material.

To ascertain to what extent the information obtained about the eight committees was in any way representative of the community relations committees as a whole, an additional special questionnaire was sent to all other C.R.O.s throughout the country in the summer of 1969. Replies were obtained from twenty-two C.R.O.s of whom three chose to be personally interviewed rather than reply by post. Information was thus obtained from thirty committees in all. Most of these committees also responded to our request to send us annual reports and other publications. Those C.R.O.s from whom no reply was secured included Teeside, where the committee's grant had been withdrawn by the Community Relations Commission, and Greenwich, Hounslow, Northampton, Oldham, and Preston, all of which had only recently appointed C.R.O.s (spring 1969). The remainder included Manchester committee whose C.R.O. and chairman had in fact been interviewed by one of the authors in the preliminary investigations in 1967–8, so that some information was available. No data were obtained from the following committees: Bolton, Bristol, Derby, Halifax, Hammersmith, Kensington, and Southwark.

A brief comment on terminology seems appropriate. When the grant structure for local committees was first developed after the 1965 White Paper on Immigration, the committees were called 'voluntary liaison committees'. The national body administering the system was the National Committee for Commonwealth Immigrants. At this stage the local committees bore a variety of names, such as International Friendship Committee, Commonwealth Citizens Consultative Committee, Council for Racial Harmony, and International Liaison Committee. From about 1967 onwards, the N.C.C.I. decided that the most appropriate name for the committees was community relations committees, or community relations councils. New committees were encouraged to adopt this kind of name, and existing committees were asked to change their names. At the time of writing most committees included 'community relations' in their titles. Thus, confusion may arise from the fact that, just after the completion of our work in their area, the Ealing committee changed its name from Ealing International Friendship Council to Ealing Council for Community Relations. At the same time as the local terminology was changed, in November 1968 the N.C.C.I. was replaced by the Community Relations Commission. These changes also had an impact upon the full-time officials of the local committees, who became known as community relations officers (C.R.O.s) instead of liaison officers. Some of the local organizations are called 'councils' and some are called 'committees'. It may be unclear whether references are being made to them as corporate entities, to their full general meetings, or to their executive committees. It might seem appropriate to talk of the full bodies as 'councils' and reserve the concept of 'committee' to specific references to their executives. We prefer to use the expression 'committees' to refer to the whole organizations, since often the use of 'councils' may lead to confusion with the local authorities. Where confusion might arise between executive committees and the full organizations we have tried to make our meaning clear by using the more elaborate terminology available.

Finally a brief note on some other aspects of terminology. As we make clear in Chapter 3, we are not at all happy about the implications of the loose use of the concept of 'community'. However, since we are dealing with a field of activity in which this sort of usage is widespread we have almost inevitably used it in a similar way. Equally, we are uneasy about the conventional terms used to distinguish ethnic groups. Throughout the book we will normally talk of white members and black or immigrant members. We have avoided as far as possible talking of 'hosts' or 'the host community' despite its popularity with some people in the community relations movement, since the opposite of hosts is 'guests'! Apart from this we have adopted the conventional terms, despite a particular unease about the word 'immigrant'. It is easier to make one's meaning clear by doing this than by insisting on formulations that may be more acceptable from the pedantic point of view but are long-winded and cannot be used repeatedly (such as 'persons born in the new Commonwealth countries and their descendants').

We would like to thank all the community relations officers, executive committee members, and other people connected with the committees who set aside a great deal of time to help us with our inquiries. It would be invidious to single out particular people for mention, but we must say that we encountered a great deal of kindness and hospitality throughout our field-work. We hope that none of these people will interpret any of our critical comments on the work of the committees as in any way reflections on the good faith and high ideals which we know many of them bring to bear on their activities.

We would like to thank the following for their helpful comments at various stages of our work: David Donnison, E. J. B. Rose, Hannan Rose, Navnit Dholakia, John Downing, Daniel Lawrence, and Juliet Cheetham. We would also like to thank the Librarian of the Institute of Race Relations, A. Sivanandan, for facilities provided.

We thank the Social Science Research Council for their support of the project, and the University of Reading for the facilities it provided. Finally we would like to acknowledge the important contribution made by our secretary, Pat Cross, and the general help and support given by Betty Hill.

During the time between formulating the study in 1967 and date of publication, one of the authors has become increasingly convinced of the irrelevancy of the whole community relations movement to the extent that it seems difficult to justify the time spent on the detailed analysis of the committees. She does not believe that the necessary comprehensive social change of a socialist kind could ever come about through the voluntary activities of a government-sponsored organization in the present society, but she hopes that there may be some value in publishing the findings as evidence of the epiphenomenal nature of the community relations movement.

MICHAEL J. HILL and RUTH M. ISSACHAROFF

CHAPTER 1

The Community Relations Movement

Almost ever since the arrival of Jamaican immigrants on the *Empire Windrush* in June 1948, voluntary organizations have been created to handle race relations in various parts of Britain. Many have had but short lives. Most of those that have lasted have become or have been merged into organizations now known as community relations committees.

Even in 1948 voluntary organizations to help tackle an 'integration' problem were not new. Before the war, attacks on the Jews had brought into being organizations of a political and educational kind to fight anti-Semitism.[1] During and immediately after the war the settlement problems of refugees of all kinds had led to the creation of welfare-oriented organizations. Even the very small coloured groups settled in some of the dockland areas had attracted the attention of voluntary workers. For example, a Liverpool Association for the Welfare of Coloured People was set up in the inter-war period.[2] In *The Coloured Quarter*, Michael Banton describes a Coloured People's Society set up in Stepney in 1951.[3]

The early initiatives came almost entirely from people responsive to welfare needs rather than to political issues. Immigrants were largely seen as strangers facing problems in settling down in Britain, rather than as citizens suffering discrimination. One of the pioneers of this kind of organization recently described the original aim of the committee of which she was founding secretary as 'to help the local coloured community to settle down as happily and as easily as possible'.[4]

[1] For example, the Council of Citizens of East London set up in the 1930s.
[2] In the evidence submitted to the Parliamentary Select Committee on Race Relations and Immigration during their visit to Liverpool on 26–7 March 1969, reference was made to a report published by this organization in 1940, entitled 'The Economic Status of Coloured Families'.
[3] Michael Banton, *The Coloured Quarter* (London, Cape, 1955), p. 230.
[4] D. M. Wood, quoted in Katznelson, op. cit., p. 282.

A typical example of this kind of committee was the Committee for the Welfare of Coloured Workers in Bristol, set up in 1952,[1] though the above quotation refers to a slightly later foundation, the Nottingham committee.

Churches played an important role in many of these early initiatives. In September 1949 the Social Responsibility Department of the British Council of Churches held a conference on the position of coloured workers and students in England. They circularized clergy in areas of immigrant settlement asking what steps had been taken by the churches to render assistance to immigrants and inquiring whether it was likely that any representative committee would be set up in these areas to consider such issues as the accommodation, employment, and recreational facilities of coloured immigrants.

One clergyman who responded to this circular was the Archdeacon of Birmingham who set up, in March 1950, what came to be known as the Birmingham Co-ordinating Committee for Coloured People. The membership of this committee initially consisted of nine representatives of churches and religious organizations, and eleven others from the British Council, Rotary, Birmingham University, Birmingham International Centre, the Ministry of Labour, the educational authority, the Colonial Office, and the Birmingham Council of Social Service. There were no immigrants on this committee, despite the fact that there already existed a thriving Afro-Caribbean Association, which was directing its efforts during this period towards combating discrimination in public houses and among Birmingham Corporation Transport Department staff.

Churches were also involved to a considerable extent in the committees set up in Bristol and Nottingham in the early fifties, and a number of Councils of Churches set up race relations committees. One such which came to our attention was in Sheffield, the main achievement of which was the setting up of a multiracial housing association.[2]

An organization which soon established itself as a leader in this field was set up in Nottingham in 1955 by the Council of Churches, the Council of Social Service, and some local immigrants,

[1] S. K. Ruck (ed.), *The West Indian comes to England* (London, Routledge & Kegan Paul, 1960), pp. 155–9.

[2] *Sheffield Telegraph* (5 February 1957).

the Nottingham Consultative Committee for the Welfare of Coloured People.[1] This organization survives to this day as the Nottingham Commonwealth Citizens Consultative Committee, one of the community relations committees. The early survival of this committee was largely due to a three-year grant from the Pilgrim Trust. From 1960 onwards the local authority, which had had little to do with it in its early days, provided support. It is therefore appropriate to regard Nottingham as the first community relations committee to achieve any degree of permanence.

The local authority did not play any part in setting up the Nottingham committee. On the whole local authorities played little part in early initiatives of this kind. One minor exception is provided by Liverpool Corporation which, in 1952, made a grant to Liverpool Personal Service Society for them to employ a welfare officer.[2] This officer was advised and assisted by a 'Colonial Welfare Committee, consisting of business men, social workers, and observers from the statutory departments. . . .' This situation still exists, yet curiously no community relations committee has been set up in Liverpool, an omission for which Liverpool Youth Organizations Committee criticized the City Council in a memorandum to the Parliamentary Select Committee on Race Relations, in March 1969.[3]

More typical was the action of Birmingham Corporation. In July 1949 the Mayor convened an informal meeting to discuss ways of setting up an official organization, inviting the Town Clerk, the Chief Education Officer, city councillors, the Vice-Chancellor of the University, and people from the same cross-section of organizations as were subsequently involved in the Archdeacon's committee. All that transpired from this meeting was an informal agreement that the City Council would co-operate with local agencies which they supposed would have information of 'impending visits', and an arrangement that Birmingham Information Bureau would send letters on behalf of the Mayor giving 'visitors' a 'civic welcome' and information about facilities

[1] Ruck, op. cit., pp. 162–7, and E. J. B. Rose and associates, Colour and Citizenship (London, Oxford University Press, for Institute of Race Relations, 1969), pp. 383–4.
[2] Ruck, op. cit., pp. 159–62.
[3] Evidence to the Parliamentary Select Committee on Race Relations and Immigration, Session 1968–9, The Problems of Coloured School Leavers (London, H.M.S.O., 1969), p. 787. (Hereafter P.S.C.)

available. Viewing that 'initiative' as we do, from the other side of a period of heavy migration, it looks quite ludicrous.

Some of the uncertainty on the part of local authorities as to what their role should be in relation to immigrants stemmed from the more general uncertainty in the early 1950s as to who was actually responsible for coloured immigrant workers. The welfare of West Indians recruited in the war to work in Britain had been the responsibility of welfare officers appointed by the Ministry of Labour, which ran several hostels in conjunction with the Colonial Office.[1]

After the war it became unclear whether responsibility for immigrant welfare belonged with the Colonial Office, or with some other central government department, or with the Commonwealth governments, or with local government, or, of course, with no one other than the few voluntary groups who sought to try to shoulder the responsibility.[2]

As late as 1955 Lambeth Borough Council regarded the Colonial Office as the appropriate place to send a deputation on this issue. Yet that department showed a continued reluctance to get involved. In April 1952 the Archdeacon of Birmingham wrote to the Colonial Office expressing anxiety at their closure of their welfare department in Liverpool and stressing the need for a welfare office and information centre in Birmingham. He received the reply that there was no possibility of such an initiative from the Colonial Office, but that they might consider the attachment of an officer to a local government department or voluntary organization. The Colonial Office made it quite clear that they regarded the responsibility for the welfare of coloured immigrants to lie with local government.

Accordingly the Archdeacon approached Birmingham City Council to urge them to appoint a welfare officer. In November 1952 the City Council agreed to send representatives from several relevant committees to the Archdeacon's committee. In September 1954, on the Co-ordinating Committee's recommendations, a former Colonial Service officer was appointed to the Town Clerk's department as 'Liaison Officer for Coloured People'.

Birmingham City Council was the first local authority to

[1] A. H. Richmond, *Colour Prejudice in Britain* (London, Routledge & Kegan Paul, 1954), Chapter 3.
[2] Rose *et al.*, op. cit., pp. 207–15.

appoint a liaison officer of this kind. Its initiative was followed in 1956 by the setting up of a consortium of fourteen other West Midland authorities to form the Commonwealth Welfare Council of the West Midlands and employ their own peripatetic liaison officer.[1]

Most of the initiatives from local authorities in the late fifties involved appointments of liaison officers on their own staffs rather than the provision of subsidies to independent bodies. For example, in 1959, Hackney appointed as Information Officer in the Town Clerk's department, a West Indian with the duty of 'assisting in providing information especially to West Indians, and to keep up-to-date detailed information of social services available to them through municipal and voluntary agencies'.[2]

In general, these early initiatives, whether from voluntary organizations or local authorities, tended to be welfare-oriented and rather paternalistic. Little attempt seems to have been made to canvass the opinions of the immigrants. The Archdeacon's committee in Birmingham had no coloured members until 1958, when a representative from the newly-opened Birmingham office of the Pakistan High Commission was invited to join.

In fact, tension seems to have occurred between the Co-ordinating Committee in Birmingham and the Afro-Caribbean Association, the former regarding the latter as too militant. In July 1953 the Afro-Caribbean Association presented a memorandum to the City Council signed by one hundred members in which they appealed for the formation of a non-party, non-sectarian 'Birmingham Inter-racial Welfare Council', to include city council representatives, co-opted representatives from English organizations, and *elected* representatives from among coloured citizens. The memorandum stated: 'We emphatically refute the statements made from time to time that there would be difficulties in finding suitable coloured representatives. Such statements are made by self-appointed representatives who have no first hand knowledge of coloured people, or by obstructionists.'

This is very interesting as one of the earliest formulations of a basis for a viable multiracial committee. Yet it came from an organization at that time regarded as militant, which was kept

[1] D. Prem, *The Parliamentary Leper* (Aligarh, U.P., India, Metric Publications, 1965), p. 30.
[2] *Hackney Gazette* (22 September 1959).

out of discussions on the welfare of immigrants. To this day no real progress has been made towards this form of organization and many immigrant groups in Birmingham have lost all patience with multiracial initiatives. (The request was rejected by the General Purposes Committee of the City Council on the grounds that the Archdeacon's committee was already in existence and doing good work.)

This exclusion of immigrant groups continued. In 1958 various West Indian organizations requested the liaison officer of the British Caribbean Welfare Services to seek greater co-ordination of organizations concerned with the welfare of immigrants. The liaison officer wrote to the Archdeacon: 'As present arrangements stand in Birmingham there appears to be an unnecessary risk of the coloured group thinking that their organizations are outside of things.'

In 1959, the Birmingham 'Liaison Officer for Coloured People', an ex-colonial policeman, reported on his job to the City Council in terms that indicated that his conception of his post was as a kind of probation officer. 'At the present time,' he wrote, 'coloured persons do not come to me for help and advice until the very last moment. They talk things over with each other, follow suggested courses of action which are ill-conceived and doomed to failure and they finish up talking colour bar when they finally come to the office.' To remedy this he recommended a scheme for home-visiting amongst those he saw to be 'at risk'.

Rex and Moore have documented how totally out of touch with immigrants this official was, and how low an opinion immigrants held of him.[1] He particularly undermined his own work by refusing to have anything to do with any organizations he regarded as in any sense 'political'.

Similar evidence of paternalism can be found in activities in Sheffield and Nottingham in the late fifties. In Sheffield, in 1959, the City Council convened a conference for those interested in the welfare of coloured people. No immigrants were invited. The secretary of Sheffield Trades Council made an eloquent plea that 'the majority of us here are not competent unless we take the coloured people themselves into our confidence. Their needs are far better spoken for by themselves. They do not want patronage,

[1] J. Rex and R. Moore, *Race, Community, and Conflict: A Study of Sparkbrook* (London, Oxford University Press, for Institute of Race Relations, 1967), p. 161.

they want help so they can help themselves.' This plea was disregarded.[1]

In Nottingham, no coloured people were present at the founding meeting of the Consultative Committee in 1954. A second planning meeting was called 'to hear from the colonial peoples what they felt they needed'. Three members of the non-political Colonial Social and Cricket Club were invited to represent West Indians. Most of the Colonial Club's approximately twenty-five members were 'old settlers' who had served in the R.A.F., settled in Nottingham after the war, and had middle-class occupations.[2]

It was only after the 1958 disturbances in Nottingham that the Indian Workers' Association and the Afro-Asian West Indian Union were invited to affiliate to the Consultative Committee.[3]

Councils of social service had been showing interest in the position of coloured immigrants throughout the 1950s, as their contribution towards the establishment and support of the Nottingham committee testifies. In Sheffield, the Council of Social Service established a Standing Conference on the Welfare of Coloured Workers which worked with the Council of Churches and immigrant organizations to establish a housing association.[4] Similarly, the International Council of Leeds Council of Social Service formed a Colonial Workers' Sub-Committee in 1956, which worked in co-operation with the Aggrey Society, a voluntary organization founded two years earlier, to help run their multiracial housing association and social centre.[5]

In July 1957, a National Council of Social Service Group on the Welfare of Coloured Workers had been set up by eight councils of social service, and Liverpool Personal Service Society, to meet once or twice a year. In London, the Council of Social Service appointed Miss Nadine Peppard as an assistant secretary to co-ordinate field-work in the London area, and act as secretary to a West Indian Advisory Committee, which subsequently became known as the Immigrants Advisory Committee.

Many councils of social service sought to sponsor multiracial liaison committees during the late fifties. A National Council of Social Service report in 1960 referred to the existence of

[1] *Sheffield Telegraph* (24 March 1959).   [2] Katznelson, op. cit., p. 282.
[3] Ibid., p. 299.   [4] *Sheffield Telegraph* (4 December 1957).
[5] *Yorkshire Post* (23 March 1956).

'co-ordinating committees' in Bath, Birmingham, Bristol, Coventry, Derby, Dudley, Gloucester, Leeds, Liverpool, Nottingham, Redditch, Sheffield, and the West Midlands, though they will have included a variety of organizations, few of which constituted elaborate organizations comparable to the community relations committees of today, under this umbrella concept.

In 1960, a report was published by the Family Welfare Association[1] which largely reflected council of social service thinking on this issue, recommending the appointment of 'community relations officers' in boroughs with 'non-European' populations of 5,000 or more. The relevant recommendations were made by Albert Hyndman, a West Indian social worker who had been working with the F.W.A. on a three-year 'Project for the Welfare of Coloured People in London'. Mr. Hyndman suggested:

Now that Britain, to all intents, has a coloured settled minority that has increased several hundredfold during the post-war years, it would be to the future advantage to carry through a programme of social engineering now, before the position deteriorates. This in our view does not demand new legislation, or a special government welfare department to be responsible for migrants. Much of this work is already being done by the British Caribbean Welfare Service and other non-governmental groups. What is suggested is that in those boroughs with a non-European population of 5,000 or more, a Community Relations Officer be appointed. This officer will have as his first responsibility to collaborate with existing organizations, both migrant and English, in the organising of activities of equal interest to the groups concerned on the basis of equal status in order to knit the disparate elements of the community together. In addition the Community Relations Officer might be called upon by existing organizations, especially Citizens' Advice Bureaux, Members of Parliament and other advisory agencies, to try to sort out those problems which may develop into racial intolerance—in particular those which arise between non-European landlords and their English tenants, as experience has shown that many of these situations can be talked over and clarified by reasoning and exhortation rather than by resort to legal action.[2]

Mr. Hyndman's proposals represented a departure from the purely welfare approach to the problems of immigrants. Another such departure was provided by Willesden Borough Council,

[1] Ruck (ed.), op. cit.   [2] Ibid., pp. 150–1.

influenced probably by the disturbing riots in nearby Notting
Hill, in 1959. The story of this venture is summarized by Davison:

Willesden has been pioneering in this field owing in no small measure
to the fact that one or two prominent people in the borough, notably
the Leader of the Council, have taken a close personal interest in the
question. At a public meeting held in March 1959, convened by the
Mayor and attended by representatives of both statutory and voluntary
bodies, a decision was taken to form a body known as the 'Willesden
International Friendship Council'. A half-yearly general meeting was
arranged, with an elected executive committee meeting monthly. A
large number of interested local organizations, both voluntary and
statutory, send representatives to the half-yearly council meetings and
the executive committee, consisting of about thirty people, is elected
annually. The membership of the executive is approximately half
immigrant and half English. The council began work by persuading
the Borough Council to make a grant to the Citizens' Advice Bureau
for a research worker to be employed to make a survey of the local
scene. At the end of the survey, which took about nine months, the
Borough Council agreed to make a grant for a full-time worker to be
appointed to work towards the integration of the English and West
Indian Communities.[1]

There are several significant aspects to this story: the key role
played by the Borough Council, the involvement of a major local
politician, Reginald Freeson, and the fact that despite local
authority involvement an organization was set up with a more
positive approach to race relations than the personal welfare
emphasis characteristic of the earlier initiatives in this field.
In the next few years, Miss Peppard, of the London Council
of Social Service, was to play a vital role in the development of
the ideas put forward by Mr. Hyndman and by Willesden I.F.C.,
into a government-backed scheme for community relations
committees.
Characteristic then of the Willesden approach in the early
1960s, an approach followed by several other committees set up
at this time (notably Southall I.F.C. and Haringey Commonwealth Consultative Council), was work to create racial harmony
through social activities and through conciliation. This work is
summarized in *Colour and Citizenship*:

---

[1] R. B. Davison, *Commonwealth Immigrants* (London, Oxford University Press, for
Institute of Race Relations, 1964), pp. 50–1.

The various local 'liaison' committees set out to promote their goal of peaceful integration by undertaking a variety of activities on a rather limited scale. Mixed social gatherings, 'international' exhibitions, or events, functioned as symbolic offers of welcome to immigrants, and could provide mild propaganda for the host population if they were attended by local dignitaries. No commitment to a policy more specific than harmony and friendship was required. The function of the social occasions whether arranged by a club or a voluntary liaison committee could vary. If organized for no particular purpose than to 'mix' people, they could become a matter of non-representative English meeting non-representative immigrants, a dilemma familiar to many middle-class voluntary workers in other fields. Collins described such an organizatory meeting in a school 'on kiddies' chairs, in which the 'middle-class elite, M.P.s, reverends and idealists . . . unblinkingly faced the robustness of the migrants, and with their beautiful English manners politely observed the invisible gulf which existed between themselves and their dark brothers; that bridge which could be crossed only by the new West Indian quasi-elite, who inserted himself in the middle, in a kind of social no-man's land.'[1] But where these meetings took place, to celebrate, for example, the opening of a new community centre for an immigrant group, they could be a kind of social sealing-wax, a friendship ritual closing a period of conflict about the establishment of the centre. Where they were for purposes of entertainment or enjoyment, they could simply provide just that.

One of the main functions of some of the committees was a kind of U.N.-trouble shooter role: harmony in action. This involved the provision of 'conciliation' officers, to go and talk to the parties when cases of personal racial friction occurred. The best example is that of Willesden Friendship Council's work, in resolving or quieting disputes between landlords and native tenants, by sending a multiracial team to discuss the grievances. The technique was extended by some committees to cases of racial discrimination, prior to the 1968 Race Relations Act. In Nottingham, lawyers attached to the Housing Association formed by the Committee, also attempted to conciliate in cases of housing discrimination. Their experience indicated that without legal sanctions, such 'persuasive' work was doomed to failure. Effective action on this front had to await the passage of legislation against discrimination.[2]

During the early 1960s this kind of work for racial harmony had increasingly to compete with two other approaches to the use

[1] Reference to W. Collins, *Jamaican Migrant* (London, Routledge & Kegan Paul, 1965).
[2] Rose *et al.*, op. cit., pp. 385–6.

of committees in the field of race relations. As local authorities grew increasingly concerned about numbers, they sought to take new initiatives to deal with welfare problems. To put it another way, they sought to shunt off problems existing officers found difficult to handle onto special welfare officers for coloured people, backed in some cases by committees. We have already referred to appointments of this kind in Birmingham, Hackney, and the West Midlands. Other examples are the 'Welfare Officer for Coloured People' appointed to Nottingham's Education Department in 1959, a West Indian who had become active in the Consultative Committee, and the liaison officers appointed in Bradford's Health Department in 1964, who were Pakistanis.

The increasing political controversy about race relations inevitably led to the creation of local organizations of a political kind, committed to work for racial equality and to fight racial discrimination. This development was partly encouraged by the emergence of virulent anti-immigrant organizations, such as the British National Party, Southall Residents Association, and Birmingham Immigration Control Association.[1] Also, it was in some respects a consequence of the failure of the existing co-ordinating committees and welfare officers to oppose these movements effectively.

In Birmingham, as early as 1958, the liaison officer made public his view that the city had reached saturation point.[2] In 1960, he proposed to the Archdeacon's committee that they should seek to secure the control of entry of Commonwealth immigrants on similar lines to the controls over aliens. The committee rejected the notion of legislative control, and the Archdeacon made this view clear to the Press, the Birmingham M.P.s, and the Home Secretary.

Another reaction to the increasing aggressiveness of the Birmingham Immigration Control Association was the setting up in 1960 of the Birmingham Co-ordinating Committee against Racial Discrimination (C.C.A.R.D.) under the presidency of Victor Yates, Labour M.P. for Ladywood. This organization was set up by representatives from West Indian, Indian, Pakistani organizations, and the Birmingham University Socialist Union.

[1] Paul Foot, *Immigration and Race in British Politics* (Harmondsworth, Penguin, 1965).
[2] *Birmingham Mail* (27 August 1958).

C.C.A.R.D. held a series of meetings in the inner ring areas of Birmingham during 1960 and 1961.[1]

In some cases more complex organizations were created by radicals who felt the need to oppose the growth of racialism. These aimed to be coalitions of local organizations, individuals, and local authorities on the lines of Willesden I.F.C. Southall International Friendship Council and Oxford Committee for Racial Integration are examples of such organizations.

At the same time many of the less political organizations, set up to provide welfare services for immigrants, found they could not avoid the growing political controversy. Debates developed for example within Nottingham Consultative Council with Eric Irons, the West Indian member employed by the local education authority, arguing that 'the consultative committee should concentrate on work in Nottingham and the matter of restrictions should be left to the politicians', a view that was opposed by another leading West Indian member. Initially the organization supported Irons but after the introduction of the first Immigration Bill the Consultative Committee did issue a public statement deploring it.[2]

In addition to the welfare and the political approaches to community relations work, about which there was to be a great deal of controversy after 1965, another approach was also developing, emphasizing the need to educate the host community. This approach was suggested in a report to Willesden I.F.C.[3] It also figured to a great extent in the objectives of national organizations such as the Society of Friends Race Relations Committee and the British Caribbean Association. Increasing attention was to be paid to this kind of work by national and local organizations.

In 1965, then, voluntary committees were concentrating upon one or more of five types of activity: conciliation; fostering social contacts; individual welfare work; political activity; educational work.[4]

We are focussing our attention on the position as at 1965 because in August of that year the Government made certain

---

[1] *Birmingham Post* (18 September 1961 and 9 October 1961).
[2] Katznelson, op. cit., p. 300.
[3] J. Maizels, *The West Indian comes to Willesden* (Willesden Borough Council, 1960).
[4] Our summary approximates quite closely to an account of fields of action of local committees prepared prior to the 1965 White Paper in consultation with Miss Peppard in R. Hooper (ed.), *Colour in Britain* (London, B.B.C. Publications, 1965), pp. 172–5.

arrangements, set out in its White Paper 'Immigration from the Commonwealth', that were to weld most of the local voluntary efforts we have been discussing into a single movement, held together by a system of grants. Before describing what was involved, it is necessary to sketch in some national developments leading up to the events of August 1965. We do not intend to chronicle the political events of this period in any detail, this has been done very fully elsewhere.[1] We want to set the development of local committees in a national context.

Alongside governmental concern about numbers of immigrants, stimulated by political agitation reaching a peak in the 1964 general election in Smethwick and elsewhere and continuing at a high level almost ever since, some small efforts were being made to study aspects of integration. In 1962, the Home Secretary appointed the Commonwealth Immigrants Advisory Council under the chairmanship of Lady Reading, 'to advise him on any matters which he might refer to it from time to time affecting the welfare of Commonwealth immigrants in the United Kingdom and their integration into the community.'[2]

On the recommendation of Lady Reading's committee the Government set up the National Committee for Commonwealth Immigrants on 1 April 1964. This committee provided advice and information to the Government, and also sought to foster the formation of local and regional organizations based roughly upon the kinds of committees existing in Willesden and Nottingham. Nadine Peppard moved from the London Council of Social Service to act as secretary to this committee, but she had next to no supporting staff and no central funds to offer to local committees. Accordingly, she sought to get local authorities and councils of social service to back local ventures.

While the Government was making faltering steps towards the recognition that there was a case for the central co-ordination and support of some of the activities of local committees, there was an increasing demand for some radical response to anti-immigrant agitation. This demand was linked with the growing interest in the case for anti-discrimination legislation. During 1965

[1] For fuller accounts see Rose *et al.*, op. cit., Foot, op. cit., and N. Deakin (ed.), *Colour and the British Electorate, 1964* (London, Pall Mall Press, 1965).
[2] *Immigration from the Commonwealth*, Cmnd. 2739 (London, H.M.S.O., 1965), para. 64 (hereafter 1965 White Paper).

this radical movement became concentrated in the Campaign Against Racial Discrimination. According to *Colour and Citizenship*:

C.A.R.D. had been set up in December 1964. The initial impetus had come from the anxieties generated by the Smethwick episode among a number of white radicals associated with the Committee of 100 and a West Indian Quaker, Marian Glean; the catalyst was provided by the visit of Martin Luther King to London en route to receiving a Nobel Prize. After a number of co-options, partly of community leaders unable to attend the initial meetings and also of sympathetic whites (who formed a minority of four on the provisional executive of thirteen members), C.A.R.D. began the painful process of defining its objectives.[1]

C.A.R.D. brought together a motley coalition of white radical organizations, immigrant organizations, multiracial organizations, and individuals, both white and black, which was to prove highly unstable. As an organization initially preoccupied by the need to lobby for effective anti-discrimination legislation, the key role played in it by intellectuals oriented towards the traditional left-wing role of a parliamentary pressure group made it naturally vulnerable to assault from black militants with a more global view of the war against racism and little patience with the liberal processes of pressurizing M.P.s. This divisive situation was reinforced by a wide range of personal rivalries and conflicts emanating from factional fights, whose bases lay in other organizations.

It is appropriate to refer to C.A.R.D. because it occupied, and still does in a nominal sense, nationally, and perhaps more significantly locally, a special place in relation to the growing community relations movement. Some of the local committees that were in 1965 evolving into the 'liaison committees' under the wing of the National Committee for Commonwealth Immigrants, were actively involved in C.A.R.D. at the outset, notably Oxford and Willesden. Yet already Miss Peppard was warning representatives of local committees that campaign committees of the C.A.R.D type offered an approach significantly different in kind from liaison committees aiming to bring a cross-section of people together to solve local race relations problems. It was symbolic of

---

[1] Rose *et al.*, op. cit., pp. 507–8. For a detailed account of C.A.R.D., see B. W. Heineman, *The Politics of the Powerless: A Study of the Campaign Against Racial Discrimination* (London, Oxford University Press, for Institute of Race Relations, forthcoming).

the ambivalence that has remained with the community relations movement that Miss Peppard appeared on the platform at the opening session of C.A.R.D.'s inaugural conference in summer 1965. Significantly, too, when, after the 1965 White Paper, the National Committee for Commonwealth Immigrants was reconstituted, both the chairman and vice-chairman of C.A.R.D. agreed to become members. While some people saw the difference between the N.C.C.I. and C.A.R.D. as a matter of difference of principle, Miss Peppard, Dr. Pitt, and Mr. Alavi, amongst others, saw any difference in terms of the use to be made of a variety of tactics.[1] As will be seen, argument about this difference has gone on to this day.

As far as many of the local committees were concerned, a variety of responses were developed. Oxford Committee for Racial Integration sought to operate more or less as a local branch of C.A.R.D. while carrying on other more 'orthodox' liaison committee activities.[2] Many London committees contained members who were also active in C.A.R.D., notably Camden. In Manchester, the local branch of C.A.R.D. affiliated to the liaison committee, but its members saw themselves as a pressure group within the committee. In some towns a hostile relationship developed between the community relations committee and the local C.A.R.D. group. For example, in Leicester two rival organizations developed, the Campaign for Racial Equality affiliated to C.A.R.D., and a liaison committee associated with the National Committee for Commonwealth Immigrants. This sort of conflict continued to build up long after the events of 1965, as the community relations movement suffered considerably on account of its association with the Government. The first blow to the community relations movement came, at what was realistically its birth as a national movement, in the double-edged nature of the 1965 White Paper.

The 1965 White Paper was in three parts. Parts I and II were concerned with immigration control and imposed a very much tighter check on inflow of immigrants than the original 1962 Commonwealth Immigrants Act. The White Paper was the embodiment of the view of the new Labour Government for which Roy Hattersley, Labour M.P. for Sparkbrook, was a typical spokesman:

[1] Heineman, op. cit.   [2] Ibid.

I was a passionate opponent of the Act (the 1962 Commonwealth Immigrants Act) and the opposition was led by the then leader of the Labour Party, a man for whom I had and still have unqualified admiration. But notwithstanding those things in the light of time and with the advantage of hindsight I suppose we were wrong to oppose the Act.[1]

and:

I believe that integration without limitation is impossible; equally I believe that limitation without integration is indefensible.[2]

These proposals were widely attacked by those involved in race relations in this country, as measures designed explicitly to discriminate against coloured entrants, in effect placing the Commonwealth immigrant in an inferior position to the alien. It was argued that such stringent control involved a breach of faith with Britain's coloured population and a capitulation to the anti-immigrant lobby that would inevitably lead to the worsening of race relations. It was portrayed as part of a political 'dutch auction' on immigrant numbers, a competition between the main political parties to see who could be 'most nasty to the immigrants'.[3]

Again, it is not our intention to discuss the political arguments about immigration control. We have drawn attention to the impact of the first two parts of the White Paper in order to explain why the organizations for whom government support was promised in Part III ran into difficulties right from the start.

Part III of the White Paper, headed 'Integration', began with a rather complacent recital of existing government policies and a 'justification' of the absence of special policies for immigrants. It also promised some special help to local authorities forced to undertake 'exceptional commitments by engaging special staff, in order to ease the pressures on the social services which arise from differences in language and cultural background and to deal with problems of transition and adjustment'. There was nothing very exceptional in this section.

The White Paper then turned to the subject of what it called

[1] Hansard, 5S H (709) 380, 23 March 1965.
[2] Hansard, 5S H (721) 359, 23 November 1965.
[3] Both these comments are taken from speeches at the time by Dr. David Pitt, chairman of C.A.R.D. and subsequently vice-chairman of the Community Relations Commission.

'voluntary liaison committees',[1] including within this concept the wide variety of voluntary committees which had been created up and down the country to co-ordinate effort and exchange information and ideas on activities designed to promote integration. It said of these committees, 'Above all they help to create a climate of mutual tolerance in which the stupidity of racial prejudice cannot survive.'[2]

It was recognized that local conditions vary and that the diversity of committees was desirable to maintain a flexible approach. The Government considered that there was a need for central intervention to provide for co-ordination, positive government support for local committees, and the creation of additional committees in areas of immigrant settlement lacking them.[3]

To this end, the White Paper announced that the Government would set up 'a new National Committee for Commonwealth Immigrants which will be composed of individuals who are able to bring special knowledge and experience to bear on the problems arising from Commonwealth immigration'.[4] This committee would replace the existing National Committee and would be much better financed than its predecessor. So it would have both staff and funds to develop the existing services to local and regional committees. The White Paper went on:

it is important that the new National Committee should be able to build up a comprehensive body of doctrine which can be flexibly applied to a variety of local situations, extend the range of existing information work, organise conferences of workers in the field, arrange training courses, stimulate research and the examination by experts of particular problems, and generally promote and co-ordinate effort on a national basis.[5]

To meet the needs of local committees, the Government stated that it would make grants available, to be administered by the National Committee.[6] These grants would provide sufficient money for each committee to employ a full-time officer as 'the direct servant of the committee'. The White Paper expressed the 'hope' that local authorities would help with the support of local committees in their areas by providing office accommodation and secretarial help, making this one of the conditions under which

---

[1] 1965 White Paper, para. 62.   [2] Ibid., para. 61.   [3] Ibid., para. 72.
[4] Ibid., para. 73.   [5] Ibid.   [6] Ibid., para. 75.

grants would be available. The National Committee was to ensure that local committees employed competent people and to assist in the training of such officers. The Government considered that this use of the National Committee as the organization directing this operation would avoid direct government control and thus 'party political pressure'. Nevertheless the Government intended to maintain close touch with the operation.

As early as 1965, however, there was quite a degree of anxiety among back-bench members of the Labour party in the Commons as to the exact relationship between the committees, N.C.C.I., and the Government. Reginald Freeson, Labour M.P. for Willesden (the founder of Willesden I.F.C.) asked:

What is to be the relationship between these Committees and Parliament and the Government? Will there be a minister or representative on the N.C.C.I. or will it be the junior minister from the D.E.A., or will there be a representative from the Ministry of Labour or the Department of Education and Science or the Home Office? Will the N.C.C.I. report direct to the Prime Minister or to Parliament? Nobody knows. There are other departments concerned like the Home Office, the Ministries of Education, Labour, Housing and Health. Where is the co-ordination to be? Is it still to be kept at junior minister level or are we to have some genuine ministerial responsibility for policy? Nobody knows the answers to these questions and it seems that no thought has been given to them. Will there be a direct line of communication between local authorities and appropriate voluntary bodies through the N.C.C.I. to the Junior Minister and thus to Parliament and the Government. . . . There is a great need for more information on what is to be the basis of work of local voluntary bodies in welfare and education as recommended in the White Paper.[1]

The question of co-ordination, location of responsibility for the community relations movement, and access to the Government proved to be crucial in the ensuing years. It is beyond the scope of this book to discuss the lack of interdepartmental co-ordination. Suffice it here to say that the location of the ministerial responsibility for community relations at junior level at the Home Office, after a brief period of responsibility by the D.E.A., provoked a certain amount of opposition from immigrant and campaign organizations, because of the Home Office's preoccupation with the control of immigration. The small size and insignificant status

[1] Hansard 5S H (721) 454–5, November 1965.

of the division responsible for community relations at the Home Office is also a matter of some importance.[1] Nor does its continued location there seem to have resulted in any gain in co-ordination after responsibility for the Urban Programme was located at the Home Office too.

To implement the proposals, the National Committee was very promptly reconstituted under the chairmanship of the Archbishop of Canterbury. The choice of such a chairman was seen at the time as a valuable means of establishing the body's respectability, but later the drawbacks of possessing such a non-political figure-head began to appear.[2] The National Committee was a large committee for which a wide cross-section of people were selected, from both the native British society and from the ranks of those who were seen as immigrant 'leaders'. The inclusion of the chairman and vice-chairman of C.A.R.D. amongst their members has already been mentioned.

The presence of the proposals for the National Committee in a White Paper primarily concerned with immigration control meant that the acceptance of positions on the committee inevitably attracted criticism from some militant quarters for some of the leaders of immigrant or multiracial organizations.[3]

Miss Peppard remained as secretary of this new National Committee and very rapidly got down to work to build a national network of liaison committees. She, some of the members of the National Committee, and Mr. Maurice Foley, the Minister at the D.E.A. designated as 'co-ordinator of policies for integration', travelled around the country stimulating local authorities to set up liaison committees or to support existing ones, and encouraging existing organizations that did not quite fill the bill as committees to reform their structures so that they might qualify for grants. In doing this they were guided by some paragraphs in the White Paper which laid down what liaison committees should be like.

A paragraph headed 'Conditions of Success' stated that a

[1] David Stephen points out that, while the Home Office employs five Assistant Secretaries and about 1,450 other Civil Servants with responsibilities for immigration control, the Community Relations Department has only eight persons on its staff, one of whom is an Assistant Secretary. *Immigration and Race Relations* (London, Fabian Research Series, No. 291, 1970).

[2] In fact, R. A. Butler was offered the chairmanship of the N.C.C.I. in 1965 but refused. See Katznelson, op. cit., p. 247.

[3] Rose *et al.*, op. cit., pp. 523-4.

liaison committee should satisfy three conditions.[1] It should be a joint project 'in which immigrant and host community are both fully involved', it should have the full backing of the local authority, and it should have the support of a wide variety of local organizations as a 'non-sectarian and non-political' body. All three of these conditions were to create problems for local committees. We will examine them more fully later as they had a crucial impact upon the committees.

Next, the White Paper attempted to make some suggestions on the functions of voluntary liaison committees. This paragraph was rather vague, containing merely a few tentative suggestions under three headings, information, education, and welfare.[2] On the last of these three it was stressed that the objectives of committees when dealing with the welfare of immigrants 'should be to help immigrants to use the ordinary facilities of social service provided for the whole community'.

Education was clearly conceived as a two-way process, and voluntary liaison committees were seen as providing a 'forum' for mutual education. Thus, while much of the emphasis was still on providing help for immigrants, there was some recognition that the attitudes of the 'host' community required attention. Discrimination was mentioned as the province of the Race Relations Board rather than of the voluntary liaison committees, a rather surprising note in view of the fact that the anti-discrimination legislation under consideration at that time did not deal with the really important fields of discrimination in housing, employment, and personal services.

The actions of the National Committee for Commonwealth Immigrants over the next three years were to be closely determined by the 1965 White Paper. The 'conditions of success' paragraph was made the basis for recommendations on the structure of local committees, and grants were only given if these conditions were considered to have been met. In particular, the N.C.C.I. only provided grants where local authorities were prepared to provide financial support too. The Government limited the grants to £1,500 per committee, a sum that had to be specifically spent on the salary of the liaison officer.

When the 1968 Race Relations Act superseded this part of the 1965 White Paper by providing for a new grant system under

---

[1] 1965 White Paper, para. 66.   [2] Ibid., para. 67.

the Community Relations Commission, the Government refrained from trying to spell out these points again in detail, thus providing a much more flexible statutory superstructure. However, by that time, the White Paper had had a crucial impact upon the structure of most committees.

The best way to convey the impact of the 1965 White Paper upon the local committees is to describe briefly what happened in the eight areas in which were committees which we studied intensively. In all but one of the eight areas, new committees were formed or existing ones reorganized in the twelve months following the White Paper. The exception was Wycombe, where the committee was founded on the Mayor's initiative in 1960. As early as November 1964 Miss Peppard had suggested that the Borough Council should appoint a liaison officer but the committee did not succeed in getting a local authority grant to match an N.C.C.I. one until 1967.

There was already a committee in the Borough of Ealing but it was based on the old Middlesex borough of Southall. Southall I.F.C., set up in 1963, sought a grant immediately after the White Paper but had to be reformed on an Ealing Borough basis to qualify for one. In fact a grant was given and an officer appointed before the new Ealing committee was properly constituted. The liaison officer was appointed early in spring 1966 and had, as his first job, to help set up his own committee.

In Hackney, a more or less inactive Consultative Committee for Commonwealth Citizens, consisting solely of councillors, had to be reconstituted. Here the N.C.C.I. pushed the Borough Council into taking the initiative to set up a liaison committee in May 1966, and a liaison officer was appointed in December.

In Tower Hamlets, there existed a Council of Citizens of East London, dating from the 1930s, which had begun to recognize that coloured immigrants rather than Jews should be its main concern in the 1960s. In order to quality for an N.C.C.I. grant this organization created at the end of 1965 a Council of Citizens of Tower Hamlets as a subcommittee, to confine its activities within the borough boundaries. The C.C.E.L. appointed a full-time officer in December 1965. Her post became N.C.C.I.-supported a few months later. C.C.T.H. became an autonomous body in October 1966.

Organizations were created in Bradford and Sheffield as a

result of pressure from Miss Peppard and Maurice Foley in autumn 1965. In both towns rudimentary and ineffectual bodies had existed for some time before, with close ties to the churches. In Bradford, the Bishop called the inaugural meeting in January 1966, and a liaison officer was appointed in January 1967. In Sheffield, the committee moved, with a great deal of local authority help, from inaugural meeting to the appointment of C.R.O. in the first five months of 1966.

In Birmingham, the N.C.C.I. experienced considerable difficulty in persuading the local authority to abandon the existing arrangement with its own social welfare-oriented liaison officer and the by now more or less moribund voluntary committee chaired by the Archdeacon. After some skilful political manoeuvres the City Council agreed that the Mayor should *appoint* a new committee responsible to him. This local committee was modelled upon the N.C.C.I., rather than a voluntary committee. However, the N.C.C.I. agreed to give it a grant. The committee was set up during winter 1966–7.

In Huddersfield, the committee emerged as a result of voluntary initiative after the White Paper, when the International Co-operation Year Committee set up in 1965 persuaded the Mayor that the setting up of a liaison committee would provide a means of continuing some of the 'inter-community' activities they had started. Their inaugural meeting was held in April 1966 and their honorary secretary was appointed liaison officer in March 1967.

This account of developments in eight specific areas gives a very good idea of what went on in towns with large numbers of immigrants after the 1965 White Paper. At the same time the N.C.C.I.'s staff grew rapidly and it set up nine advisory panels to examine some of the issues and problems at a national level. Many individuals who played key roles in local committees served on these panels, yet on the whole a clear relationship between the N.C.C.I.'s national activities and the local activities which it supported did not grow up. A standing conference of voluntary liaison committees was set up which, proving to be a rather large affair, was forced to delegate responsibilities to a Central Advisory Group, selected by the N.C.C.I. on a regional basis. The latter body was never allowed to have any real impact, and with the setting up of the Community Relations Commission, both the 'standing conference' and the Advisory Group were disbanded in favour of more *ad hoc* arrangements for consultation. In the last year of the N.C.C.I., relations with the committees became highly charged with controversy, as we shall see.

The growth of what we have called the community relations movement is recorded in Tables 1.1 and 1.2. Table 1.1 charts the growth in the number of local committees recognized by the N.C.C.I./C.R.C. Table 1.2 gives the annual grants awarded to the N.C.C.I. and C.R.C. which further illustrates the rate of growth.[1]

TABLE 1.1
GROWTH OF COMMUNITY RELATIONS COMMITTEES

	No. of committees	No. with N.C.C.I. grants
April 1964	15	—
End of 1965	32	—
End of 1966	42	12
End of 1967	50	32
March 1969	78	42

TABLE 1.2
GOVERNMENT GRANTS TO N.C.C.I./C.R.C.

1965–6 (six months)	£70,000
1966–7	£120,000
1967–8	£170,000
1968–9	£200,000
1969–70	£300,000

This transformation from a number of entirely autonomous committees loosely co-ordinated by the N.C.C.I. to a network of committees all subject to a certain amount of supervision by that body, in order to qualify for grants, did not occur without a certain amount of tension. In some cases friction arose merely from a general suspicion of a government-controlled body operating from London. In other cases conflict occurred between local committees and the N.C.C.I. over specific constitutional points such as the balance to be achieved between individuals,

[1] These tables are based upon information provided in the *Report of the Community Relations Commission for 1968–9* (London, H.M.S.O., 1969), and *The National Committee for Commonwealth Immigrants Reports for 1966 and 1967* (London, N.C.C.I.).

organizations, and local authorities in the membership of committees. The enlistment of substantial local authority support in this enterprise also proved difficult in many areas. Local authorities were only too ready to seek financial help from the Government to help them cope with what they saw as the problems created by immigrants. They were not so happy about making a contribution to a largely independent local committee, whose government money would come from a new national agency whose respectability was suspect.

In practice the changing climate of race relations and the sensitivity of the Government to the demands of the anti-immigrant lobby placed the National Committee in a very difficult position. The situation became particularly difficult in 1968, as the Community Relations Commission made clear in its report. We quote from this report at length, as this passage provides a particularly clear statement of the N.C.C.I.'s point of view in the face of its difficulties:

The period since the beginning of 1968 has been eventful for community relations in this country with much to record on both the debit and the credit sides of the account. Many knowledgeable observers and many workers in this field no doubt write 1968 down as a year of deterioration in community relations. Perhaps the worst feature was that for the first time opinion in this country appeared to accept as socially respectable the use of blatantly hostile language in public utterances on the subject of race and minority ethnic groups. Certainly also the strong feelings aroused among the immigrant communities and in circles sympathetic to their interests by the enactment of the Commonwealth Immigrants Act 1968 have left a legacy of suspicion and mistrust which can only add to the difficulty of promoting harmony in community relations. Subsequent developments, such as the recent restrictions on the entry of fiancés of British subjects already established here, have had the effect of strengthening suspicion and resentment regarding official policy. Certainly also much publicised statements which were made during the year suggesting that coloured immigrants were an undesirable and burdensome element in the population and the reaction which these statements inevitably provoked among both the host community and the minority ethnic groups did incalculable harm to the cause of good community relations. For those concerned with the difficult day-to-day work of helping society to recognise, provide for and come to terms with the multi-racial character it has already acquired, it was a year of anxiety and uncertainty. In particular some loss of momentum in the work of community relations was an unavoidable consequence of the transition from the National Committee to the Commission. Understandably the Committee was reluctant during its last months in office to take decisions by which it might appear to be committing in advance the new Commission. On the other hand the Commission, on taking over, felt the need to spend some time in taking stock and reviewing policies, objectives and priorities, before undertaking any new initiatives.

In February, 1968, the publication of the Commonwealth Immigrants Bill confronted the National Committee with an acute problem. There was no doubt in the Committee's mind that the enactment of this measure would make the task of promoting good community relations immeasurably more difficult. But the question was whether, in the situation which had thus arisen, the Committee would be serving the purpose of good community relations better by resigning in protest against the measure or by carrying on and doing what it could to mitigate the harmful effects. The advice it received from many different quarters was conflicting and indeed opinion within the Committee and among its staff was divided. In the event the Committee concluded that it was its duty to carry on, but two of its members and two members of its staff felt compelled to resign as a result. A number of the members of Advisory Panels also resigned at this time. Having decided however to continue in office, the Committee considered it was in duty bound to make its views about the enactment known to the Prime Minister and at the same time to urge the need for better provision to be made for community relations work and for the enactment of strong and effective race relations legislation.[1]

The inability of the N.C.C.I. to effectively anticipate or lobby against the Government's proposals to restrict entry to Britain of Kenya Asians with British passports deeply disturbed many of the local committees. It reminded many that the whole structure had been built up after the restrictive immigration measures of 1965, and that many of the efforts of the N.C.C.I. to influence government policies in other ways (such as their attempt to get the Government to curb local housing authorities with discriminatory policies) had also been unsuccessful.[2] In other words it suggested that the whole N.C.C.I./local committee structure was being used as a smoke-screen by the Government to create the illusion that

[1] *Report for 1968–9*, pp. 6–7.
[2] J. Rex, 'The Race Relations Catastrophe' in T. Burgess *et al.*, *Matters of Principle: Labour's Last Chance* (Harmonsworth, Penguin, 1968).

it was working for integration while in practice it was more responsive to the racialist point of view.

Quite a few local committees felt the N.C.C.I. should resign over the treatment of the Kenya Asians. A meeting of the standing conference of voluntary liaison committees in the spring of 1968 proved a very unhappy encounter between the N.C.C.I. and the local committees. Many representatives expressed bitter feelings about the ineffectiveness of the N.C.C.I., and the whole system came very close to breakdown. The cynical interpretation of its survival is that there were sufficient committees of a totally unpolitical, welfare-oriented kind unwilling to let this event destroy their work, and that the militant committees had too much at stake financially to go all the way. A more charitable interpretation is that the Race Relations Bill, with its promise both of reasonably effective anti-discrimination legislation and a new body, with wider powers and a statutory basis, to replace the N.C.C.I., offered just sufficient hope to keep the movement going. Obviously the truth lies in a combination of these interpretations.

Inevitably, this situation created ripples that were to affect many of the local committees. Some of the committees lost members, notably immigrant organizations. Many more found that immigrant members became much more suspicious of the whole set up and much more liable to resign over other issues.

Having decided to remain in the structure and pin their hopes on the Community Relations Commission proving a much more effective body, the dissident committees turned their attention to a close scrutiny of the proposals for the new Commission. Under the leadership of the Rev. Wilfrid Wood, chairman of the new Hammersmith Council for Community Relations, some proposals were drawn up suggesting new approaches to the relationship between the central body and the community relations committees (as the voluntary liaison committees were now called). These proposals were:

That the advisory functions of the N.C.C.I. should be taken over by a National Commission for Racial Equality comprising twenty-eight to thirty members. One quarter of these members should be nominated by the Government, one quarter should be elected representatives of the community relations committees, and the remaining half should be representatives of the ethnic minority groups elected by immigrant organizations, with their voting strength determined by their registered

memberships. Included in the community relations committee representatives there should be one full-time community relations officer
elected by his fellow C.R.O.s.

Funds should be paid direct to community relations committees, in
conjunction with their local authorities, on an expressed statutory basis.
Reserve funds should be available in each area to finance 'grass-roots'
schemes not initiated by the community relations committees, and
appeals about refusal of funds at the local level should be heard by the
National Commission for Racial Equality.

The Government rejected these proposals, making one small
concession. It suggested that three members of the twelve-man
Community Relations Commission could be selected from a list
of people nominated by local committees.

The Government's arrangements for the Community Relations Commission to replace the N.C.C.I., were set out in the very
short Section 25 of the 1968 Race Relations Act.[1] Following as
they did the controversial anti-discrimination proposals in that
Act they received scant Parliamentary attention. Their importance
lies in the fact that the N.C.C.I. was replaced by a body possessing
statutory recognition. Its duties were set out very briefly indeed.
The Community Relations Commission was 'to encourage the
establishment of . . . harmonious community relations and to
co-ordinate on a national basis the measures adopted for that
purpose by others', and 'to advise the Secretary of State on any
matter referred to the Commission by him and to make recommendations to him on any matter which the Commission consider
should be brought to his attention'.[2]

The Act goes on to permit the Commission to give financial
assistance 'to any local organizations appearing to the Commission
to be concerned with community relations'. In theory, then, it
has a much more flexible brief than the N.C.C.I. had in trying
to work within the terms of the 1965 White Paper.

Before the vesting day for the Commission, representatives of
many of the local committees sought to secure discussions with the
N.C.C.I. about future arrangements, fearing that they were
merely going to get the N.C.C.I. under a new name. As the
quotation from the 1968–9 report indicates, the N.C.C.I. would
not enter into any discussions on future arrangements.

[1] *Race Relations Act 1968* (London, H.M.S.O.), part III, Section 25.
[2] Ibid.

So, at the time of the abolition of the N.C.C.I. in November 1968, many local committees remained uneasy about the system in which they operated, and particularly about its relations with the Government. This hiatus proved even more damaging since the period of silence during which the N.C.C.I. made way for the C.R.C. coincided with the first of the many widely publicized vociferous outbursts of Enoch Powell. The Government could not live down the Commonwealth Immigrants Act despite both the Race Relations Act and the formulation in summer 1968 of an Urban Programme of help for underprivileged inner city areas. David Ennals, the Home Office Minister with the incompatible tasks of responsibility for immigration policies and integration policies, received a hostile reception from the standing conference of voluntary liaison committees despite his attempt to stress the positive side of government policy; the negative side had done too much damage. However, those still active in local committees remained hopeful that the Community Relations Commission under the chairmanship of Frank Cousins, a man with a record of standing up to the Government, would produce a new dawn. The growing recognition of the case for community action in decaying urban areas would make new initiatives possible.

Before examining what followed the setting up of the Commission, it is appropriate to examine first some criticisms of the liaison committee system which developed after the 1965 White Paper. We will then take a look at the evolution from liaison committees to community relations committees, a change intended to be something more than just a change in name. Indeed, one may suggest that this represented an attempt by the N.C.C.I. to meet its critics. This account is only intended to give some idea of the kind of argument going on at the national level. The relevance of the criticism, and the effectiveness of the transformation as far as local committees are concerned, will be our concern throughout the rest of this book.

Perhaps the most sophisticated critique of voluntary liaison committees can be found in Dipak Nandy's attack on the inadequate approach of the British Government to policies for integration in the Fabian pamphlet 'Policies for Racial Equality'. In it he suggests that the voluntary liaison committee system was developed largely by Councils of Social Service. After referring briefly to the standard criticism of social work as oriented to helping the underprivileged to adjust to the *status quo*, he goes on to argue:

It is not surprising, then, that the V.L.C.s see the problems of race relations as being, in the first place, *individual* problems, and, in the second place, as *welfare* problems. There is a persistent tendency to shy away from problems of *discrimination*, to forget that the 'problem' is not a person, whatever his personal qualities may be, but the denial of equal rights to a person, and to a whole group.

Voluntary liaison committees have always had a choice, one which has been masked by the imprecision of the concept of 'liaison' (for it suggests a symmetrical, two way relationship which does not obtain in real life). The choice is between interpreting the demands for equal opportunities of the minority to the dominant white society and, on the other hand, acting as spokesmen of that society to the minority group. In effect, the V.L.C.s have uniformly chosen the second alternative.

The predictable, if regrettable, consequence is that very few of the V.L.C.s command the confidence of the immigrant communities. Those immigrant organizations which 'participate' in the work of the V.L.C.s have little sense of involvement in an organization whose objectives and methods they have had a share in deciding. As a result, immigrant participation is limited to the 'Uncle Toms'.[1]

Nandy argues that these 'Uncle Toms' are unwilling to jeopardize their positions as accepted spokesmen of the minorities in a society dominated by a white majority by making demands for their own groups which challenge the *status quo*. He goes on to suggest that there are some significant weaknesses in the approaches of local authorities towards the needs of immigrants, and that V.L.C.s need to seek to alter these attitudes. He says: 'I am not convinced that they have even recognized the need for it; nor am I convinced, even if they had, that they possess the appropriate equipment for undertaking the task.' He concludes:

At the moment the machinery for integration seems to be working satisfactorily, but this is an illusion. It is largely an illusion of competence, generated by the fact that the political exploitation of racial tensions (which is where the current interest in race relations originated) has for the time being been neutralised. But should that change, I believe we shall find our present arrangements woefully inadequate.

[1] D. Nandy, 'An Illusion of Competence', in A. Lester and N. Deakin (eds.), *Policies for Racial Equality* (Fabian Research Series, No. 262, June 1967), p. 38.

For none of these arrangements is designed to cope with the fundamental causes from which racial tension, and discrimination stem. Both
at the local and at the national level, the dominant attitude to race
relations is one of paternalism. Attention is invariably focussed on the
minority groups: it is *they* who must be educated, improved, brought
up to acceptable British specifications. In this obsession with remedial
measures for the immigrants, what is forgotten is the society which has
found in immigrants a convenient way of explaining its own weakness
and failures. What is forgotten, too, is the relevant conception of
'integration', as in Roy Jenkins' succinct formulation, which involves
the acceptance simultaneously of equality and diversity.
We have a duty to be pessimistic, for an illusion of competence is, in
the long run, costlier and more dangerous than simple incompetence.[1]

Rather similar points to Nandy's are made by John Rex
though his attack is purely upon the failure of the N.C.C.I. to
lead an attack on local authority policies, or the Government to
comprehend it.[2] Rex implicitly expounds the view that the
development of policies for racial integration in close alliance with
local authorities will severely limit the room for manoeuvre open
to the new agencies.

An attack on the N.C.C.I. and the local committees by
Michael Dummett at an Institute of Race Relations conference in
September 1968 took a rather different line. Dummett saw the
community relations movement as a means by which the Government sought to divert the activities of immigrants and their
supporters into non-political directions to prevent the development of an effective protest movement.

Dummett's argument is that by selecting, in 1965, the less
militant multiracial organizations for support, the Government
emasculated 'the embryo civil rights movement'. It sought to
stimulate the development of a safe kind of organization and
ignore the 'campaign' committees and immigrant organizations,
with serious effects upon the development of ventures that could
really have an impact upon racialism in Britain. He particularly
suggests that the setting up of the N.C.C.I. had a damaging effect
upon C.A.R.D.

The existence of the N.C.C.I. crucially affected the newly formed
Campaign Against Racial Discrimination in two quite separate ways.
First, it prevented most of the liaison committees from joining C.A.R.D.

---

[1] Lester and Deakin (eds.), op. cit., p. 40.   [2] Burgess *et al.*, op. cit.

By this I am not chiefly referring to the N.C.C.I.'s active efforts to dissuade liaison committees from taking this step: it did this, indeed, when it had to, but the necessity seldom arose. I mean that most of these bodies would, sooner or later, feel the need of a central body to which to turn for help and advice, or simply to put them in touch with other organizations elsewhere. It is certainly true that, on many liaison committees, C.A.R.D. sounded frighteningly militant to many of the members; but, if there had not existed an official, Government-sponsored body, perhaps a number of them would eventually have swallowed their fears and joined. As it was, the N.C.C.I. appeared to provide the link with other organizations, the help and advice; and so it became an excuse for not joining C.A.R.D.[1]

Accordingly, he sees the whole official community relations structure as a confidence trick. While he recognizes that so harsh a judgement is unfair to a minority of the local committees, in general he sees the committees as irrelevant to 'the struggle against racialism' and relevant only 'as a means of deceiving the general public' and as a means of camouflaging 'the actual voice of the black people in this country'. He says of the committees:

. . . a considerable proportion can now only be described as propagators of a moderate racialism, a great many more are shackled to local authorities determined to treat them as a department of the Council, and of the bulk of the rest the most charitable thing one can say is that they have no conception of what an adequate response to the current racial situation would constitute; further, even if individually effective in their local areas, collectively they have lost all resolution or capacity for initiative.[2]

Dummett's view is that this situation has arisen out of the fact that the Government's 'fundamental aim is to keep the black minority under control, not to give them a part in determining how things are run'.

Nandy and Dummett provided the most coherent written critiques of the voluntary liaison committees, but it would be wrong to imagine that they alone expressed doubts about the system. As pointed out earlier, the association of the grant system with the immigration restrictions proposed in the same White Paper immediately created doubts in some people's minds.

[1] M. Dummett, 'Immigrant Organizations' (Background paper for a talk given at the Third Annual Race Relations Conference, Queen Elizabeth College, London, 19–20 September 1968), p. 8.
[2] Ibid., p. 15.

Community relations committees are not unlike quasi-official biracial committees in the United States which had, by 1965, come under similar attacks as organizations which cannot effectively challenge the *status quo*.[1] There seems some basis for suspecting that the 1965 White Paper suggestions may have been partly derived from Dean and Rosen's *Manual of Intergroup Relations*,[2] a book which has been criticized in the United States for naive consensual assumptions.[3]

If we turn now to the attitude of the N.C.C.I. we will see that, whatever else can be said about the N.C.C.I., it can never be claimed that they were insensitive to their critics. Right from the start the N.C.C.I. recognized the difficulties in establishing coherent roles for local committees, and the need for diversity and a wide range of experiment. They were seldom dogmatic about activities deemed appropriate or inappropriate to local committees, and they rarely went beyond the lines laid down in the White Paper in prescribing the exact form a V.L.C. should take. In their second annual report they show some sensitivity to the arguments going on about the roles of local committees. In it they discuss the methods appropriate to local committees, pointing out the futility of trying to make these organizations all-embracing, and the need to recognize that there is scope for a variety of organizations to work together, some using more direct approaches and others being less direct in 'persuading a society which has become multi-racial in fact that it must also become so in spirit'.

They go on to emphasize that the liaison committee should opt for a subtle approach, but recognize that this involves walking a 'tightrope':

A body dedicated simultaneously to liaison, conciliation, the eradication of injustices and the propagation of a new spirit is constantly confronted by choices which seem impossible to make. Success depends on retaining the confidence of the authorities in order that one's views will be heeded when it comes to policy-making. No less important, however, is the confidence of immigrants, who may often interpret

---

[1] L. Killian and C. Grigg, *Racial Crisis in America* (Englewood Cliffs, N.J., Prentice Hall, 1964).

[2] J. P. Dean and A. Rosen, *A Manual of Intergroup Relations* (Chicago, University of Chicago Press, 1955).

[3] J. N. McKee, 'Community Power Strategies in Race Relations', *Social Problems* (Vol. 6, No. 3, 1958–9).

co-operation with the authorities as condonation of what may be discriminatory policies and who, like any other man in the street, are inevitably unaware of many of the victories achieved by intensely difficult and intricate operations, some of which must inevitably take place behind the scenes.[1]

They recognize that local committees will have to decide when it is best to remain working behind the scenes and when, for tactical reasons or to retain the confidence of members, it is necessary to protest publicly. They also point out that organizations 'balanced on this tightrope' will be 'vulnerable to criticism from others whose contribution is equally important but who do not carry the same responsibility'.

Their answer to Nandy and Rex's criticisms is that backdoor lobbying may be more valuable than outspoken criticism of local authorities, and if this fails there may be situations which justify outspoken criticism. In any case the N.C.C.I. certainly shows an awareness of the pressure group role for local committees which was lacking in their previous year's report or in the 1965 White Paper. Whether by this time the structures and relationships with local authorities developed by most committees made it possible for the latter to adopt such a role in any effective way is another matter, with which we will be concerned later. The above quotations show that the N.C.C.I. recognized that the 'determination of role' problem was still a very real one. Much of our research is concerned with the way in which the local committees have sought to meet this problem.

Towards the end of their short life, the N.C.C.I. began to grope towards an approach to the role problem. This was symbolized by the change of the name used for local committees from 'voluntary liaison committees' to 'community relations committees', and ultimately in the transformation of the N.C.C.I. into the Community Relations Commission.

Several different developments contributed to this change of emphasis. First, clearly, it owed a great deal to events in the United States during this period. During the early 1960s Americans began to recognize that the plight of the Negro was not one that could be removed merely by bringing an end to discrimination. Attention began to turn from the legal issue of civil rights to the

---

[1] *Report for 1967*, pp. 13–14.

problems of poverty, unemployment, and urban decay. This awakened concern was evidenced in the poverty programme, in the writings of Kenneth Clark,[1] and in the Moynihan[2] and Kerner[3] Reports. The next stage in the battle for Negro equality was seen to involve something more than the provision of equal opportunity in the strict legal sense. It involved an assault on the problems of the Northern cities, in which the underprivileged Negroes themselves would need to be involved, if possible in alliance with other underprivileged groups.

Such a development in thinking in the United States corresponded well with a line of thought which had been pursued for some years by some English radical intellectuals, particularly by Professor Titmuss[4] who had long recognized the weakness of the 'equality of opportunity' concept of equality and who had criticized the *status quo* approach to social work described by Nandy. Between 1965 and 1968 English radicals of this persuasion were going through the traumatic experience of discovering that the election of a Labour government was in no way producing the kind of radical social changes they had looked for. Many of them turned their attention to the development of pressure groups to work for social changes. The Child Poverty Action Group and Shelter were typical creations of this period. These pressure groups discovered that to operate merely as a group of intellectuals, influential in enlightened middle-class circles, and sometimes able to gain the attention of Parliament was not sufficient. Some of them began to try to organize the poor and the underprivileged to agitate for their own rights. Good examples of this are the Notting Hill Summer Project and Community Workshop and the squatters' movement.

Hence, when Nandy reviled the social work approach in 1967, it was already under attack from within the social work professions. In the United States a substantial branch of social work concerned with community development had already grown up, trying to face up to political realities and to recognize that its role might be to create social change rather than simply to reform

---

[1] K. Clark, *Dark Ghetto, Dilemmas of Social Power* (London, Gollancz, 1965).

[2] *The Negro Family: the Case for National Action* (Office of Policy Planning and Research, United States Department of Labour, 1965).

[3] *Report of the National Advisory Committee on Civil Disorders* (Washington, United States Government, 1968).

[4] R. M. Titmuss, *Commitment to Welfare* (London, Allen & Unwin, 1968).

individuals.[1] In England, the Gulbenkian Foundation had agreed in 1965 to finance an 'enquiry into the nature and extent of community work with a view to making proposals for training'.[2] Just as 'participation' was becoming the slogan for the young political activist, so social work agencies were increasingly beginning to talk of 'community work', 'community development', and 'community organization'. When the Gulbenkian committee reported in 1968, they entitled their report 'Community Work and Social Change'. Even though it is reasonable to suggest that they had not fully thought out the political implications of this kind of community work, they had begun to recognize the close connexion between community work and social change.

The report which the Community Relations Commission published a few months after it was set up seemed to appreciate the need for new approaches, without spelling out with any clarity what these approaches really involved. The Commission defined 'two major challenging tasks':

to plan for itself and for the local councils associated with it a consistent course of action which can be clearly seen to serve the basic aim of promoting harmonious community relations and which can be pursued steadfastly in the face of what ever tensions and conflicts may arise in future from various sources.

And:

the development of a new professional discipline and expertise for social workers specialising in the field of community relations.[3]

These tasks seem to involve the achievement of a sense of purpose within the community relations movement that would enable it to put itself out of reach of the controversy that had so damaged the N.C.C.I. They suggest that there is work to be done which will enable the Commission to be judged by other criteria than its success or failure in influencing government policies, and that this work will involve laying the foundations of a new and sophisticated form of social work. Our study was largely carried out at about the time this first report of the C.R.C. was written. This book will be concerned with examining the implications of the way in which the C.R.C. defined and implemented its tasks.

[1] B. J. Frieden and R. Morris (eds.), *Urban Planning and Social Policy*, Parts IV and VI (New York, Basic Books, 1968).
[2] *Community Work and Social Change* (London, Longmans, 1968), p. 1.
[3] *Report for 1968–9*, p. 13.

CHAPTER 2

The Eight Areas

This chapter provides a brief profile of each of the eight areas covered by the community relations committees we studied, to form a background against which their operations can be seen in perspective. An attempt has been made to portray the social and political climate of the 'communities' in which the community relations committees are working and to give an indication of the explicit or overt support or opposition which the committees have to take into consideration.

The local authority areas served by the eight committees vary to quite a considerable extent. The whole of Tower Hamlets could be classified as a twilight urban area with advanced decay centred on the western boundary. In the bigger county boroughs, the contrast in the provision of services and the social composition of the inner city wards and the suburban areas, is more marked. The proportion of black immigrants in the local population is not of itself an indicator of the social needs and deprivations of an area. This is a fallacy which the then Prime Minister, Harold Wilson, helped to perpetuate when he announced the Urban Programme in the backwash of the Powell debate, and described it as a programme of assistance to immigrant areas, in which the problem to be relieved derived quite simply from the presence of immigrants in those areas.[1] Nor is the measure of the percentage of coloured immigrants in the local population any indicator as to whether immigration and race have become a local political issue.

A description of each of our eight areas including an outline of the social composition of the resident population, the size and general location of the immigrant 'communities', the style of local politics, and the nature of the main local social, economic, and political problems should serve to clarify these points further.

[1] Rose *et al.*, op. cit., p. 622.

TABLE 2.1

SOCIAL COMPOSITION OF THE EIGHT AREAS

according to the Registrar-General's classification of socio-economic groups for economically active males

	Tower Hamlets %	Hackney %	Birmingham %	Bradford %	Sheffield %	Huddersfield %	Wycombe %	Ealing %
Professionals, employers, and managers S.E.G. 1, 2, 3, 4, 13	5·4	8·5	10·1	11·0	12·9	14·4	14·0	16·8
Skilled manual S.E.G. 8, 9, 12, 14	41·9	44·9	44·8	40·3	45·8	42·0	46·1	38·4
Semi-skilled manual S.E.G. 7, 10, 15	19·3	18·2	20·5	24·5	16·1	20·3	15·4	14·4
Unskilled manual S.E.G. 11	18·2	10·9	8·8	8·6	10·1	7·5	6·9	7·0
Total S.E.G. 7, 8, 9, 10, 11, 12, 14, 15	79·4	74·0	74·1	73·4	72·0	69·8	68·4	59·8
No. of economically active males	63,760	77,670	344,310	89,860	153,190	41,030	17,740	98,100

Source 1966 Census, Economic Activity Tables

Table 2.1 shows that London boroughs, one inner and one outer London borough, represent the two extremes in the social composition of the eight areas. Tower Hamlets has both the lowest proportion of its economically active males in professional, managerial, and employing occupations, and the highest proportion in manual work. It also has the highest proportion of male workers in unskilled manual work. Ealing stands at the other end of the spectrum with a higher proportion of its working males in professional, managerial, and employing categories, and a lower proportion than any other area of its men in both manual work and unskilled manual work.

The new London borough of Ealing is made up of three former non-county boroughs in Middlesex: Acton, Ealing, and Southall. The borough is a long one running east–west along the main railway line to the West Country. Acton and Southall are both industrial areas containing a wide range of modern factories, many of which were established in the inter-war period. By contrast much of 'old' Ealing is a favoured middle-class residential area. It is fair to say that the new borough of Ealing lacks any over-all common identity. All three old boroughs approached their 'marriage' under the London Government Act of 1963 with considerable misgivings.

Immigrants have moved in fairly large numbers into Southall and to a lesser extent into Acton, but are largely absent from the Ealing area. Southall is notable for the fact that it contains the largest Punjabi community in Britain.

The 1966 Census estimates (which do not identify coloured children born in Britain, and which underestimate immigrants)[1] offer the following figures for the Borough of Ealing:

| Population | Numbers born in | | |
	West Indies	India	Pakistan
292,750	4,550	8,700	570

Persons born in West Indies, India or Pakistan form, according to this estimate, 4.9 per cent of the population.

Because the inadequacy of the 10 per cent census figures are recognized, there is a tendency for extravagantly high estimates

---

[1] Rose *et al.*, op. cit., Chapter 10, for a discussion of underenumeration.

of the 'actual' number of the coloured population to be bandied around to serve the particular purposes of certain political groups. The Department of Education and Science gave the following figures for 'immigrant' pupils—their definition of 'immigrant' is someone born abroad or whose parents have been here for less than ten years—in maintained primary and secondary schools in Ealing, for January 1968, as 17·3 per cent and 14·6 per cent respectively.[1] Generally the Caribbean population is to be found in the Acton part of the borough and the Sikhs in the Southall part.

Punjabi Sikhs began to settle in Southall in the mid-1950s.[2] By July 1960, the Indian Workers' Association in Southall claimed a membership of 900 and in December 1962 opened their own welfare centre in Featherstone Road. By 1961, there were 2,259 persons born in India, Pakistan, and West Indies in the borough of Southall's population of 52,983, according to the Census. In 1964, the Town Clerk's department in Southall estimated the borough's coloured population at 6,500.

By 1961, a certain amount of agitation began to develop about immigrants in Southall. The *Middlesex County Times* Southall column 'Notes and News' reported that 'the growth of the coloured population in Southall is causing concern among residents' according to council election canvassers and that some members of Southall Chamber of Commerce felt that 'Southall has its fair share of coloured people'.[3] In August 1961, Martyn Grubb, later to become Ealing I.F.C.'s community relations officer, attacked colour prejudice in Southall. The report of his sermon at St. John's Church was inevitably given the misleading headline: 'Southall has serious colour problem—priest.'[4] In the autumn of 1961, the Labour-controlled Southall Borough Council was attacked for not doing enough to prevent overcrowding. One of the Labour members, Councillor Steele, expressed hostility towards immigrants at a council meeting. In November 1961, however, George Pargiter, the town's Labour M.P., attacked the Commonwealth Immigrants Bill and during 1962 engaged in continuing controversy over it with the prospective Tory parliamentary candidate, Barbara Maddin. In April 1962, the Divisional

---

[1] P.S.C. (13 February 1969).
[2] P. Marsh, *Anatomy of a Strike* (London, I.R.R. Special Series, 1967).
[3] *Middlesex County Times* (April 1961).   [4] Ibid. (August 1961).

Education Executive decided to admit no more Indian children to Beaconsfield Road School, a decision which marked the beginning of their subsequent policy of dispersal.

In 1963 the British National party began to organize in Southall. Judging from the *Middlesex County Times*, it was from then onward that anti-immigrant activity really began to build up in the town. In the Southall Borough Council elections in May 1963 the B.N.P. contested two Labour-held wards, getting 479 votes in Hambrough Ward and 257 in Glebe Ward. Labour's Councillor Steele, who was becoming increasingly noticeable for his anti-immigrant statements, commented: 'The B.N.P. votes are resentment votes. Our ward (Hambrough) is rapidly turning into a slum area and people have voted for the B.N.P. to register their protest.' During the mayoral year 1962–3, Councillor Steele was leader of the Labour group on the Council, in place of Alderman Hopkins who was Mayor that year.

The early months of 1963 also saw the beginning of agitation by the white residents in the Burns Avenue–Palgrave Avenue area who wished to prevent Indians moving into their part of town. The movement was to grow into the notorious Southall Residents Association. In July, Southall Borough Council agreed to a proposal for a subcommittee of the health committee to study problems arising from multi-occupation. In August, the Council considered a petition presented by 625 white residents urging them to buy vacant properties in Dormers Wells Ward to prevent the 'silent invasion' of immigrants. After a meeting which ended in an uproar from petitioners, the Council agreed to set up a special committee to look into allegations made in this and two other petitions, to accept an Indian Workers' Association request for a meeting 'to discuss urgent problems being faced by the Indian community in Southall', and to consider the Southall Trades Council's request for the local authority to join the newly-established International Friendship Committee. Towards the end of September, the Borough Council's subcommittee submitted its first report, agreed to meet the I.W.A. and to send observers (Alderman Hopkins, Labour, and Councillor Ward, Conservative) to the I.F.C. meeting, and reported it could not buy houses to prevent immigrants doing so. The subcommittee also proposed to ask the Government for stricter legislation on overcrowding and a total ban on immigration. This last point is significant coming from a subcommittee with five Labour members, including Alderman Hopkins and deputy leader Steele, to three Conservatives. Presumably because it was totally at variance with the line taken by George Pargiter and the Parliamentary Labour party, the Labour group secured the dropping of this recommendation at the Council meeting in favour of a resolution requesting the M.P. to ask for legislation to prevent immigrant entry to towns such as Southall. This 'walls round Southall' policy recommended by the Labour Borough Council was to be echoed five years later by the Tories in Birmingham.

Under the London Government Act, Southall was to be absorbed into the Greater London borough of Ealing in May 1965. During the Greater London Council election in April 1964, the election for the new Ealing Borough Council in May 1964, and the general election of October 1964, the B.N.P. was active and the Southall Residents Association, set up in October 1963, produced a mass of anti-immigrant propaganda. It can be fairly said that with the exception of one unsuccessful Labour candidate in the borough election, none of the candidates really opposed this standpoint. Some, including notably the Conservative Parliamentary candidate, gave implicit support to it.[1]

Anti-immigrant agitation was conducted by the B.N.P. and the Southall Residents Association through meetings, deputations, petitions, and an incessant stream of letters to the Press focussing on issues of health and housing. The attempt to keep immigrants out of the Dormers Wells area continued, the Southall Residents Association first trying to influence local estate agents and later investigating the possibility of entering the business themselves.

Education too became an increasingly controversial issue. Having earlier decided to try to keep down the proportion of black children in Beaconsfield Road school, the Divisional Executive initiated a policy of dispersal. One of the more unsavoury consequences of this was that the parents of children at a number of schools to which black children were sent, notably Lady Margaret Primary School, in autumn 1963 organized a protest and made allegations about the standards of health and cleanliness of Indian children. By 1965 the Divisional Executive was beginning to look outside its area for new schools to which it

[1] Deakin (ed.), op. cit., and Foot, op. cit.

could disperse 'immigrant' children and it was agreed that the new Ealing Borough education authority should be asked to formulate a policy on this matter. Meanwhile, Southall Borough Council continually insisted to its critics, the Southall Residents Association and others, that it was dealing as firmly as it could with overcrowding and other alleged breaches of the law by immigrants. It was during this period that George Pargiter, Southall's Labour M.P., changed his position on immigration control to conform with Labour's impending White Paper. Although Ealing's community relations committee originated in the voluntary Southall I.F.C. set up during this turbulent period, the close involvement of the committee in local politics belongs to the years since 1965. The above account gives the flavour of Southall politics. The interrelations of politics and race in this area will be discussed in Chapter 8.

Tower Hamlets presents a very different picture as an area. Composed of the former boroughs of Stepney, Bethnal Green, and Poplar, the borough of Tower Hamlets contains extensive warehouse and docking facilities and a still thriving though gradually declining industrial sector comprising in particular cloth manufacturing in the west side of the borough, food distribution based on Spitalfields Market, docking and shipping, furniture manufacturing, and brewing. The area has experienced a drastic decline in population during the course of the century. In 1901 the total population of the three boroughs was 597,106. By 1951 it was 229,118, and by 1966, 196,830.

The East End's squalor and poverty, graphically documented since Charles Booth's day, and its centuries-old tradition as a reception area for immigrants are well known. The first influx of Huguenots followed the Massacre of St. Bartholomew in 1572, but the largest influx was caused by the Revocation of the Edict of Nantes over a century later. Between 1685–7, over 100,000 Huguenots fled to England and Ireland, and 15,000 settled in London, mainly in the East End where they re-established their silk weaving industry in the Spitalfields area.

From the 1840s onwards the Irish began to come to St. Georges in the East, Whitechapel, in significant numbers.[1] The great influx of East European Jews began in the 1870s. After

---

[1] K. Leech, 'Ghettoes in Britain', *Institute of Race Relations Newsletter* (July 1965).

1880 their geographical concentration in Whitechapel became more intense.[1]

	Stepney			London
Year	Population	Aliens	Russians and Poles	Russians and Poles
1871	275,567	14,030	3,435	5,294
1881	282,676	15,998	6,682	8,709
1891	285,225	32,374	22,029	26,742

By 1901, 42,032 of the 53,537 Russians and Poles in London were living in Stepney. Between 1891–1901, the proportion of aliens in Whitechapel had risen from 21·4 per cent to 31·8 per cent. Some streets in Spitalfields had become 95–100 per cent Jewish, e.g. Old Montague Street and Goulston Street.[2] Sir William Marriott, Conservative M.P. for Brighton, observed in the Commons after a day's excursion to the East End: 'There are streets you may go through and scarcely know you are in England.'[3]

Leech has demonstrated how the most cohesive immigrant group in East London today, the Pakistanis, are living in precisely those areas and streets in Spitalfields previously inhabited by Jews and Huguenots, in particular Old Montague Street, Princelet Street, where Muslim names on the electoral list for 1964 accounted for 44·4 per cent (132 out of 195) and 60·9 per cent (92 out of 151) of the total, and other streets off Brick Lane.[4] John Garrard has pointed out the similarity in the protests levelled against Jewish immigrants at the turn of the century and those levelled at present-day Commonwealth immigrants.[5] But Elizabeth Burney has emphasized: 'It is important to realise that in sheer numbers, immigrants in the East End in the 1960s are nothing like so significant as those of 60–80 years ago, although they appear more clearly in the shrunken population.'[6] The ratio of the sexes in the Russian–Polish immigration was surprisingly close to even,

---

[1] Lloyd P. Gartner, 'Immigrants in London in the 1880s', in J. L. Blau *et al.*, *Essays on Jewish Life and Thought Presented to Salo Baron* (New York, Columbia University Press, 1959), p. 237.   [2] Leech, op. cit.

[3] Hansard, 4S H(8) 1205, 11 February 1893, quoted by J. Garrard, 'Parallels of Protest', *Race* (Vol. 9, July 1967), p. 49. See also Foot, op. cit., Chapters 1 and 2.

[4] Leech, op. cit.   [5] Garrard, op. cit.

[6] E. Burney, *Housing on Trial* (London, Oxford University Press, for Institute of Race Relations, 1967), p. 82.

whereas this is not the case with the Pakistani community in East London.

The 1966 Census classifies 17,420 people in Tower Hamlets as born outside the British Isles. Of these, 11,270 come from Commonwealth countries, colonies, and protectorates. The main Commonwealth immigrant groups are as follows:

| | Numbers born in | | | % total | |
Population	West Indies	India	Pakistan	population	Cyprus
196,830	3,580	2,100	2,040	3·9	1,410

Asians and Cypriots are living mainly in the Spitalfields (western) end of the borough, West Indians in the Tredegar Square, Bow, and Mile End area.

Political life in the East End has always been very alive. Extreme right and left-wing groups have expressed their opinions of the East End community and its poverty in very different ways during the century. In the 1920s, Poplar was the first borough to elect a wholly Labour Council. In 1933 Stepney Borough Council included twelve Communist party members. In 1945 Mile End sent one of the only two Communist M.P.s to Westminster. The 1930s witnessed the mobilization of the para-military British Union Movement by Oswald Mosley, and the 'battle' of Cable Street in 1936. In the 1937 municipal elections, the British Union of Fascists candidates polled a higher proportion of votes in Bethnal Green than in any other part of Britain.[1]

Currently the Council in Tower Hamlets is Labour-controlled. It is one of the only metropolitan boroughs to have resisted the 1968 swing to the Tories. Social problems remain very acute in the area. Despite considerable amounts of building by the local authorities (one-third of all the slum clearance undertaken by the L.C.C. between 1945 and 1964 took place in the East End although this area formed only 6·5 per cent of the county),[2] housing problems still remain acute.[3] In January 1967 Bob Mellish, Joint Parliamentary Secretary to the Ministry of Housing and Local Government, stated that the borough had 13,854 slum

---

[1] J. H. Robb, *Working Class Antisemite* (London, Tavistock, 1954), p. 207.

[2] *East End Housing, 1964* (London, L.C.C., 1964).

[3] *Report of the Committee on Housing in Greater London* (Milner Holland Report), Cmnd. 2605 (London, H.M.S.O., 1965), p. 88.

terraced houses: 8,354 more than any other borough in London.[1] In addition 8,166 tenement dwellings were recognized as substandard, of which only a half were suitable for improvements.

The metropolitan borough of Hackney, formerly the boroughs of Hackney, Shoreditch, and Stoke Newington has also served as a reception area for immigrants, in many cases as a second stage after initial settlement in Aldgate, Whitechapel, and Stepney. In the early part of the century, Jews from Russia and East Europe were by far the largest group of immigrants. Immigration from the Commonwealth is a relatively far more recent phenomenon. Unlike Ealing and Tower Hamlets, Hackney is an area of predominantly West Indian immigration. The 1966 Census gives the following figures:

Population	Numbers born in West Indies	India	Pakistan	% of total population	Cyprus
244,210	14,640	2,340	420	7·1	3,400

Department of Education and Science figures give the proportion of 'immigrant' schoolchildren in maintained primary and secondary schools in the borough, at January 1968, as 26·2 per cent and 19·6 per cent.[2] Unlike Ealing Borough Council, the Inner London Education Authority has never implemented any 'dispersal' policy.

With a large proportion of Jewish people living in the borough in the past, Hackney has had experience of right-wing racialist propaganda since before the war. Even the more visible immigration of West Indians in the 1950s did not altogether change the focus of fascist attack. Disturbances occurred occasionally in the Ridley Road area of Dalston and elsewhere. In July 1965 Lea Bridge Road Synagogue was one of the targets of widespread incendiary attacks on North, North-West, and East London synagogues by the National Socialist Movement.[3] In January 1966 a gang of thirteen Hackney boys stabbed a young orthodox Talmudic student and an old Jewish man.[4] In the

---

[1] Quoted in F. W. Skinner (ed.), *People Without Roots* (Tower Hamlets Council of Social Service), and Burney, op. cit.
[2] P.S.C. (13 February 1969).   [3] *Hackney Gazette* (12 September 1967).
[4] Ibid. (21 January 1966).

March 1966 general election, Sir Oswald Mosley tried to make a political comeback as Union Movement candidate in neighbouring Finsbury and Shoreditch but lost his deposit.

Nevertheless the political *élite* in Hackney took a less ambiguous line than in Ealing. The Labour party had control of Hackney Borough Council uninterruptedly from the Second World War until 1968 and local Labour politics has been characterized by a disproportionately large Jewish participation. Reference has already been made in Chapter 1 to the appointment of an information officer in the Town Clerk's department by the Borough Council in 1959. More recently, Borough councillors have not hesitated to express their viewpoint both in an official and unofficial capacity on the subject of race relations. David Pitt, one of the G.L.C. members for Hackney, a West Indian who is now vice-chairman of the Community Relations Commission, strongly condemned the Government 1965 White Paper on immigration and resigned from the London Labour party executive in protest.[1] Councillor Clinton Davies, Mayor of Hackney during 1968–9, moved a resolution at a Council meeting in November 1965 urging the Government not to act on proposals set out in Part 2 of the White Paper, requesting the strengthening of the Race Relations Act 1965, and the sponsoring and financing by the Government of vastly increased research into all aspects of immigrant welfare. The motion was carried by 30–1.[2] David Weitzman, Labour M.P. for Stoke Newington, joined Norman Atkinson, Labour M.P. for neighbouring Tottenham, in calling for the abandonment of the 1965 White Paper on the grounds that it was based on muddled thinking.[3] In a Commons debate on the Race Relations Act Amendment Bill, Weitzman asserted that the Act had not gone any great distance towards achieving the desired objectives.[4] In December 1966, Hackney Borough Council decided it would not in future offer work to contractors operating a colour bar. A clause was inserted in all subsequent contracts that there must not be discrimination on grounds of colour, race, ethnic national origin, religion or sex.[5] On 29 February 1968, the Council passed a motion urging the Government to 'withdraw the Commonwealth Immigration Bill,

---

[1] *Hackney Gazette* (10 August 1965).   [2] Ibid. (26 November 1965).
[3] Ibid. (28 September 1965).   [4] Ibid. (30 December 1966).
[5] *Stoke Newington Observer* (30 December 1966).

embodying as it does the principle that different standards are to be applied to white and coloured holders of British passports'.[1]

There had not been complete unanimity during the period of a 100-per-cent Labour Council, but voices of dissent were restricted to one or two. For example, in 1965, in opposition to Councillor Clinton Davies' proposal, condemning the controls proposed in the 1965 White Paper, Councillor Lee maintained that immigration should be banned for five years to give England a breathing space.[2]

Labour's monopoly in Hackney was brusquely brought to an end in the May 1968 elections which returned thirty-one Conservative, twenty-seven Labour, and two Liberal Councillors. In Dalston Ward, an area of heavy West Indian concentration, three Conservatives (including one Independent Conservative) stood on a racialist platform and two were returned.[3]

Hackney is a borough with severe social problems. It was described as an area of worsening housing stress by the Milner Holland Committee.[4] Hackney's tradition of absorbing immigrants is in some ways both a strength and a weakness. The avoidance of trouble in the past is too much of an inducement to remain complacent in the present, an attitude sometimes typified in the columns of the local *Hackney Gazette*. At a conference of editors of London papers organized by the N.C.C.I., the editor of the *Hackney Gazette* maintained that East London had a 'traditional spirit of give and take', that it had come sensibly through many large-scale influxes of immigrants, but that the process was above all a gradual one which could not be accelerated by legislation against discrimination. The 'Viewpoint' column of the *Gazette* maintained that 'even with the acceleration of immigration from Commonwealth countries in the post war years, East London has not been conscious of any pressing problem' and that 'with a little more patience and a good example, it (the objectives of the Street Report) could be achieved without starting up the chilly processes of the law'.[5]

Moving on now to Birmingham, it is very difficult to convey a clear picture of this vast city, lying as it does at the centre of a

---

[1] *Hackney Gazette* (1 March 1968).   [2] *Hackney Gazette* (26 November 1965).
[3] Ibid. (5 March 1968) and also *Stoke Newington Observer* (15 September 1967) for a statement by one successful candidate, Councillor G. Jones.
[4] *Report on Housing* . . ., p. 90.   [5] *Hackney Gazette* (3 November 1967).

growing conurbation. The report on the region by the Department of Economic Affairs provided what is perhaps the best brief
pen portrait of this complex area:

The conurbation itself is a pepperpot mixture of Nineteenth and
Twentieth century, with renewal and dereliction and industrial and
residential areas often cheek by jowl. Some parts are pleasant, especially
on the fringes. Some of the town centres, especially the city centre of
Birmingham, are being extensively modernised. But there are also
widespread areas of mean streets, twilight housing and plain slums.
The atmosphere is one of activity, prosperity and growth, but a great
deal of congestion and decay as well.[1]

These contrasts strike the visitor to Birmingham rather forcefully.
It is hard to apply the concept of 'community' to this area of
51,600 acres and over a million inhabitants, governed by the
largest single all-purpose local authority in England and Wales.
     The D.E.A. report also contains a perceptive comment on
the impact of immigration upon this area:

Insofar as this immigration has had its problems, particularly in the
field of housing, education and health and welfare, these have been
mainly, in areas where difficulties in these fields have already been
fairly marked. From the point of view of a general study of the region,
they can be regarded as an additional symptom of an existing and
more general problem—that of labour shortage, housing deficiency and
general social stress, arising from continued concentration of employment and population in and around an already big, crowded and
partly outworn urban complex.[2]

     The West Midlands conurbation contains the next largest
proportion of the total Commonwealth immigrant population in
Britain, after London. The 1966 Census gave the following figures
for Birmingham:

Population	West Indies	Numbers born in India	Pakistan	% of total population
1,064,220	23,580	10,590	10,280	4·2

In 1968 the C.R.O. estimated the number of Commonwealth
immigrants and *their children* to be about 82,000. About 75 per
cent were living in the hitherto undeveloped middle ring of the

[1] *The West Midlands: A Regional Study* (London, Department of Economic Affairs,
H.M.S.O., 1965), p. 5.   [2] Ibid., p. 53.

city in the large Victorian houses built between 1860–1900 in Aston, Handsworth, Soho, Balsall Heath, Edgbaston, Moseley, and Sparkbrook. D.E.S. figures for the proportion of 'immigrant' schoolchildren in 1968 were 9·6 per cent and 8·0 per cent in primary and secondary schools respectively. This is an over-all figure which conceals the concentration at over 90 per cent to be found in some schools such as Grove Park in Handsworth, since the Education Department does not practise a dispersal policy.

Sporadic racialist activity had been occurring in Birmingham in the 1950s. In 1955, a 'Nationalist Association' was reported to be handing out leaflets demanding action against the 'coloured invasion'.[1] In 1955, Charles Collett, Conservative Councillor for Acocks Green, instigated his private 'investigation' into complaints of exploitation of Birmingham's housing shortage.[2] He was reported as stating: 'If we can make out a strong enough case we could ask the Government to control immigration.'[3] In November 1956, the Birmingham Citizens' Association was formed on non-party lines to seek legislation to restrict immigration. Their object was to ensure that an immigrant had a job to come to, means of support, no police record, and a clean bill of health.[4] By 1959 Councillor Collett was asserting that he would permit immigrants to come to Britain if they contributed more than they took out and if they had a coherent understanding of English, but that they should not have a vote for at least ten years nor be considered for a council house for at least five years, after which they should have a trial period in a substandard house.[5] In 1960 he was warning Birmingham of the 'menace of coloured immigration and a piebald population'.[6] In October 1960 the inaugural meeting of the Birmingham Immigration Control Committee (later called the Birmingham Immigration Control Association) was convened on Stroud council housing estate.[7] Councillor Collett became its chairman and a massive lobbying campaign was directed at councillors and Birmingham M.P.s, of whom Harold Gurden (Conservative, Selly Oak) and Martin Lindsey (Conservative,

---

[1] *Birmingham Evening Mail* (22 April 1955).
[2] *Birmingham Evening Despatch* (8 November 1955).
[3] *Birmingham Evening Mail* (9 November 1955).
[4] *Birmingham Evening Despatch* (9 November 1956).
[5] Ibid. (12 December 1959).   [6] Ibid. (7 January 1960).
[7] *Birmingham Evening Post* (29 October 1960). See also Foot, op. cit., pp. 195–206, for a description of growth, splits, and offshoots of B.I.C.A.

Solihull) had been among the most vociferous supporters of Cyril Osborne's call for immigration control since 1955. In the autumn of 1960 the *Birmingham Evening Despatch* attached a note to its correspondence columns stating that 'letters on the racial problem in Birmingham have produced the heaviest mailbag for some considerable time'.[1] Donald Finney's formation of a B.I.C.A. group in neighbouring Smethwick and his support for Peter Griffiths in the 1964 general election have been well documented elsewhere.[2]

In April 1965 the Conservative minority group on the City Council issued a statement drawn up for the Conservative candidates in the forthcoming municipal elections, stating that there was an estimated 70,000 coloured immigrants and children in Birmingham and that 'in our view this figure is too high. It ought not to be increased and if possible it should be reduced.' They called for closer health checks, strengthening of deportation provisions, a just repatriation scheme for workless immigrants, practical government assistance, and a council standing committee to review all matters arising from immigrant settlement.[3]

After the 1968 local elections, Birmingham's Conservative majority requested the Government either to restrict the flow of immigrants into their area or to stop them coming to England altogether for some years. The Tory group then set up a working party to prepare a brief showing that local bans on further immigration were not impracticable. On 19 June, a four-point plan presented by Council officers was put forward to the General Purposes Committee including demands for a further restriction of numbers coming in, and more government financial assistance to meet expenditure incurred in dealing with the immigrant population. During the Council debate following the General Purposes Committee report in July 1968, there was all-party support for the request for increased governmental financial aid. Argument was largely confined to the practicability of the call to restrict the inflow of immigrants to Birmingham. An amendment put forward by Labour to delete the request for restriction of immigration was heavily defeated.

---

[1] *Birmingham Evening Despatch* (14 October 1960). The letters published by Birmingham papers accounted for half of the newspaper clippings received by I.R.R. on subjects related to race in October 1960.

[2] Foot, op. cit., and Deakin (ed.), op. cit.　　[3] *Guardian* (1 April 1965).

On 20 April 1968 Enoch Powell used Birmingham as a platform for his first speech on immigration. His sentiments and misleading statistics had already been anticipated by the Conservative chairman of the Health Committee, Councillor E. Franklin, during the Council debate on the Kenya Asians Bill, on 28 February 1968,[1] and were echoed in January 1969 when Franklin alleged that the health services were in danger of breaking down and that people were not buying houses in Birmingham because of the presence of immigrants.[2] The gross inaccuracies of his statistics were exposed by the local Press,[3] but an attempt by the Labour minority on the City Council to force Franklin's resignation was unsuccessful.

Bradford provides a great contrast to Birmingham as far as open debate on race relations is concerned. Certainly, until recently, it would be fair to say a complacent view of race relations prevailed in Bradford. One author, commenting on the absence of immigration as a political issue in Bradford in the 1964 general election wrote:

Bradford must be unique among the centres of immigrant settlement in Britain. In a period of mounting interest in racial problems, the city continues to be the standing refutation of the argument that multiracial communities are inevitably beset by racial troubles. . . . A number of factors now widely recognised in the city and among interested commentators have been mentioned to explain this situation. The important economic role of the immigrants (for instance the virtual dependence of nightshift textile work on immigrant labour), the wise and tolerant attitude of the Telegraph and Argus, the long tradition of immigration to the City; the largely male social composition of the Pakistani group coupled with the declining English population acting to minimise pressure on housing, language and cultural barriers keeping contact and possible points of tension to a minimum, all these have combined to produce a situation of interracial stability.[4]

An examination of the *Telegraph and Argus* in 1964 and 1965 supports Spiers' account of the absence of political conflict on race but it also reveals an alarming complacency. Spiers' essay was reviewed in the local paper and his compliments to Bradford highlighted, but a correspondent subsequently pointed out that all that was benig demonstrated was that the communities

[1] 'Birmingham's Failure of Leadership', *New Statesman* (15 March 1968).
[2] *Tribune* (3 January 1969).   [3] *Birmingham Evening Post* (3 January 1969).
[4] M. Spiers in Deakin (ed.), op. cit., pp. 153–4.

'co-existed' but could hardly be said to be 'integrated'. There seems little doubt that many immigrants, and particularly Pakistanis, have been compelled to accept low wages, semi-segregation in industry, and poor housing. Several factors suggest they will be less inclined to tolerate such conditions in future. They are increasingly bringing wives and children here, the cultural and linguistic barriers which cut them off initially are inevitably falling as time passes, and a new generation is growing up much more conscious of inequalities. A complacent view based on interracial accommodation of a highly unequal kind is thus inherently dangerous.[1]

Bradford, like the East End boroughs of London, is not experiencing heavy immigration for the first time. In the years after the Irish famine it received a heavy influx of migrants from Ireland. There is in fact evidence of a certain amount of segregation of, and hostility to, the Irish during the nineteenth century.[2] Just as Irish labour helped to build up the wool textile industry, Pakistani labour has helped to keep it going. The problem today is that Bradford is still highly dependent upon its Victorian legacy. Its prosperity is very dependent upon the declining textile industry,[3] and it has a great deal of Victorian working-class housing which is undoubtedly substandard and subject to high private loan rates for purchase.[4] The textile industry has been eager to employ them, but Bradford is surely building up problems for the future.

The 1966 sample Census provided the following figures for Bradford:

---

[1] In fact, during the past few years, there have been various examples of racialist statements by politicians, not only from the extreme Tory fringe. For example, in November 1968, the leader of the Tory group on the Council, Alderman Horsfall, supported Birmingham's call for a complete ban on any more dependants. *Yorkshire Post* (18 November 1968).

[2] C. Richardson, 'Irish Settlement in Mid-Nineteenth Century Bradford', *Yorkshire Bulletin of Economic and Social Research* (Vol. 20, May 1968). In 1851, 26 per cent of the population of Bradford was Irish-born.

[3] Cohen and Jenner have shown that the willingness of migrants to work shifts, accept low rates of pay, and work with new equipment has enabled extensive new capital investment in the textile industry. 'The Employment of Immigrants: A Case Study Within the Wool Industry', *Race* (Vol. XI, July 1968).

[4] The National Building Agency reported that of a total stock of 100,000 Bradford houses, 40 per cent (all pre-1900) were unfit and recommended a 20-year clearance programme, and an annual rebuilding rate of 1,400 dwellings. *Telegraph and Argus* (29 April 1968).

Population	Numbers born in Pakistan	Numbers born in India	West Indies	% of total population
290,310	7,030	3,600	1,690	4·2

Underenumeration undoubtedly occurred, most acutely in the case of Pakistanis.[1]

The existence of underenumeration was so widely recognized that it was used as a reason to oppose the reduction of Bradford's Parliamentary representation proposed by the Boundary Commission.

Arrivals since 1966 have been quite considerable as many Indians and Pakistanis have brought families here recently. In a paper published in 1968, Bradford's Director of Education reported an influx of thirty to forty children per week.[2] An attempt to estimate the number of coloured Commonwealth immigrants and dependants including those born in Britain has been made since:

The exact number of coloured Commonwealth immigrants in the City is unknown but a recent survey by the Yorkshire Committee for Community Relations (January 1968) estimated a total of 38,000. This is thought to be somewhat on the high side and a figure of around 26,000 would probably be more realistic. Pakistanis predominate with some 18,000 and Indians (mostly Sikhs) about 6,000 and there are about 2,000 West Indians.[3]

Proportions of 'immigrant' schoolchildren have been given as 7·5 per cent and 9·2 per cent in primary and secondary schools respectively.[4]

Huddersfield presents a similar picture.[5] After the war, like Bradford, it attracted considerable numbers of central European refugees. More recently there has been a steady influx of immigrants from Eire and the coloured Commonwealth.[6] According

[1] D. Eversley and F. Sukdeo estimated underenumeration over the whole country as follows: Jamaicans, 10·2 per cent; rest of the Caribbeans, 12·2 per cent; Indians, 4·6 per cent; Pakistanis, 29·5 per cent. *The Dependents of the Coloured Commonwealth Population* (London, Oxford University Press, for Institute of Race Relations, 1969).
[2] Presented to I.R.R. conference, September 1968.
[3] G. Moore, 'One Step East', *Probation* (Vol. 14, No. 3, 1968), p. 79.   [4] P.S.C.
[5] For a picture of life see B. Jackson, *Working Class Community* (London, Routledge & Kegan Paul, 1968), and B. Jackson and D. Marsden, *Education and the Working Class* (London, Routledge & Kegan Paul, 1962).
[6] T. Burgin and P. Edson, *Spring Grove: the Education of Immigrant Children* (London, Oxford University Press, for Institute of Race Relations, 1967).

to the 1966 Census the total proportion of West Indians, Indians, and Pakistanis in the population are the same in Bradford and Huddersfield, but West Indians predominate in Huddersfield:

Population	West Indies	Numbers born in India	Pakistan	% of total population
130,210	2,390	1,570	1,330	4·1

The C.R.O. in January 1969 put the total coloured population including children at 10,500, comprising 5,000 West Indians, 4,500 Pakistanis, and 1,000 Indians, i.e. 8 per cent of the town's population. Residentially, coloured people are to be found primarily in the central areas of the city. A high concentration of Asians are in the Bradford Road and Lockwood area. Huddersfield has a large amount of cheap late-Victorian housing and, with a more or less static population, a lack of housing shortage. The C.R.O. has estimated that over 10 per cent of all council houses in Huddersfield are occupied by coloured families.

Huddersfield is perhaps more fortunate than Bradford in that it is not so highly dependent upon one industry, but has acquired large-scale engineering and chemical industries in addition to its textile industry. In general, the problems of change and decay seem more manageable in Huddersfield than in Bradford partly because of its continuing prosperity[1] and perhaps partly because it is a considerably smaller town.

Until recently there has been an absence of political controversy about immigration in Huddersfield. It is a strong Liberal-Labour area. Huddersfield's own M.P.s, J. P. W. Mallalieu and K. Lomas, are both Labour, and the nearby Colne Valley seat was the solitary Liberal gain from Labour in 1966. Until 1967, Labour was the largest single party on Huddersfield Town Council with a Liberal group holding the balance between them and the Conservatives. Since 1967 the Tories have the majority. During 1968, however, there were signs that the political silence on immigration was being broken. In April 1968 there was an unprecedented outburst of controversy about immigration in the letter pages of the *Huddersfield Examiner*. The National Front has been holding meetings in the town, writing to the Press, and put

---

[1] For a comment, but perhaps a rather exaggerated one, on Huddersfield's prosperity, see Jackson and Marsden, op. cit., p. 18.

up candidates for the Borough Council elections in May 1969. The major political parties have refused to debate with the National Front so as not to give them a platform but some of the newer Tory Councillors are known to have Powellite views and to sympathize with the National Front.

Our third Yorkshire city, Sheffield, differs from the other two in that it is not associated with a declining textile industry, although it has suffered from net losses of population since before the war. World-famous for its cutlery, the city is still flourishing industrially and is not faced with the labour shortage which has produced large-scale immigration elsewhere.

Another feature of Sheffield is the extent to which it has coped with its problems of urban decay. Since the Second World War Sheffield has made great strides both with the redevelopment of its city centre and with the clearance of its slums.

The 1966 Census gives the following figures for immigrants:

		Numbers born in		% of total
Population	West Indies	India	Pakistan	population
482,540	2,820	1,300	1,360	1·1

The C.R.O. in 1969 estimated that coloured immigrants and their children comprised 7,000 Pakistanis, 5,000 West Indians, 750 Arabs, and about 400 Africans and Indians. Most of the Asians live in the Attercliffe and Darnall areas at the east end of the city, and this settlement spreads into the adjoining County Borough of Rotherham. West Indians are primarily in the area of Pittsmoor, Crookesmoor, and Burngreave in the central, northern, and western parts of the city.

Four of Sheffield's constituencies are safe Labour seats (Attercliffe, Brightside, Hillsborough, and Park). One was a Labour gain in 1966 (Heely), and one is Conservative (Hallam). Sheffield Borough Council was Labour-controlled for many years, marginally lost to the Conservatives in 1968 but surprisingly regained by Labour against the national tide in 1969. There has been no substantial attempt to exploit race in Sheffield politics. Although the last year or two has seen some National Front activity this has had no real impact on local politics. There has been no attempt by Conservatives to exploit racialism. When the

P.E.P. Report implied that Sheffield's housing policy was discriminating in putting more emphasis on waiting time than on need,[1] the Conservative leader Alderman Hebblethwaite said his party would allocate on need alone.[2] When in power, the Conservatives gave local authority backing to a youth campaign against racialism. The only public major outburst to disrupt race relations was the speech of the Master Cutler in April 1969 in which he aligned himself with Enoch Powell.

Wycombe committee is based upon a non-county borough and its surrounding rural district. These two local authority areas contrast quite strongly. High Wycombe has a substantial working-class population and a significant urban core of small Victorian houses. The rural district contains largely modern middle- to upper-middle-class dwellings. The working class in the Wycombe area, and therefore the immigrants, are largely employed in local industries. Many of the middle-class people commute to London to work. It has the smallest population of all the eight areas studied. The 1966 Census gives the following figures for High Wycombe:

		Numbers born in		% of total
Population	West Indies	India	Pakistan	population
53,920	1,600	350	680	4·9

The local Conservative M.P., John Hall, disputes these figures and has suggested a proportion of 8–10 per cent. The Town Clerk considers this estimate to be an exaggeration and considers 7 per cent to be a reasonable estimate. Presumably this figure is meant to include immigrants and dependants.

Migrants have always been attracted to High Wycombe by its flourishing engineering works, light industry, and especially its furniture industry. An influx of people from Wales and Durham were attracted by the low unemployment rate in the 1930s. Recognition was made of the increasing number of Commonwealth immigrants to the area by 1960 in *The Times*,[3] and an

[1] Quoted in W. W. Daniel, *Racial Discrimination in England* (Harmondsworth, Penguin, 1968), p. 185.

[2] Despite this statement the Conservatives do not appear to have altered housing allocation policies while they were in power. We will show in Chapter 8 just how housing allocation policies remained a matter for concern in Sheffield which the community relations committee ignored.

[3] *The Times* (23 December 1960).

A.T.V. programme.[1] The letter pages of the *Bucks Free Press* were beginning to show a degree of unambiguous hostility towards coloured newcomers,[2] emanating in particular from Roberts Road residents, an area into which West Indians were then currently moving.[3] As far as local politics are concerned, race has not been an issue. The local Conservative M.P., John Hall, however, is a professed supporter of Enoch Powell, as is Ronald Bell, Conservative M.P. for the neighbouring South Buckinghamshire constituency.

Coloured immigrants are currently settled in the Bowerdeen and Priory Road areas and Desborough Road area in the central west and south-east of the town.

[1] In 'Gallery' series (9 February 1961).
[2] *Bucks Free Press* (21 April 1961, May 1961).
[3] Ibid., letter signed by one on behalf of 92 residents of Roberts Road. (Also 13 October 1961, July 1962.)

CHAPTER 3

The Concept of Community and Community Organization

When we started this project, we saw it primarily as a study of localized organizations setting out to try to formulate activities in a conflict-ridden situation, rather than as a contribution to the sociology of race relations. Our main hypothesis was that community relations committees would face problems arising from conflict between local authorities and other powerful institutions in the native British community on the one hand, and immigrants and their supporters on the other.

In the course of our researches we became increasingly aware of three things. First, a meaningful analysis of the relations between ethnic groups in any particular British town must rest upon a wide appreciation of the social situation of black people in the world today and of the British colonial legacy. Any belief that particular communities or localized areas can be regarded as islands, unaffected by the wider world, is a delusion. Second, any account of local power in Britain will be highly misleading if the dominance of central government over local government is not fully appreciated. This second proposition is also concerned with the impossibility of trying to examine local communities as isolated entities. Our third important consideration concerns the need to recognize that the local political units that do exist do not correspond with social units of any kind, and certainly not with units that might be dignified with the name 'communities'.

It was not part of our task either to provide an examination of race relations on a global or national basis, or an account of the structure and power of local government. These were underlying facts that had to be taken into account. What we will try to do in this book is to show that the formulation of policies designed to ameliorate race relations on the basis of narrow and misleading views of the nature of local social structures, and the positions of immigrants within those structures, leads to a situation in which those policies will tend to be irrelevant.

At the centre of our scepticism about the micro-sociological approach to race relations adopted by the community relations movement lies a view that there has been a failure to understand the social and political structure of the urban areas which are the so-called 'communities' to which community relations committees direct their attention. The concept of 'community' is altogether a problematical one to apply to the urban social structures within which most immigrants are found; lacking clarity of meaning, turning attention away from the wider problems of social power, and leading to erroneous assumptions about social cohesion.

The concept of 'community' has been the subject of much controversy among sociologists and has been used to mean an assortment of qualitatively different phenomena.[1] In 1955 George Hillery examined 94 definitions of 'community' and found that over three-quarters agreed that social interaction, geographic area, and common ties were commonly found in 'community' life.[2] Controversy still revolves around the element of geographic area in the definition. Don Martindale has removed the geography from the concept and equated community with a total social system and a total way of life.[3] Stein, on the other hand, has defined community as an organized system on a local basis standing in a determinate relationship with the wider environment and with large parts of the social system living outside the community so defined.[4] The question of the importance of the geographic element is closely connected with the issue of size and the rural-urban continuum in social relationships which has itself provoked much controversy.[5] The first urban sociologists, particularly Robert Park and the Chicago School, conceived the city as an anonymous social collection in which the traditional intimacy

[1] Margaret Stacey, 'The Myth of Community Studies', *British Journal of Sociology* (Vol. 20, No. 2, June 1969), and R. Pahl, *Patterns of Urban Life* (London, Longmans, 1970), Chapter 7.

[2] G. Hillery, 'Definitions of Community', *Rural Sociology* (Vol. 20, 1955).

[3] 'The Formation and Destruction of Community', in G. Zollschan and W. Hirsch (eds.), *Explorations in Social Change* (London, Routledge & Kegan Paul, 1964).

[4] M. Stein, *The Eclipse of Community* (Princeton University Press, 1960), pp. 100–1.

[5] R. Pahl, 'The Rural Urban Continuum', in R. Pahl (ed.), *Readings in Urban Sociology* (London, Pergamon Press, 1968), pp. 263–300.

and community of rural areas were minimal or not existent.[1] Sanderson, writing in 1919, argued that the term 'community' should be reserved completely for rural life.[2]

The notion of the 'rural urban continuum' whereby some have attempted to explain social characteristics by spatial location alone, appears to us to be virtually useless for the purpose of analysis, and has misled many of the authors of earlier studies of 'small communities' into assuming the integration of the community as if it were a matter of course and examining all other problems from that precondition.[3] In general the concept of community has been criticized for being 'a static concept containing no insights or guiding principles for the analysis of social change because it is basically descriptive rather than analytical.'[4]

The idea of 'community' underlies the theory of the 1965 White Paper on Immigration from the Commonwealth, and the recommendations of both the N.C.C.I. and the C.R.C. For this reason we cannot dismiss the notion without examining what relevance it may have. The third section of the White Paper, headed 'Integration', advocated that, to be successful, liaison committees must first satisfy the condition of being 'a joint project in which immigrant and host community are both fully involved'.[5] It is unclear what exactly is meant by 'community'. The structure which the C.R.C. prescribes for local committees implies what we shall call an '*élite* strategy', community involvement through securing the support of all the 'most powerful elements in the community'. On the other hand, the C.R.C. expects the local committees to be engaged in working with the 'community' in a much wider sense. The concept is used to refer to the whole population, white and black, in the area in which the committee is operating, for whom the committee will provide services or help to organize themselves. For example, in the notes for guidance for the formation of the committees, the general secretary of the

---

[1] L. Wirth, 'Urbanism as a Way of Life', *American Journal of Sociology* (Vol. 44, July 1938), and P. Sorokin and Zimmerman, *Principles of Urban–Rural Sociology* (New York, Henry Holt, 1929).

[2] D. Sanderson, 'Democracy and Community Organisation', *American Sociological Society*, quoted by Hillery, op. cit., and a view which Hillery shares.

[3] R. Redfield, *Tepoztlan, A Mexican Village* (Chicago, University of Chicago Press, 1931), and Oscar Lewis, *Tepoztlan—Village in Mexico* (New York, Henry Holt, 1960).

[4] R. Morris and J. Mogey, *The Sociology of Housing* (London, Routledge & Kegan Paul, 1965), p. 103.   [5] 1965 White Paper, para. 66.

N.C.C.I. stressed: 'It should be emphasised that this is not a committee to serve the interests of one section of the community but a committee to promote racial harmony. It is therefore beneficial to all.'[1]

We have mentioned how the word community has been used to refer to qualitatively different things. Dennis has argued that the term has been variously defined as 'Community meaning locality', 'Community meaning social intercourse' (as measured by the strength of interaction of members of the group), and 'Community meaning social control' (the community in this sense is delineated by common culture, the community group has common opinions and autonomous social control).[2] We will argue that all three aspects are embraced in the C.R.C.'s usage of the word. The community relations committees are locally based and refer to a specific geographic area. They are intended to promote harmonious relations in the 'community' in social interaction. They may also be used in some cases to try and persuade immigrants to 'conform' to the 'British way of life', and to channel and control incipient discontent.[3]

The concept of community has many potential ambiguous inferences and it is not surprising that the 'quest for community' has had an appeal to both Conservatives and to some on the radical left in the U.S.A.[4] It can connote a return to tradition-bound society[5] and an attempt to resist change and to buttress the existing power and authority structure.[6] But also, some radicals look forward to the achievement of a new sense of community, a new social order in which solidarity is achieved within small units of the population by a re-ordering of social relationships.[7] 'Community organization', the mobilization of groups of people to secure more power over their destinies is seen by some as a move in this direction. This is what Saul Alinsky,

[1] 'Notes for Guidance', circulated in April 1967.
[2] N. Dennis, 'The Popularity of the Neighbourhood Community Idea', *Sociologica Review* (Vol. 6, No. 2, 1958).
[3] I. Katznelson, 'The Politics of Racial Buffering in Nottingham 1954–68', *Race* (Vol. XI, No. 4, April 1970).
[4] D. P. Moynihan, *Maximum Feasible Misunderstanding* (New York, Free Press, 1969), Chapter 1.
[5] F. Tonnies, *Community and Association* (Transl. C. P. Loomis, London, Routledge & Kegan Paul, 1936).
[6] R. A. Nisbet, *The Quest for Community* (New York, University Press, 1953).
[7] P. Goodman, 'In Search of Community', *Commentary* (February 1960).

for example, has been trying to do for over three decades in the U.S.A.[1] But what the usage by both the Right and the Left have in common is the emphasis on the microlevel and to that extent they both represent what A. H. Halsey has called:

The persistent residue of a romantic protest against the complexity of modern urban society—the idea of a decentralised world in which neighbours could and should completely satisfy each others needs and legitimate demands for health, wealth and happiness.[2]

To return to the first approach envisaged by the C.R.C., how feasible is their recommendation that the *élites* in local communities—the commercial and industrial interests, the unions, the political parties—should be involved in the community relations committees?

In considering the idea of community in relation to community relations committees we are concerned solely with the urban community, albeit with urban communities ranging from small towns to large conurbations. Ceri Peach has pointed out that whereas 53 per cent of the population as a whole in England and Wales lived in towns of 50,000 or more in 1961, 89 per cent of the West Indians, 77 per cent of Indians, and 84 per cent of Pakistanis did so. Ranking towns with 50,000 or more people in three categories according to size, he also shows that the proportion of towns having West Indians, Indians, and Pakistanis increased with size and that the proportion of that population made up of West Indians, Indians, and Pakistanis also increased with size.[3] Community relations committees are thus inevitably operating in large urban areas.

Roland Warren defined 'community' in terms of local autonomy, coincidence of service areas, psychological identification with a community, and the strength of the 'horizontal pattern' (i.e. the relationship across the many different subsystems of the community to each other). The effect of what he calls the Great Change (the division of labour, the differentiation of

---

[1] C. Silberman, *Crisis in Black and White* (New York, Random House, 1964), pp. 318–45, and S. Alinsky, *Reveille for Radicals* (Chicago, Chicago University Press, 1945).

[2] 'Government against Poverty', unpublished paper presented to the Anglo-American Conference on the Evaluation of Social Action Programmes (1969).

[3] C. Peach, *West Indian Migration to Britain* (London, Oxford University Press, for Institute of Race Relations, 1968), pp. 76–9.

interests and association, the growth of bureaucratization, urbanization, the increasing systemic relations to larger society) has been the weakening of these four dimensions of community and the greater orientation of local community units to extra-community systems of which they are part, i.e. an increasing emphasis on vertical patterned relationships.[1] Stein similarly emphasizes the extent to which the processes of urbanization, industrialization, and bureaucratization have increased interdependence and decreased local autonomy.[2]

Margaret Stacey has pointed out that the presence or absence of certain institutions produce critical differences in the type of local social system that can be found.[3] Economic influences on community life may be locally sited but are often not locally controlled and are administered by a new managerial class which is in turn very mobile. The topic of 'community power' has provided a subject of controversy far more for American social scientists[4] than for their British counterparts, for whom it is a relatively neglected field. American studies have suggested that as a city grows from an isolated self-contained entity to one interrelated with the larger economy of the country, its power structure changes from a monolithic one dominated by persons with great economic power to a bifurcated structure comprising two critical and relatively discrete power sets, the economic dominants and the public leaders. Economic dominants appear to have reduced their ties to the political leadership and to a lesser extent they have also reduced their participation in civic associations especially where there is more absentee ownership.[5] Rose concludes: 'While community power structures seem to vary somewhat this is the pattern which is increasingly being revealed for industrialized cities, whereas the pattern of economic *élite* dominance is characteristic only of smaller towns and cities.'[6]

[1] R. Warren, *The Community in America* (Chicago, Rand McNally, 1963), p. 93, p. 161.
[2] Stein, op. cit.   [3] Stacey, op. cit.
[4] For a summary of the American debate, see A. Rose, *The Power Structure* (New York, Oxford University Press, 1967), pp. 255–98.
[5] British studies appear tentatively to confirm this. G. W. Jones, *Borough Politics* (London, Macmillan, 1969), A. H. Birch *et al.*, *Small Town Politics* (London, Oxford University Press, 1959), and F. Bealey, J. Blondel, and W. P. McCann, *Constituency Politics* (London, Faber & Faber, 1965). See also D. S. Morris and Ken Newton, 'Profile of a Local Political Elite', *The New Atlantis* (No. 2, winter 1970).
[6] A. Rose, op. cit., pp. 296–7.

The interlocking nature of these changes is well summarized by N. Dennis:

The typicality presents a picture of geographical specialisation. The form and contents of those activities which remain in the residential locality generally speaking are progressively less locally determined. Educational and industrial decision become increasingly centralised. Shops are managed by people who administer policies decided elsewhere with very little reference to the locality as such. The same is true of the field of local politics. Some activities remain in the locality . . . but each of these remains attached to the bottom of its own encapsulated hierarchy and is neither individually autonomous nor linked in any organic way to other institutions at this level.[1]

A strategy that advocates organizing local *élites* must come up against the problem that critical decisions for any locality are taken by people many of whom are unconnected with or uninterested in that locality. The fate of a local area is determined increasingly by changes in the urban infrastructure at the macro level.

We have consequently in our urban areas a situation in which the controllers of economic institutions continue to have a critical impact upon the quality of life in the towns, but play little part in the political institutions concerned with the social problems for which they and their predecessors are largely responsible. In the past economic dominants took an interest in local affairs to block interference with their activities. Today much of industry and commerce is too strong and insufficiently localized to have much to fear from local authorities. In this situation, the inevitable impotence of local government has led to increasing central government intervention.

Recognition of such developments is implicit in comments such as the following one on national influence on local action:

What is new is not the plight of cities however increasing their deterioration but rather . . . the locus of reform initiatives and resources is increasingly found on the level of national politics and foundations rather than in the political vitality, economic resources or the zealous initiatives of elites with local roots.[2]

---

[1] Dennis, op. cit.
[2] A. W. Gouldner, 'The Sociologist as Partisan, Sociology and the Welfare State' *American Sociologist* (Vol. III, No. 2, May 1968).

Though originally made in an American context this comment sums up the genesis and inspiration behind the British urban programme too.

We will consider in more detail further issues entailed in the Community Relations Commissions' recommendation of an *élite* strategy at the local level in our chapter on the relationship between the committees and the local authorities.

To return to the second aspect of the approach envisaged by the Commission, how feasible is their postulate of the existence of a 'community' white and coloured in the areas in which the community relations committees operate?

The 'meaningful' social area which people inhabit depends on class, life-cycle characteristics, length of residence, career pattern, and type of social network. The same physical situation will appear differently to different configurations of people with different social characteristics.[1] Several writers have emphasized that propinquity may be an initial cause of friendship formation but cannot be the final or sufficient cause and is outweighed in importance by factors such as homogeneity in social class, life-cycle stage, and ethnic origin.[2] Gans has shown how the rate of propinquity in friendship formation varies with sex and class. Children choose playmates on a propinquitous basis, though decreasingly as they get older. Women find female friends nearby, especially if they are mothers whose mobility is restricted. The higher the social class measured in terms of income, occupation, and education, the greater usually the physical mobility for visiting and entertaining.[3] In addition to having the means to maintain friendships over wider spatial areas, higher social classes may have moved more in the past and therefore their friends are likely to be scattered over a wider area.[4] Social mobility is likely to be an important variable explaining spatial mobility and consequently the spatial distribution of friends. The Community Attitudes Survey conducted for the Royal Commission on Local Government pointed out that:

[1] Pahl, *Patterns of Urban Life*, p. 106.
[2] H. Gans, 'Planning and Social Life', *Journal of American Institute of Planners* (Vol. 27, No. 2, May 1961), and 'The Balanced Community, Homogeneity or Heterogeneity?', ibid. (Vol. 27, No. 3, August 1961).
[3] Ibid.
[4] *Community Attitudes Survey*, Research Study No. 9 for Royal Commission on Local Government (London, H.M.S.O., 1969), p. 38.

6

There is a tendency for a greater proportion of electors of a lower socio-economic status to have lived in the 'home' area for over 20 years.[1]

and:

Informants in lower socio-economic groups, of a lower level of educational attainment and in particular of the greatest length of residence tend more frequently to have a larger proportion of their total circles of relatives and friends, living within the boundary of their 'home' area. Thus they may be said to possess more clustered community patterns.[2]

Clusters of social networks may in certain circumstances coincide with a temporarily limited area, such as old mining or dockland communities, but the more complex methods of production and distribution in highly industrialized societies, as well as the possibilities for physical mobility, have accelerated the disintegration of locally-based social networks. Ruth Glass pointed out that only the poorest area in Middlesbrough would be considered a 'neighbourhood' in this sense. It was an area which was also geographically rather isolated and socially homogeneous, which she saw as contributory factors.[3] More recently Pahl has asserted:

'Community' is simply a constraint on the less privileged, and with greater affluence and more 'choice' there has been a slow and steady move from community to social network as the meaningful area for social relationships.[4]

He sees the mobile middle class as being able to escape 'the community of common deprivation' and to inhabit a non-place community based on their loose-knit social networks and careers.[5] He concludes:

The constraints of locality are less the higher an individual is placed on the occupational hierarchy. However the locality constraints increase until we reach those who are completely trapped in the so-called twilight zone of rented rooms in the centres of large cities. Unable to change jobs because of their lack of training, their inability

---

[1] *Community Attitudes Survey*, p. 35.
[2] Ibid., pp. 45–6, and Table 43.
[3] R. Glass, *The Social Background of a Plan* (London, Routledge & Kegan Paul, 1948), pp. 39–41.
[4] Pahl, *Patterns of Urban Life*, p. 105.
[5] Pahl, *Patterns of Urban Life*, p. 106, and 'Social Differences between Urban and Rural Societies', *Whose City* (London, Longmans, 1970), p. 100.

to get dwellings elsewhere and perhaps the colour of their skin, a pattern of cumulative and circular causation creates ghetto conditions unless there is vigorous intervention with social policies aimed not so much at the physical environment, but more specifically at ways of increasing social mobility.[1]

Paradoxically, as Pahl has also pointed out, if community activity is measured by involvement in more formal voluntary associations, the mobile middle class may in this sense be highly locality-conscious, with specific demands and expectations.[2] This paradox implies that dependence on wider professional and other non-locality-based social networks may have become *relatively* more important but that the geographic area of residence still retains some importance, for example in its symbolic value as an indication of social status[3] given the residential segregation of different social classes in British cities.

Various studies have shown that people conceptualize a 'home' area. Four-fifths of the respondents to the Community Attitudes Survey provided affirmative replies to that question. The size of the area postulated by respondents increased with social class. But three-quarters of the respondents living in urban areas defined their 'home' area as no larger than an average local government ward.

The authors of the Community Attitudes Survey distinguish between two types of community involvement. 'Social attachment', which they relate to patterns of kinship, extended relationship, and acquaintance in the 'home' area, and 'interest in local affairs', as manifested by interest and participation in local government, local public service, and events in the 'home' area.[4] The typical person most likely at present to be highly socially attached to his community area was young and of a low level of education and socio-economic status.[5] Length of residence was especially strongly associated with such social attachment:

The importance of this factor length of residence lies partly in the fact that it allows for a wider opportunity to form ties, experience social activities and assume familiarity with the area in its several physical

---

[1] Pahl, *Patterns of Urban Life*, p. 135.

[2] Ibid., p. 107. See also *Community Attitudes Survey*, p. 28, p. 165.

[3] Ibid., p. 23. See also John Rex, *Race Relations in Sociological Theory* (London, Weidenfeld and Nicholson, 1970), p. 96.

[4] *Community Attitudes Survey*, p. 144.   [5] Ibid., pp. 146–8.

and personal respects. It also implies a deeper and more qualitative form of commitment to the area though this may be manifested in tangible forms (house ownership, dependence on business customers and contacts or even a position of employment) as well as for example patterns of friendship among people in the area or simply attachment in a vague form to the area as a whole.[1]

The highly involved informant on the scale relating to interest in local affairs is by contrast more likely to be older, of a higher or secondary level of education, and of a higher socio-economic status.[2]

Informants of higher social status and a higher level of education may be considered to be more 'knowledgeable' in the wider sense, they are more closely peers of the managers, elected representatives and decision-makers in local government; they are more frequently involved themselves in community and local governmental affairs. They represent more than their proportionate numbers would suggest, a larger part of the highly active, highly interested group in terms of involvement with the community. Their greater mobility, complementarily implying shorter and weaker ties of residence and relationship within the community means that they are much less involved in the manner which is characterised by the social attachment form of community feeling.[3]

Thus, a sense of 'community' can exist for some individuals as the product of social, economic, and educational constraints. A different kind of community involvement can characterize the activities of others as a result of their socio-economic status and educational equipment. This demonstrates how the paradox described by Pahl earlier is reconcilable.

Even if individuals do conceptualize a 'home' area, it does not follow that any 'collective' expression of a neighbourhood exists even in a passive sense. In distinguishing the 'home community' area from surrounding areas, respondents to the Community Attitudes Survey had considerations of physical appearance uppermost in their mind. Mental distinctions in human terms were less evident.[4] The authors assessed that only a small minority could be considered very socially attached to their home area or interested in local affairs.[5] Moreover, the fundamental variables in determining styles of life in an area in Britain will be class and

---

[1] *Community Attitudes Survey*, p. 164.   [2] Ibid., pp. 146–8.
[3] Ibid., p. 165.   [4] Ibid., p. 17.   [5] Ibid., p. 145.

life-cycle stage, not the locality *per se*.[1] Wider societal divisions along class and ethnic lines will be reflected at the local level.

It is possible for 'community consciousness' to be engendered by a specific issue, either a threat from without, conflict within or common experiences of deprivation. Much has been written about the initial 'neighbourliness' of new arrivals to a new settlement, but social contacts initially based on propinquity usually give way in the face of population turnover and a gradual tendency with time to find other friends outside the immediate area with common interests and a common social background. Ruth Durant explained the initial co-operation she observed among newcomers to the new estate of Watling in terms of their homogeneity in social class and stage in the life-cycle, the simultaneous time of arrival, the hostility of their surrounding privately-housed neighbours, and the lack of near and convenient facilities. This 'community co-operation' was however a feature of the estate only in its early stages. Once the main problems had been solved, after two or three years, it significantly subsided as a steady turnover in population took place and new arrivals made their own adjustment to the estate.[2]

The situation in which the locus of economic power is changing is also one in which the nature of social identifications is likely to be changing too. Exposure to mass media may contribute to a situation in which national identifications may be replacing local ones, or the relevant identifications may be wider still embracing 'the West', or the 'white Anglo-Saxon world'. In as much as such identifications are growing in importance they may be more powerful than local 'community' ones, so that attachment to and solidarity with a wider nationally or racially defined society may be more significant than acknowledgement of community interests with multiracial neighbours.

Issues can just as easily cause divisions among a locally-based population dependent on its social composition and characteristics.[3] Joint tenants' and residents' associations in proposed clearance areas in St. Ann's, Nottingham, and Rye Hill (Newcastle) have been split by disagreement on whether they wanted

[1] Pahl, *Whose City*, p. 101.

[2] R. Durant, *Watling, A Survey of Social Life on a New Housing Estate* (London, P. S. King & Sons, 1939), p. 116, and also pp. 42–3, p. 119.

[3] Lisa Peattie, 'Reflections of an Advocate Planner', *Journal of the American Institute of Planners* (Vol. xxxiv, No. 2, March 1968).

improvement and rehabilitation of the houses (which owner-occupiers frequently preferred) or demolition (which tenants often wanted instead).[1]

We will return to these themes and their implication for community development or community action strategy towards the end of this chapter. We will proceed now to consider what significance these comments have for the urban areas in which community relations committees are operating.

When considering areas of large-scale coloured immigration, we are primarily talking about inner ring areas whose population is perhaps the least homogeneous in all respects. These are areas of a high degree of population movement. Ceri Peach has shown that Commonwealth immigration to England prior to control in 1965 was highly sensitive to labour demand, and immigrants were compelled to act as a 'replacement population'. Thus, in those non-growth industries into which they moved in substantial numbers, West Indians were twice as numerous as in the growth industries in which they were found. Geographically, 'they have been drawn to those regions which in spite of demand for labour have not been able to attract much net population from other parts of the country. In towns they are proportionally twice as numerous in those that lost population between 1951–61 as those which increased. They have gone to the decreasing urban cores of expanding industrial regions.'[2] Over 75 per cent of West Indians in Great Britain live in towns which have lost population and within these towns they are settled predominantly in areas showing net decreases in white population. For example, in Birmingham, 70 per cent of the West Indian population was located in wards in which there was a net decrease in population between 1951–61. In London, 80 per cent of West Indians lived in metropolitan boroughs which had lost population. In both London and Birmingham the percentage of West Indians living in wards or boroughs which had net losses of white population was over 86 per cent.[3]

Analysis of 1961 and 1966 Census material undertaken by the authors of *Colour and Citizenship* showed that the numbers of Asians and West Indians in seven selected London boroughs increased

---

[1] K. Coates and R. Silburn, *Poverty—The Forgotten Englishmen* (Harmondsworth, Penguin, 1970), pp. 228–31.
[2] Peach, op. cit., p. 82.   [3] Ibid., p. 97.

from 46,700 to 81,600 between 1961–6. These areas also experienced an over-all decline in population of 15,000, chiefly made up of an increase of 35,000 coloured immigrants and a decline of 50,000 English.[1] Since the decrease in population is in the central areas of towns and since coloured immigrants do not appear to be rehoused in public and private suburbia in due number, it is likely that this tendency will increase.[2] In Bristol nearly half the West Indian population was concentrated in the St. Paul's Montpelier district, an area of depressed and dilapidated housing on the edge of the central business district, at the time of the 1961 Census. By 1965 their number had increased by over 40 per cent.[3]

As Rex and Moore have pointed out, the constraints inherent in the way the existing housing market, public and private, operates means that the inhabitants of the 'twilight zones' tend to be a motley assortment. Rex and Moore agree with Park, Burgess, and Mackenzie in their recognition of the differentiation of the various residential zones of the city produced by an over-all competition for land use. They differ from the Chicago School in denying that each zone consists of a relatively self-sufficient and internally integrated subcommunity.[4] The zone of transition is distinctly different from the traditional working-class zone in many cases even when both appear to be undergoing processes of urban decay. Gittus points out there are two types of decaying urban areas.[5] The *residual area* characterized by the inadequacy and obsolescence of the buildings, such as the terraced cottages of the mid-, or late nineteenth century or the grim Victorian tenements. The *transitional area* in which the decay is preceded or accompanied by change in the occupancy of buildings and the essential character of their use.[6] The zone of transition in particular is distinctive

---

[1] Rose *et al.*, op. cit.

[2] Ibid., p. 125.

[3] A. Richmond and M. Lyon, 'Study of St. Paul's Area and of Three Housing Estates in Bristol', quoted in Rose *et al.*, op. cit., p. 425.

[4] Rex and Moore, op. cit., p. 273, p. 277.

[5] E. Gittus, 'Sociological Aspects of Urban Decay', in D. F. Medhurst and J. Parry Lewis, *Urban Decay* (London, Macmillan, 1969).

[6] This difference is brought out too in the Milner Holland Committee Report on housing in Greater London (*Housing in Greater London*, op. cit.) where a distinction is made between housing stress engendered by multi-occupation and overcrowding (concentrated in western and northern parts of inner London), and that caused in single household poor quality dwellings by the lack of basic amenities, a situation more prevalent in the East End and the boroughs south of the Thames.

not only in that it contains a large number of lodging-houses but that it contains residents in each of the housing classes.[1]

The zone of transition is therefore much less homogeneous than many other parts of the city.[2] The residents will include:

Newly-formed native households consisting of temporary residents who will eventually accumulate sufficient money or 'points' to become owner-occupiers or be rehoused by the Council. Their commitment to the local community is therefore minimal.[3]

Native isolates and tenants who prefer the advantages of anonymity which the area offers.

Native English older residents with children who have grown up and left home. They will be concerned to maintain the standards in the area and will be strongly motivated to demand that newcomers conform to old standards, if not to agitate for their restriction.

Rex and Moore observed that nostalgia for the past glories of the neighbourhood added to the resentment of older people in Sparkbrook.[4] Similarly, in Southall, it was found that the longer the residents had lived in the area the more often they tended to mention immigration as a problem. This was especially noticeable in the group that had lived in Southall for over twenty years.[5] Anthony Richmond and Michael Lyon found in their study of the

---

[1] Rex and Moore, op. cit., p. 274, distinguish the following housing classes:
   outright owners of a whole house;
   owners of a mortgaged house;
   council tenants in (a) houses with long lives
                          (b) houses awaiting demolition;
   tenants of whole houses owned by private landlords;
   owners of houses bought with short-term loans who are compelled to let rooms
      in order to meet repayment obligations;
   tenants of rooms in lodging-houses.
Valerie Karn in 'A Note on Race, Community and Conflict', *Race* (Vol. IX, No. 1, July 1967), pp. 101–4, pointed out that Rex and Moore underestimated the number of privately-rented whole houses including those occupied by immigrant families.
   Robin Ward in 'Discrimination, the Market and the Ethnic Colony' (paper presented to British Sociological Conference, 1969), pointed out that owned property also normally comes right into the zone of transition. Both these points reinforce the view of the heterogeneity of the area.

[2] For a similar analysis of heterogeneity in an inner American city situation see H. Gans, 'Urbanism and Suburbanism as Ways of Life' in Pahl (ed.), *Readings in Urban Sociology*, pp. 97–103.

[3] Rex and Moore, op. cit., pp. 281 onwards, from whom this analysis has been borrowed.

[4] Ibid., p. 60.

[5] D. Woolcott, 'Southall', in Deakin (ed.), op. cit.

St. Paul's area of Bristol that the majority of the English residents were skilled artisans or clerical workers and that many identified themselves with the middle class and voted Conservative. They found that the feelings of loss of status experienced by the English in this area produced great antipathy towards West Indian neighbours.[1]

The heterogeneity of the English population appears to be still greater in certain areas, especially in certain inner London boroughs such as Islington, Kennington, and Camden where middle-class professionals or students appear to be moving in through the process which Ruth Glass has termed 'gentrification'.[2] Twilight area renewal policies of selective rehabilitation and redevelopment adopted by some inner urban local authorities may exacerbate this tendency.[3]

There will be considerable differences too among the immigrants to the area. Single immigrants, using the area as a temporary dormitory, will have little interest in conforming to the values of local society or preserving the amenities of the area. Some of these will either marry or bring families over and resemble the next group.

Permanent immigrants will first use the area as an 'ethnic colony' for cultural familiarity and personal security and then as a base for exploring the possibilities of contact with the English. Those who eventually assimilate will tend to be usually white English-speaking or professionally qualified.

The remainder, the overwhelming majority, because of discrimination will be forced to use the colony as a base for organizing to obtain entitlements, unless they can find some solution for improving their housing situation by home purchase or in public housing.[4]

The differences in immigrant residents' points in the life-cycle, their differing intentions regarding permanency of residence in that area, as well as the varying cultural and religious

[1] Rose *et al.*, op. cit., pp. 425–6.

[2] R. Glass and J. Westergaard, *London's Housing Needs* (London, Centre for Urban Studies, 1965). Gittus, in Medhurst and Lewis, op. cit., p. 30, describes the same tendency in Liverpool and Newcastle.

[3] T. Blair, 'Twilight Area Renewal', *Official Architecture and Planning* (November 1969).

[4] Rex and Moore, op. cit., pp. 14–18, p. 283, and J. Rex, 'The Sociology of the Zone of Transition', in Pahl (ed.), op. cit., pp. 219–21.

prescriptions for conducting life which characterize the different
ethnic groups will add to the diversity of ways of life in the zone of
transition. Each group will have a subcommunity of differing size
and cohesiveness to which to relate. There will be no over-all
'community' corresponding to the boundaries of the area.
Proximity in the absence of other factors creates only quite loose
relationships.[1] Often cultural and social affinities cancel out
physical proximity and will replace initial neighbourhood
relations. Proximity can also aggravate existing tensions. This is
well documented for ethnically similar groups, for example white
council house tenants, and obviously equally applies to ethnically
diverse groups.[2]

Margaret Stacey has pointed out that where the majority of
the population of a locality do not share to any considerable
extent common groups, institutions, beliefs, and expectations
there can be no one local social system for that locality.[3] Ray
Pahl's comment that 'any attempt to tie particular patterns of
social relationship to a specific geographical milieu is a singularly
fruitless exercise',[4] seems most fitting in the case of the 'zone of
transition'. We have pointed out that the occurrence of a 'crisis' or
an 'issue' need not necessarily induce co-operation in a locality.
What constitutes an 'issue' and 'why' will depend largely on who
is defining and is affected by it.

There is in general a dearth of voluntary organizations in
inner ring areas. Such organizations as exist are often dominated
by middle-class or more prosperous working-class people from
outside the area, such as the political parties and churches, or not
really concerned with local community issues, such as trade

[1] L. Festinger, S. Schachter, and K. Back, *Social Pressures in Informal Groups* (New
York, Harper, 1950), p. 163. The authors analysed the relationship between ecological
factors and the formation of friendship groups in two housing projects, Westgate and
Westgate West, occupied by a group of similar ex-servicemen students at M.I.T.
The authors emphasized that in the case of a heterogeneous community, 'one would
expect the ecological factors to have considerably less weight than they do in communities where there is a high degree of homogeneity and common interests among
the residents'.
[2] T. Simey (ed.), *Neighbourhood and Community: The Liverpool Estate* (Liverpool,
Liverpool University Press, 1954), p. 74; L. Kuper (ed.), *Living in Towns* (London,
Cresset Press, 1953), p. 116, p. 159.
[3] Stacey, op. cit.
[4] 'The Rural Urban Continuum', *Sociologia Ruralis* (Vol. 16, Nos. 3–4, 1966).

unions, or are merely social organizations, such as working men's clubs. Organizations concerned with specific community issues are sometimes set up, but very often these are ephemeral and decline once controversy dies down.[1] Some organizations may be concerned with opposing particular changes in the character of their areas rather than with seeking improvements. They may tend to be dominated by people unsympathetic to immigrants whom they see as another source of change. Sometimes this kind of community organization is specifically anti-immigrant. In Southall the Indian Workers' Association sought to explore areas of common interest with Southall Residents Association when the latter was first set up. Some members of the Residents Association were sympathetic, but they were rapidly driven out of the organization and it became more explicitly racialist. Thus Southall International Friendship Council found that there was little scope for a common front with S.R.A. on the social and amenity problems facing the district.

An optimistic view of the possibilities of community co-operation has been offered by Rose *et al.*, which includes a specific reference to Sparkbrook.[2]

Local associations which are formed to cater for the welfare of all the people in an area, irrespective of their origins, can arouse a response from old and new alike. They are effective if they can create a sense of purpose and make people believe that it is possible to get things done to improve the conditions in which they are living. The most disparate elements in a neighbourhood, who would not otherwise feel any sense of community, can be brought to co-operate in projects which are seen to be needed. These associations have a double value. They preserve the morale of the native, by providing an effective channel of action for people who might otherwise have found no outlet for their frustrations except in some anti-immigrant Association, they declare racialism to be an illegitimate response and offer alternative solutions to the problems which it purports to solve.[3]

However, it is the goals and objectives of the organization which will determine who in the long run participates and whether

[1] See for example the account of various tenants associations on council housing estates in W. J. H. Sprott, *Human Groups* (Harmondsworth, Penguin, 1958).

[2] Rose *et al.*, op. cit., p. 20.

[3] Rex and Moore, op. cit. Rex develops this point of view further in 'The Sociology of a Zone of Transition', in Pahl (ed.), *Readings in Urban Sociology*.

conflict will develop within the organization. One would expect the objectives of an organization to dictate its structure. If, instead, structure is determined first, this will have a constraining impact upon the setting of objectives. As far as community relations committees are concerned, the objectives of the movement were not explicitly formulated before the structure of the organizations was prescribed. This theme which is central to the whole argument of this book will be developed in Chapter 7 when we attempt to assess the 'achievements' of the community relations committees. The Community Relations Commission was not sure whether the prime purpose of the committees should be to promote change or co-ordinate efforts made by existing local statutory and voluntary agencies in the provision of social services in the widest sense to be used by a multiracial local clientele. The main concern in the formative years of the Commission and its predecessor, the N.C.C.I., was the detail of the structure of the committees rather than the consideration of the implications and reconcilability of different sets of objectives. The prescribed structures which will be described in Chapter 4, became more rigid and bureaucratized over time (Chapter 10), and came to dominate and determine the objectives of the committees.

Morris and Rein have argued that success in achieving a goal in community organization depends on the use of a structure and strategy appropriate to that goal. Certain strategies and structures are more appropriate for goals of change while others are more consistent with goals of co-ordination.[1] They identify two types of strategy: 'co-operative rationality' and 'individual rationality'. 'Co-operative rationality' is the kind of strategy adopted when it is believed that different interest groups can work together towards common goals. In this case, 'a search for common values can be initiated with a tacit understanding based on implicit rules that non-shared ends, which can embarrass the participants or cause conflict, are assiduously avoided'.[2] Consensus is sought, conflict is avoided. To facilitate reaching conclusions based on common aims, a great deal of emphasis is placed on procedures for ensuring that participants have a stake in any decision outcome. Hence,

[1] R. Morris and M. Rein, *Social Work Practice* (New York, Columbia University Press, 1962), pp. 127–45, reprinted in M. Rein, *Social Policy—Issues of Choice and Change* (New York, Random House, 1970), pp. 178–91. (Pagination quoted here from the latter.)

[2] Ibid., p. 182.

the committee mechanism is crucial, and the whole process is legitimated by reference to the 'community'.

An integral part of the search for shared goals and the use of democratic procedures is legitimation by the community. This is achieved in part by the requirement that the set goals must favor no special interest, must be non-controversial, and must be in the community's best interest; that is, they must contribute to increasing community solidarity and to reducing community conflict and strain. Thus, the goals emanate from a now legitimate source—the community itself, further buttressed by the use of democratic process so important in our culture. Characteristic of this strategy is the indefiniteness with which the term 'community' is used. The term is meant to cover all persons and interests, but it is not defined. Nor are mechanisms available which permit us to reach such an ideal community, so that it remains vague and general.[1]

'Individual rationality' by contrast does not involve an attempt to embrace a diversity of points of view. It is based upon the 'tough-minded pursuit of specific interests: starting with firm specific goals, the sponsors ask, what is the most rational means of accomplishing their aims?'

Morris and Rein go on to suggest that a strategy of 'individual rationality' is best suited for goals of change, while 'co-operative rationality' approaches are most appropriate where consensus and conformity exist.

They go on to describe two ideal types of organizational structure:[2] the federated structure, an association of agencies primarily accountable to themselves and only secondarily to the federation; the 'simple structure', composed of a simple relatively homogeneous group of persons with similar ideological beliefs and likemindedness of purpose in their commitment to the goals which they are trying to follow. In addition they argue that the basic goal orientations of change and integration/co-ordination are incompatible and that a choice must be made between them. The organization's structure and major type of strategy is critical to the realization of its goals. They argue that a federated structure and a co-operative rationality are most consistent with goals of

---

[1] Morris and Rein, op. cit., p. 183.

[2] These, they stress, are ideal types and are seldom found in a pure form—'simple or federated structures form a continuum and only at the extremes are they most clear cut'. Ibid., p. 184.

integration/co-ordination. A simple structure coupled with an individual rationality is most congruent with the achievement of goals of change.

They illustrate the relationship which they see between goals, structures, and strategies, as follows:[1]

	Federated	Simple
Co-operative rationality	Integration	Ritualism
	1	2
Individual rationality	Survival	Change
	3	4

(Cells 1 and 4 on the diagonal represent goals while Cells 2 and 3 involve potential goal displacements.)

The situation portrayed in Cell 1 occurs when a federated structure such as a community council employs a strategy of consensus and maximizes this likelihood by limiting the membership to agencies subscribing to values which will promote harmony. When organizations employ inappropriate structures or strategies they are in danger of displacing or diluting their goals. In the case of both kinds of organizations ritualism may set in. An organization committed to the achievement of action goals may become concerned with securing the aid of other community agencies and in so doing focuses on winning co-operation rather than achieving its aims. Slowly goals change to adapt to co-operative means and co-operation becomes an end in itself. Ritualism may develop when a change-oriented agency shifts its structure from a simple to a federated type and membership is recruited from different community subgroups (often in the name of being democratic) who have only minimal commitment to the objective. Significantly, as an example, the authors quote the Urban League:

We would expect an organisation like the Urban League to be most susceptible to the problem of ritual because it is comprised of representatives of both the white and the negro communities. Fear of offending either subgroup can lead to inaction and avoidance of aggressively pursuing its aims.[2]

A co-ordination-oriented organization may be prone to ritualism when it abandons its federated structure for a simple one in order

---

[1] Morris and Rein, op. cit.   [2] Ibid., p. 189.

to maintain harmony and thereby abrogates its co-ordination role, but cannot act as a change agency because of its overstress on co-operation and avoidance of conflict.

When at the cost of constituent agencies, an integrative organization exerts its primary energies in maintaining and enhancing itself, goal displacement in the form of 'survival' results.

The authors conclude that: 'The very nature of innovation or planned change produces resistance in some quarters. To overcome such opposition organizations must be willing to engage in controversy.'[1]

Community relations committees are on the one hand committed to integrative and co-ordinating goals. They are advised by the Commission to secure and involve all the powerful elements in the community in participation in the committee. We will show how the White Paper regarded the exercise of participation in the committee as educative and a goal in itself in this respect. On the other hand, the committees are theoretically change-oriented as well, since their very *raison d'être* arose out of the awareness of the discrimination which coloured immigrants encounter when confronting both public and private institutions. The fact that the emphasis on objectives was not explicitly stated from the beginning meant that the committees were more prone to be diverted by other factors such as their structure. In addition, the Commission recommended that the prescribed structure of the committees should be a federated one. The committees were to be primarily organizations of organizations. However, as we shall show in Chapter 4, the committees are not a 'federated' structure in the 'purest' form postulated in the Morris and Rein typology. The individuals representing voluntary organizations in many cases conform to the 'simple structure' pattern, in that they are often self-selected because there is usually little competition in the sending organization for the position of delegate to the community relations committee. Often the 'representative' is the only person in the sending organization who considers it necessary to affiliate to the community relations committee. In this respect they often share similar ideological beliefs with other organization 'representatives', and a commitment to a vague notion of racial equality. In addition, there are always a minority of individual

[1] Ibid., p. 190.

members, self-nominated, and sharing broadly similar values. The exception to these are very often the local authority officials, councillors or police who have been invited on to the committee so that the committee can act as a forum within which to influence such institutions. Committees will also exclude organizations whom they consider would be too disruptive because of their militancy.

In subsequent chapters we shall show how the goals of the community relations committees are neither clearly co-ordinative–integrative in orientation, nor change-oriented, how the structure is 'federate', yet with characteristics of the 'simple' structure, and how the strategies different committees adopt vary from 'co-operative rationality' to 'individual rationality'. It should not come as a surprise when we describe the end results in terms of action, as often oscillating between 'ritualism and survival'.

CHAPTER 4

The Structure of Community Relations Committees

In Chapter 3 we raised some of the problems entailed by the commitment of the community relations movement to organizing on a 'community' basis, particularly in the light of the fact that the tendency is to equate local authority areas with 'communities'. Naturally enough this particular commitment is reflected in the prescriptions for the structure of local committees provided initially in the 1965 White Paper and subsequently elaborated by the N.C.C.I./C.R.C.

The following structural features for a local committee are recommended by the C.R.C.:

> A general council, meeting at least twice a year, consisting of representatives from a cross-section of local organizations (including, of course, immigrant organizations), representatives of the local authority (or authorities), and individual members. Individual members with voting rights should not exceed a quarter of the total full membership. Individuals in excess of this quota should be enrolled as 'associate' members.
> Officers and an executive elected by the general council.
> Subcommittees appointed by the executive.

In the light of what we have said earlier about the relationship between the community relations committees and the 'communities' or areas which they serve, the crucial points to discuss about their structure are:

> In what ways is the membership of the committees related to the wider 'communities'? In particular, what arrangements are made to proportion individual membership and organizational membership?

7

What kinds of inner-organizational democracy are achieved within such structures? Who controls the organizations and how do they control them?

Seven of the eight local committees follow the pattern laid down in the White Paper fairly closely, though there are subtle variations in approach to individual membership, executive relations with subcommittees, and the representation of local authorities. The committee which markedly differs from the normally accepted form is Birmingham.

The members of Birmingham Community Relations Committee are all appointed by the Lord Mayor of Birmingham, in consultation with interested organizations. It has no executive, merely a single committee, modelled upon the Government-appointed N.C.C.I. Like the N.C.C.I., too, it has power to set up panels, and at the time of our study was taking steps to set up an 'education' and a 'religious-education' panel. These were seen as semi-autonomous organizations free 'to report to the Community Relations Committee, to the public, to their constituent organizations or not to make a report at all'.

The Birmingham committee lacks the normal membership structure because, in order to set up a community relations committee at all, efforts had to be made to appease opponents of the idea who were dominant in both political parties. The committee was set up on the initiative of its present chairman, Corbyn Barrow, who was Lord Mayor of Birmingham at the time, but who had considerable difficulty in obtaining the acquiescence of the then dominant Labour group, of which he was a member.

At the same time as the community relations committee was set up, the Mayor also set up an 'Advisory Council' to represent more widely immigrant organizations, the City Council, churches, and voluntary bodies. It was felt that at this initial stage it would be unwise to make the Birmingham C.R.C. the servants of the Advisory Council in the way that elsewhere general councils of community relations committees elect their executive committee. The function of the Advisory Council was to advise B.C.R.C. and it was to be independent and with power to act autonomously.

While in formal terms the Birmingham committee differs markedly from the other seven, in practice this difference is not so significant because most of the other committees are effectively dominated by their executives, and because the Birmingham Advisory Council proved to be a far from passive body.

We have already pointed out that the N.C.C.I. recommended that the committees be primarily organizations of organizations: at least 75 per cent of the members representing organizations, and only a quarter at the most being individual members. One of the chief problems posed for the committees by the White Paper formula, lies in deciding what kind of balance to achieve between organizational and individual membership, since the N.C.C.I. formula was more a recommendation than a prescription.

Apart from Birmingham, of the committees we studied, three have no rules restricting individual membership except for a general control over the admission of members. The other four all restrict individual membership to a greater or lesser degree.

Bradford does not restrict individual membership, but has never sought to encourage wide individual participation. However, five members of the eleven-person executive committee are 'individual members'.

Hackney's constitution leaves the control of the inflow of individual members to its general council, stating: 'The Council may from time to time co-opt as members of the Council, persons who are specially qualified to further the objects of the Council.' In fact it has interpreted this clause very liberally and has on its council 147 individual members in addition to representatives from fifty-five organizations (each of which are allowed to send two members). The executive includes nine individual members and nine organization representatives (including four local authority representatives).

One executive member of H.C.R.C. said he thought there should be no limit at all on individual participation. (One wonders how much check he thought there was.) No other members volunteered views on this aspect of Hackney's structure. However, Hackney had an argument with the N.C.C.I. on this point as they were considered to be too ready to welcome individual members. They justify this policy in terms of the absence of organizational life in Hackney and the need to achieve the maximum possible participation from immigrants.

Tower Hamlets' constitution simply states: 'The Council or the Executive Committee may also admit to membership any suitable persons who support the aims and objects and signify their desire to become members.' The distinction between individual and organization membership has become very blurred in practice by designation of people as organizational representatives when they regard themselves merely as individual members (this is a result of an effective campaign to get a wide cross-section of useful people into the organization), and the acceptance of people as representatives of organizations based outside Tower Hamlets and with no real connexions with the borough. This characterizes the 'social welfare' approach adopted in this London borough where, for years past, middle-class people from outside the borough have been dominant in voluntary welfare activities.

Ealing's constitution is also fairly lenient on this point, providing for 'Individual members who are accepted by the Executive Committee . . . (whose numbers shall not exceed one half of the total membership)'. This provision obviously allows for a very large number of individual members. At its 1969 annual general meeting, E.C.R.C. had seventy-nine organizations affiliated, supplying 149 representatives, and 149 individual members. This left merely twenty-six members who were only allowed to be non-voting 'associate members'. Two members stated, when asked whether they regarded E.C.R.C.'s structure as satisfactory, that they would like to see the number of individual members cut down. One other member said he would like to see unlimited individual membership.

E.C.R.C. imposes no restrictions on the nomination of individual members to offices and executive. Nine of E.C.R.C.'s executive of thirty, during 1968–9, were individual members.

Huddersfield's general council may 'co-opt to membership persons having special knowledge or experience provided that the number of co-opted members shall not exceed one-fourth of the number of representative members of the Committee'. By the 1968 A.G.M. there were only nine such members, four of whom were members of Huddersfield's ten-person executive. Forty-four organizational representatives belonged to the organization.

The remaining two committees control very strictly individual participation. In Sheffield the general committee may appoint up to six individual members. Four members of the seventeen-person executive were appointed to the general committee in this way.

No member of the executive criticized this rule in any way, when asked to comment on the structure of S.C.C.R.

In Wycombe, on the other hand, the position of the individual members was a source of some controversy. Wycombe's constitution gives their general committee 'power to co-opt from time to time persons not being nominated representatives, but such co-opted persons shall not at any time exceed ten in number'. The elected members of the executive have to be organization representatives, but oddly this rule does not apply to the officers. As a consequence both chairman and treasurer are individual members. The only other way individual members can get on to the executive is by co-option. The executive has power to co-opt up to four people and can also fill casual vacancies. Four of Wycombe's twenty-one-person executive are individual members.

Three members of the executive said they would like to have more individual members. One member wanted to reduce the influence of individual members. He was particularly concerned about the occupancy of the chairmanship by an 'individual' member.

A consequence of the restriction of individual membership is low participation of immigrants because of the lack of immigrant organizations. Sheffield has specifically formulated a co-option rule to try to overcome this problem. It gives its executive power to co-opt to the executive 'to the extent necessary to secure that at least one-third of the members of the Executive shall be members of minority ethnic groups of Sheffield citizens'. This clause has been used to draw immigrants into the organization. However, it suggests a rather paternalistic approach to immigrant participation.

Wycombe overcomes the difficulty with a very curious section in its constitution: 'Each immigrant community recognised by the Committee shall be entitled to be represented by five of its members chosen by it from amongst its number.' Again we may note the paternalism, inherent in the expression 'recognised by the Committee', a feature the White Paper formula makes it almost impossible to avoid.

Perhaps we may digress here to mention one other facet of the formal organization of community relations committees which reflects their domination by the white middle class and tends to reduce immigrant participation, that is the time and place of meetings. All the committees except Birmingham, which meets in the afternoon, arrange their council and executive meetings on weekday evenings at a central place, usually a civic building. This must have some marginal impact in cutting down the participation of shift-workers and of persons who feel uneasy in surroundings in which British middle-class people feel at home. Many immigrants do shift work, particularly night shifts, and significantly one immigrant member of the Wycombe committee whom we interviewed was about to resign because he had changed to night work. Yet we have no evidence that any of the committees we studied had considered holding week-end meetings, an arrangement that is commonplace for the Indian Workers' Association (Southall), for example, or of locating its council meetings in the areas of high immigrant settlement. Immigrants were in the minority on all eight executive committees with the exception of Hackney.

We were able to look at the constitutions of fourteen community relations councils in addition to the seven discussed above. The way in which all twenty-one councils handled this issue of individual membership is summarized in Table 4.1.

TABLE 4.1
CONTROL OF INDIVIDUAL MEMBERSHIP BY COUNCIL OR EXECUTIVE COMMITTEE

	Membership unrestricted	Unrestricted*	Restricted to half	Restricted to a quarter	Restricted to ten or less	No full individual membership
The seven councils	1	2	1	1	2	–
The other fourteen councils	2	3	–	6	2	1

* The difference between this and the previous category is that individual members are only admitted in this case at the invitation of council or executive.

The unusual rules in the constitutions of the thirteen community relations councils which are worthy of further comment come from Bolton whose constitution simply provides for membership by 'Any individual citizen who accepts the Objects of the Council'; Wolverhampton which accepts unlimited individual membership but limits individual membership of its executive committee; Slough which allows its associate members to elect two of its number to the executive and accords full membership status to those two; and Keighley which has no 'full' individual members.

Manchester has a very complicated constitution which, in addition to allowing for individual members up to one-quarter, provides for blocks of up to fifteen each on its council as 'representatives from the various immigrant communities' defined as West Indians, Indians, Africans, Pakistanis, and others. This curious rule, like Wycombe's rather similar one, provides for extensive participation by individual immigrants and supposedly survives because no attempt is made to encourage large-scale immigrant participation. Presumably if someone tried to pack a meeting with West Indians, for example, then all the members of that 'community' in attendance would be asked to select fifteen of their number to 'represent' them.

Manchester's organizational representation is arranged in a similar way, allowing for limited numbers of delegates from 'religious bodies', 'Chambers of trade and commerce', 'trade unions', and so on. The composition of its executive is determined in the same way, the various sectional groups on its council being required to elect executive members.

This ingenious scheme rests upon the maintenance of the original composition of the organization, together with acceptance that invitations to people to participate will in some measure be controlled by those running the organization. If it became subject to competition for office, of the kind which we will describe for Birmingham Advisory Council, it could hardly survive.

Most community relations councils refrain from trying to balance participation in this subtle way. They have no special rules regarding immigrant membership of their general council but use a clause based upon a model constitution provided by the N.C.C.I. to try to ensure a substantial immigrant group on the executive. For example, the version of this clause used in Rugby's constitution reads as follows:

In seeking candidates for election to the Executive regard shall be had so far as practicable to the desirability of procuring at least one-third of the elected membership of the Executive for the time being consists of persons representing minority ethnic groups in the said area of Rugby and District.

This kind of clause is widely used, though the stated proportion varies between half, a third, and a quarter. Its success depends upon white members taking the hint, since it has no force in the event of hotly contested elections. Rules like these survive because the active workers of local committees are self-perpetuating minorities. They could not survive in an organization where there was competition for office, stimulated by the expectation of the acquisition of real power.

Having said this, however, there are circumstances in which it would be misleading to see the process by which people attain office in community relations councils in terms of a polite middle-class charade in which people are embarrassed about competing and always ready to make way for the 'stranger'. Several immigrant members we interviewed expressed considerable concern about the way immigrant members of executives are selected. It would seem to rest upon indignation that self-selected individuals assumed the right to speak for all West Indians, Indians or Pakistanis, or even *all immigrants*; or an interest in the status and influence to be acquired as a member of a committee containing white middle-class influentials; or a feeling that the white members fail to recognize the subtle differences between and within different immigrant groups and have preconceived ideas about how immigrant representatives should be selected. That there is considerable strength in these viewpoints will be demonstrated when we discuss the characteristics of executive committee members.

The suggestions that were made as to how to overcome this problem were of dubious practicality and could only lead, if elections were taken seriously (and the schemes aimed at creating systems that could be taken seriously), to considerable constitutional wrangling of the kind that we have already suggested could arise over the Manchester scheme. Among these suggestions were the idea of 'card votes' for organizations, so that their strength was taken into account. Concern was expressed in Ealing, for example, about 'paper' organizations from within the Indian community. The difficulty would be that the onus would be on the community relations committee to ascertain the size of constituent organizations. It cannot devise a system of affiliation fees to determine the issue, this would drive too many organizations away. Similarly its general weakness *vis-à-vis* some of its more powerful constituent organizations would hardly make such an arbitrator role viable.

Another suggestion was that there should be 'communal' elections for executive positions in the community relations committee. This would be difficult to operate in view of the amorphous nature of the so-called 'immigrant communities' and the absence of clear-cut 'communal' areas of residence. Local committees set up under the Poverty Programme in the United States have organized localized elections of this kind, but with only very low electoral participation.[1] If community relations committees set out to draw people from areas and not from ethnic groups, and if they had a great deal more money and power than they have today, such a system might be feasible.[2] An experiment of this kind has recently been tried with some success in Golborne Ward, North Kensington, where there was a percentage poll half as high again as that in the previous borough election.

For the moment we will call this type of strategy a 'citizen participation' strategy. We have shown that the C.R.C. recommends a strategy based on an *élite* consensus, whereby the object is to involve all the powerful elements of the community in the workings of the committee. No community relations committees have adopted a 'citizen participation strategy' in any long-term or meaningful sense. We will show what occurred when a community relations committee attempted to pursue both strategies simultaneously (see pp. 92–5).

Another development which may foreshadow experiments of this kind has been the organization by some of the community relations committees of subcommittees based upon smaller localities within their areas. The Ealing committee has set up an Acton subcommittee. The Sheffield committee has experimented with local subcommittees, one of which, the Attercliffe committee, functions effectively but primarily as a base for local social events. These experiments are at present fairly small in scale and aimed at providing for locally-based discussion or social events. No real concern has been expressed about the way in which these local

[1] Moynihan, op. cit., p. 137.
[2] Kramer describes some examples involving some success in achieving such participation in the War on Poverty in California, but the sums of money involved were astronomical by comparison with the grants acquired by community relations councils, and as a consequence there were large numbers of jobs at stake. R. M. Kramer, *Participation of the Poor* (Englewood Cliffs, N.J., Prentice Hall, 1969).

committees, like the subcommittees, are subject to the central executive.

It would be misleading to present these developments as at present anything more than *ad hoc* arrangements to try to cope with the fact that the community relations committees serve large amorphous areas. However, several of the more thoughtful committee members we interviewed saw a need for developments along these lines. One of the Birmingham members suggested that a federation of local committees would be more appropriate than the present organization in that vast city. Such a development would cut across the 'organization of organizations' principle applied at the moment since many of the now significant organizations in the membership of community relations committees are not localized in this way. If this kind of experiment was carried through, it might lead to demands for area elections, to replace the present organizational representation, since with this formula there is no likelihood that the community representation problem can be overcome by formal means.

Community relations committees do not control only the admission of individuals to membership. Some committees also control the entry of organizations to membership. For example, Sheffield rejected a membership application from the National Front. It is perhaps to be expected that committees will seek to prevent disruptive organizations of this kind from joining them, but some take this position further. Sheffield seems particularly committed to maintaining its establishment image in this way and vets all membership applications. Thus, an application from the local Pakistani Welfare Association was only accepted after an investigation of its credentials by the C.R.O. The Sheffield committee also refused to try to see if it shares common ground with the local branch of the Campaign Against Racial Discrimination, which asked to meet it in July 1968.[1]

In Hackney political parties are excluded from membership of the general council. It is curious that an organization which accepts individual members almost unrestrictedly should seek to limit organization members. Apparently the measure was originally adopted to minimize the party political content in any

---

[1] We will describe in Chapter 8 how Sheffield's policy of excluding organizations they consider potentially disruptive from membership coincides with, and serves to maintain, their advocacy of co-operation with the local authority.

controversy, but of course party politicians enter H.C.R.C. as representatives of the local authority. In a sense, since when H.C.R.C. was set up the membership of the Borough Council was 100 per cent Labour, the regulation originally excluded the representatives of all parties other than the Labour party. Since 1968 there have been Conservatives amongst the local authority representatives on H.C.R.C., but the Liberals are still excluded from joining as anything other than individual members.

This situation may have deprived H.C.R.C. of some valuable energy in the community, which might have been profitably harnessed. For example, in 1965 Hackney Young Liberals mounted a campaign to combat ignorance regarding the facts on immigration, as part of a national campaign by the League of Young Liberals. In 1968, Hackney Youth Vietnam Solidarity Campaign organized a series of talks against racialism in Ridley Road market, Dalston, to counteract the 'dockers' march' in support of Powell. And as part of International Co-operation Year the Hackney Cooperative Party had a meeting at the Town Hall opposing racialism, which attracted a multiracial audience of three hundred.

Another problem about organizational membership is the extent to which the people concerned can really be said to 'represent' their organizations. There are grounds for suspecting that only in very few cases do organizational representatives really help to create a two-way communication process between community relations committee and their organization, and that as volunteers from their organizations most of them are really in effect only 'individual members'.

The woman who 'represents' the Red Cross on Wycombe's committee was the only Red Cross member who considered it necessary for the Red Cross to affiliate to the committee. Another Wycombe member originally represented Rotary on W.D.I.C. and became an 'individual' member on leaving Rotary. No other representative from Rotary was appointed in his place. As far as the committees which were set up on voluntary initiative are concerned, many members had become committed to getting a community relations committee going and then persuaded some other organization to which they belonged to send them as a delegate.

Few organization representatives regularly report back to their organizations. One Indian member of Ealing's committee who is nominally a delegate from the Electrical Trades Union told us that he was unable to get his branch to take an interest in his reports on the work of E.I.F.C.

We will demonstrate further in Chapters 4 and 5 that many of the organization representatives are not typical members of the organizations they represent on the community relations committees. All the committees we studied, except of course Birmingham, had, on paper, achieved considerable success in acquiring affiliations from a wide range of local organizations. One would expect therefore that their executives would contain a wide cross-section, at least of middle-class people, from their districts. For example, amongst Ealing's seventy-nine organization members there are three local Conservative parties, two Rotary Clubs, and two Chambers of Commerce. Yet these powerful organizations do not really play any part in the work of Ealing's community relations committee and their representatives do not form more than a very small element on its executive. In fact there is a Southall Rotary member on the executive but he is a very untypical member, a radical Jewish lawyer. There is also a Southall Chamber of Commerce member, but he is inactive in the community relations committee. Apart from the councillors the latter is the lone Conservative supporter on the Ealing executive.

The Birmingham Advisory Council faced the problem of how to accommodate organization members within its formal structure in a form that has not so far troubled any other committee. As we have said, many committees have sought to develop devices to deal with the fact that they have a lack of immigrant organizations in their areas. By contrast, Birmingham's troubles arose largely from an inability to cope with the presence of a wide range of immigrant organizations, all interested in playing a part in the Advisory Council. Accordingly the arguments over representation on the Advisory Council were intertwined with the arguments about the relationship between the Council and the Birmingham committee.

Unlike other community relations committees, the B.C.R.C. executive was not responsible to the Advisory Council, whose function was only to 'advise', not to elect the B.C.R.C. At the first meeting of the Advisory Council[1] it was apparent that there was suspicion among immigrant groups because their representatives expected to be outnumbered by the representatives of local white organizations. Accordingly, two additional clauses were inserted in its constitution:

Immigrant organizations were to be allowed to send five representatives each to the meetings, as against one from each non-immigrant organization.

Immigrant groups should have the power of veto over resolutions in the Council.

The potential attendance figure could then be 450, of whom 350 would be immigrant representatives.

In April 1967 David Ennals addressed the B.C.R.C. and expressed the view that 'the committee should ask itself whether there ought not to be the closest possible liaison between the Advisory Council and this committee, perhaps by means of the election of three or four members of the Advisory Council to this committee'. By December 1967, mention was made in the B.C.R.C. minutes of 'different feelings on various matters' that had 'been fully expressed at the Advisory Council meeting', and the C.R.O. expressed the fear that 'if the different opinions were expressed in future in too hostile a manner, the Advisory Council could lose the participation of several representatives of the host community'. Also in December, the Advisory Council raised the issue of West Indian representation on the community relations committee. The committee, according to their minutes, 'discussed the advisability of asking for an election for a representative but agreed that this procedure in this instance might raise as many problems as it solved.' By the summer of 1968 the C.R.O. wrote in his report that the Advisory Council 'has succeeded in providing a platform upon which immigrant leaders can express their dissatisfaction with the situation in their communities. . . . Many white representatives question the usefulness of attending the meetings of the Advisory Council because of the destructiveness and mutual abuse of different immigrant groups.' The C.R.O.

[1] This account of the Advisory Council is partly based upon 'Liaison Committees —Who Keeps Control of What', *Institute of Race Relations Newsletter* (Vol. 2, No. 9, November–December 1968).

recommended the continuation of the appointment of B.C.R.C. members by the Mayor and also an increase in immigrant representation on the Committee by seeking three nominees from the Advisory Council and by co-opting three extra members.

In September 1968 the Advisory Council passed a motion forcing the resignation of Dr. Dhani Prem, vice-chairman of the Advisory Council who was also vice-chairman of the B.C.R.C., on the grounds that he no longer had any contact with the 'grass roots'. The annual general meeting of the Advisory Council, on 24 October 1968, at which the new chairman of the Advisory Council was to be elected (according to the constitution, the chairman was to be alternately an English person and an immigrant, for one year) turned into complete chaos. Six weeks before the meeting all member organizations of the Advisory Council were informed by circular of the impending elections and nominations were requested to be sent one week before to the C.R.O., who acted as secretary of the Council. The outgoing chairman, the Deputy Mayor of Birmingham, was unable to attend the annual general meeting and the chair was therefore taken by Corbyn Barrow, chairman of the B.C.R.C., who suggested that nominations be taken from the floor. This was vigorously opposed. Allegations were then made that Mihir Gupta, an Indian teacher and one of the two nominees for chairman, had packed the meeting with his supporters. Corbyn Barrow asked the C.R.O. to check the credentials of those present, but no interpreter could be found who was acceptable to all sections of the meeting. An attempt to adjourn the meeting was overwhelmingly defeated and Mihir Gupta was unanimously elected chairman, the other candidate, Gurdev Singh Chana, having walked out, claiming that the majority present were not entitled to vote.

In the autumn of 1968, the Advisory Council theoretically comprised 105 organizations of the English community and integrated organizations, and seventy-three immigrant organizations. When it had been inaugurated, thirty-five immigrant organizations sat on it. In the month before the A.G.M., eleven new immigrant organizations had requested membership. Approximately two hundred people attended the A.G.M. of whom a large number could not understand English and relied on friends to translate. The C.R.O. in his report on the fiasco stated: 'Those supporting one candidate were very well organized and some may not have been entitled to vote, but certainly this did not apply to the majority of his supporters.'

However, B.C.R.C. decided unanimously that 'the Advisory Council no longer represented a reasonable consensus of immigrant opinion' and withdrew services (secretarial facilities and premises) from it. B.C.R.C. was powerless to dissolve it constitutionally. A small subcommittee was set up to reconsider the best way of devising consultative procedures between the future B.C.R.C. and immigrant communities. In November 1968, the B.C.R.C. decided that its immigrant membership should be increased by four; that the committee should call together a number of panels which would include representatives of English and immigrant communities; and that a 'community relations conference' should be called at least once a year to discuss community relations in the city. The conference should include representatives of English organizations and of the larger immigrant organizations. Some 'objective' criteria for organizations to be invited to the conference (e.g. a membership of at least one hundred) would be devised. The chairman of the conference would be the chairman of B.C.R.C. or his nominee and the conference was to have no constituency.

The interesting feature of this story is that, because of its inability to create a viable structure for the representation of immigrant opinion, the B.C.R.C. was forced to remove its support from the Advisory Council, and to propose in its place a new organization which it would effectively control. Any pretence at the achievement of a situation in which the appointed B.C.R.C. was advised by a quasi-democratic body was swept away. The patently non-representative B.C.R.C. proposed to judge whether any immigrant organization wishing to send delegates to its community relations conference deserved to be regarded as 'representative'.

Ironically, the Birmingham Advisory Council was more or less the only general council of the eight we studied which really sought to control the organization with which it was connected.

Martin Rein has discussed the various sources of legitimacy which agencies intent on social innovation can employ to authorize their actions.[1] He argues that each strategy is insufficient by itself

---

[1] M. Rein, 'Social Planning, the Search for Legitimacy', *Journal of the American Institute of Planners* (Vol. 35, No. 4, July 1969).

for each has inherent limitations. The first source of legitimacy is *élite consensus*: having the proposed social reform endorsed and supported by the leadership of the major institutions in the community. The greater the diversity of institutional interest that is embraced within such a planning structure, the greater can be the claim for legitimacy since it can be claimed that most of the 'total community' is represented.[1] But as legitimacy is strengthened, Rein suggests, innovation will probably be foresaken in favour of maintaining a consensus on which these divergent interests can agree. Invoking an *élite* consensus is the method recommended by the Community Relations Commission, and in Chapter 3 we began to outline some of the shortcomings of relying on an *élite* strategy to bring about change at the local level. We will demonstrate in Chapters 7 and 8 the fallacies inherent in the C.R.C.'s assumptions that *élite* consensus is compatible with significant social innovation.

The second important source of legitimacy quoted by Rein is *citizen participation*: the mobilization of low-income or under-privileged groups to protest. In his article, Rein discusses inherent problems in this approach, which has been used by Saul Alinsky, among others.

Efforts to organise low-income communities encounter difficulties in sustaining a high level of participation especially when programmes have only marginal meaning for the residents and offer little opportunity for changes in jobs, housing, and other amenities. There is also the danger that issues are selected more for their capacity to rally interest than for their intrinsic merit. Protests can become ends in themselves instead of platforms for bargaining and negotiating. But without an issue for protest organisations are likely to succumb to the meaningless ritual of organisation for its own sake.[2]

When protest groups are sponsored by social welfare organizations they may rapidly lose their authenticity as grass-roots movements and be used to promote bureaucratic goals.

A third source of legitimacy which Rein identifies, is 'rational analysis': the results of research. This too has its limitations in so far as claims cannot validly be made about the existence of a 'value free' social science. The power of knowledge cannot surmount political problems of implementation.

Though each strategy has inherent limitations, Rein suggests

[1] Rein, op. cit.   [2] Ibid.

that this cannot be avoided by simultaneous pursuit of all three strategies. In fact he argues that if all three are employed by the same organization, internal conflict will follow. We would suggest that what happened between the B.C.R.C. and the Advisory Council can be explained in these terms. The dilemmas are inherent in the structure of community relations committees. Only the fact that the committees have virtually no power or resources prevents the occurrence of competition or conflict within the organizations.

Except Birmingham, the community relations councils we studied have general councils or committees, executive committees responsible to those general councils and wholly or partly elected by them, and subcommittees or panels responsible to their executives.

TABLE 4.2
COMPOSITION OF THE EXECUTIVES OF SEVEN COMMITTEES

Committee	Officers elected by A.G.M.	Members elected by A.G.M.	Members nominated by local authority	Co-opted members	Subcommittee representatives serving ex-officio	Others
Bradford	3	8	–	–	–	–
Ealing	3	20	3	1	3	1
Hackney	3	12	4	1	–	3
Huddersfield	4	6	–	–	–	–
Sheffield	2	5	4	4	2	2
Tower Hamlets	3	14	–	–	–	–
Wycombe	2	12	–	4	–	1

The status of those in category 'others' is generally ambiguous. Included in it are police representatives and local authority officials (including the secretary and treasurer of the Sheffield committee) whose formal position in the organization is not made wholly clear by the constitutions. In general, one can say that little attention is normally paid to the actual 'rights' of these people. If the committee had to make a specific decision on their voting rights, it is to be expected that they would be classed as non-voting members. Normally, as with local government committees, this ambiguous situation does not preclude such people from playing a major part in decision-making on issues which directly concern them.

8

CHAPTER 5

The White Membership of the Executive Committees

Sociologists for a long time have realized the connexion between urbanization and voluntary organizations. Wirth for example maintained:

Being reduced to a stage of virtual impotence as an individual the urbanite is bound to exert himself by joining others of similar interests into organized groups to obtain his ends. This results in an enormous multiplication of voluntary associations directed to as great a variety of objectives as there are human needs and interests.[1]

But since then W. G. Mather,[2] Geraldine Knupfer,[3] Mirra Komarovsky,[4] and Floyd Dotson[5] among others have drawn attention to the low levels of organization participation on the part of many urban populations. There is still much controversy over the actual extent of membership of formal organizations.[6]

[1] Wirth, op. cit., pp. 1–24.

[2] W. G. Mather, 'Income and Social Participation', *American Sociological Review* (Vol. 6, June 1941), pp. 380–4.

[3] G. Knupfer, 'Portrait of the Underdog', *Public Opinion Quarterly* (Vol. 11, 1947), pp. 103–14.

[4] M. Komarovsky, 'The Voluntary Associations of Urban Dwellers', *American Sociological Review* (Vol. 11, 1946), pp. 686–98.

[5] F. Dotson, 'Patterns of Voluntary Associations among Urban Working Class Families', *American Sociological Review* (Vol. 16, 1951), pp. 687–93.

[6] For example, on the one hand C. Wright and H. Hyman, 'Voluntary Association Membership of American Adults', *American Sociological Review* (Vol. 23, 1958), pp. 284–93, found that only 36 per cent of their sample of the American population belonged to any voluntary groups, whereas John C. Scott, Jr., 'Membership and Participation in Voluntary Associations', *American Sociological Review* (Vol. 20, June 1957), pp. 315–26, found that 64 per cent of his sample in Bennington, Vermont, were members of at least one association other than the church. The Detroit Area Study, *A Social Profile of Detroit* (Ann Arbor, University of Michigan, 1952), found that 63 per cent of the Detroit population belonged to at least one organization. H. Goldhamer, 'Voluntary Associations in the U.S.A.' (Ph.D. thesis, University of Chicago, 1943), found that 70 per cent of his Chicago sample belonged to at least one. N. Babchuk and A. Booth, 'Voluntary Association Membership', *American Sociological*

There seems to be general agreement that membership of voluntary organizations is positively correlated with the socio-economic class of the individual whether measured by income, education or occupation,[1] as is membership of more than one organization. The economic status of the neighbourhood also appears to exert some influence on participation when individual economic status is held constant.[2] More striking correlations have been shown between socio-economic class and active participation in voluntary associations as measured by frequency of attendance and in particular by office-holding. T. Bottomore[3] for example found in his examination of organization membership in the 125 voluntary associations in 'Squirebridge', a country town of about 15,000, that Class A (professional, managerial, technical) comprised 16·6 per cent of all members but 62 per cent of all officials, Class B (other white-collar workers) formed 23 per cent of all the members and 19·8 per cent of office-holders, whilst Class C (routine non-manual and manual) provided 60·5 per cent of all

---

Review (Vol. 34, No. 1, February 1969), and W. Bell and M. T. Force, 'Urban Neighbourhood Types and Participation in Formal Associations', *American Sociological Review* (Vol. 21, 1956), both give some reasons for this discrepancy in results. As far as England is concerned the findings of the 'Community Attitudes Survey', pp. 53–5, appear to be closer to those of the latter group in that 35 per cent of their sample belong to no organization at all and 47 per cent belong to none in the local authority area in which they live.

[1] Komarovsky, op. cit., found 60 per cent of the working-class men, 53 per cent of the white-collar men, and 2 per cent of the professional men in her sample had no organizational affiliation apart from the church. Similarly, Dotson, op. cit., found in his sample of fifty working-class families in New Haven that three-fifths of the men and four-fifths of the women did not participate in any formally organized association. On further investigation it was found that ten out of the twenty-nine memberships held by men and three out of the fifteen held by women were inactive. Mather, op. cit., found that only 3·1 per cent of the higher class in his sample did not belong to any organization as compared with 25·7 per cent of the lower class, and 72·5 per cent of the upper class belonged to more than one compared to 34·4 per cent of the lower class. See also L. Reissman, 'Class, Leisure and Social Participation', *American Sociological Review* (Vol. 19, 1954), and M. Axelrod, 'Urban Structure and Social Participation', *American Sociological Review* (Vol. 21, February 1956), pp. 13–18, and 'Community Attitudes Survey', p. 57. Even those studies concentrating on other determinants of participation refer to the pre-eminence of socio-economic class as a determinant, e.g. E. Littwak, 'Voluntary Associations and Neighbourhood Cohesion', *American Sociological Review* (Vol. 26, 1961), Babchuk and Booth, op. cit., and Bell and Force, op. cit.

[2] Bell and Force, op. cit.

[3] T. Bottomore, 'Social Stratification in Voluntary Organizations' in D. V. Glass (ed.), *Social Mobility in Britain* (London, Routledge & Kegan Paul, 1954), p. 359.

members but only 18·2 per cent of office-holders. Members in Class A had thus a one-in-six chance of being an office-holder, in B a one-in-twenty-eight chance, and in C, a one-in-eighty-one chance. Similar results have been documented in other investigations.[1]

The label 'voluntary organization' embraces associations of very different type and function. Several writers have attempted to categorize associations.[2] One particular typology employs a three-fold classification of: special individual interest associations such as recreational associations; special stratum organizations such as employers associations and trade unions; general interest organizations such as fraternal organizations, civic societies.[3]

Various studies have shown the relationship between the types of organization and the characteristics of the membership. A study of high- and low-income neighbourhoods in San Francisco found that the high-income areas had a higher percentage of members in what the authors termed 'general interest' associations such as civic societies. Members living in low-income level areas were more likely to be found in 'special stratum' organizations such as trade unions.[4] Similarly, Rex and Moore found in their sample of English people in Sparkbrook, that though about half attended no formal political, social or recreational organization, the largest group of those who did went to working men's social clubs.[5] Socio-economic class largely determines the type of organizations which individuals belong to as well as the rates of membership.[6] As a corollary, organizations which embrace all social classes in their membership are few.[7]

We have already pointed out that the role and function of the community relations committees has been the object of

[1] Bell and Force, op. cit., M. Stacey, *Tradition and Change* (Oxford, Oxford University Press, 1960), J. H. Goldthorpe *et al.*, *The Affluent Worker in the Class Structure* (Cambridge, Cambridge University Press, 1969), p. 93.

[2] C. Wayne Gordon and N. Babchuk, 'A Typology of Voluntary Associations', *American Sociological Review* (Vol. 24, No. 1, February 1959).

[3] W. Bell and M. Force, 'Social Structure and Different Types of Formal Associations', *Social Forces* (Vol. 34, 1956).

[4] Ibid.   [5] Rex and Moore, op. cit., p. 78.

[6] Goldthorpe *et al.*, op. cit., Appendix B, pp. 198–9.

[7] Bottomore, op. cit. He found that of the 125 organizations he examined only 70 had members from all classes and only 57 of these were organizations whose members actually got together. Also, W. M. Williams, *The Sociology of an English Village* (London, Routledge & Kegan Paul, 1956), pp. 121–3.

vagueness and confusion. The C.R.C. have prevented committees from being agencies committed solely to the securing of rights for Commonwealth immigrants. They are meant to act as a forum for discussion and mutual education and the end result is meant to be 'beneficial to the community as a whole'. The White Paper recommended that the committees be dominated by representatives of organizations already in existence rather than 'individual' members. Bearing in mind the relationship between income, education, and occupation and organizational membership office-holding, we would expect the membership of a community relations committee to be predominantly middle class. This is not only because they are participating in this 'general interest' organization with its formal constitutional procedures and committee mechanisms, but also because they usually belong to, at least, one other organization which partly provides their *raison d'être* at the community relations committee. Seventy-five per cent (67 out of 89) of the white members of the eight committees studied represented organizations in the locality. But within organizations a process of self-selection operates and delegates will be more likely to be those committed to a 'liberal' cause of this kind. This is not to say that the membership on the white side should be considered as really radical, for certainly as we have shown in Chapter 1 the progress of the official community relations movement has done much to discourage radical participation and has disillusioned many of the more militant in both the white and immigrant communities. Nevertheless one would expect the present membership of the community relations committees to be more concerned over social issues than the average. It is also likely that they will have been further educated than the average.[1] On the other hand, although it is unwise to exaggerate the importance of the organization-individual member alternatives, it is possible that the involvement of people as representatives to the community relations committee by virtue of their prior primary interest in another organization may lead in some cases to a membership lacking in motivation, especially if the community relations committee is only a secondary or at worst an *imposed* interest, which we shall see is the case with some nominated local

---

[1] M. Abrams, 'Politics and the British Middle Class', *Socialist Commentary* (October 1967). Also F. Parkin, *Middle Class Radicalism* (Manchester, Manchester University Press, 1968).

authority representatives. Some diversity in attitude and commitment is therefore to be expected.

At this point we can analyse the social characteristics of the English executive members of the eight committees to see to what extent they conform to the hypothesized characteristics outlined above. Factors determining the nature of the immigrant representation on the community relations committees will be considered separately in the next chapter.

The eight executive committees of the community relations committees comprise 144 members, eighty-nine British, and fifty-five immigrants.

TABLE 5.1
COUNTRY OF ORIGIN OF EXECUTIVE COMMITTEE MEMBERS

Committee	British Isles	West Indies	India	Pakistan	Africa	Total
Birmingham	11	4	2	2	1	20
Bradford	5	–	2	4	–	11
Ealing	21	3	4	1	1	30
Hackney	9	9	–	–	–	18
Huddersfield	6	2	–	2	–	10
Sheffield	11	2	–	3	1	17
Tower Hamlets	12	2	–	3	–	17
Wycombe	14	3	1	3	–	21
Total	89	25	9	18	3	144

One hundred and thirty-three interviews were carried out with fifty immigrants and eighty-three white members. When additional factual information has been obtained about non-respondents, this has been included in the tables.

One hundred of the 144 are organization representatives, sixty-five white members and thirty-five immigrants. The organizations which the white members represent are set out in Table 5.2.

An analysis of the social class of the white members confirms the hypothesis set out above, as can be seen from Table 5.3.

Table 5.2 shows an over-all number of seven white members coming from trade unions and trades councils. These however do not contribute significantly to the manual categories because in Birmingham, Bradford, and Sheffield the Trades Councils were

TABLE 5.2

ORGANIZATIONS REPRESENTED BY WHITE MEMBERS

	Birmingham	Bradford	Ealing	Hackney	Huddersfield	Sheffield	Tower Hamlets	Wycombe	Total
Local authorities	2	—	3	4	1	4	2	2	18
Churches	2	1	7	1	1	2	—	3	17
Trades Councils and unions	1	1	1	—	—	1	1	2	7
Community organizations	2	—	—	—	—	1	3	1	6
Political parties	—	—	1	—	—	—	—	2	3
Business organizations	1	—	1	—	—	1	—	—	3
Women's organizations	—	1	—	—	1	—	—	—	2
Councils of Social Service	1	—	—	1	—	—	—	—	2
Police	1	—	—	—	—	—	1	—	2
Others	—	1	3	—	1	1	—	1	7
Total	10	4	16*	6	4	10	7	10	67*

* This includes two persons representing two organizations each.

represented by their full-time general secretaries, all of whom had held that position for a considerable part of their working life. Furthermore, one of the two representatives from trade unions on the Wycombe committee belongs to a white-collar union, the N.U.T. In Tower Hamlets the T.G.W.U. representative is a full-time officer at Headquarters dealing with insurance claims. Thus, five of the seven 'trade union representatives' are 'white-collar men'. The remaining two consist of a foreman builder, member of the N.F.B.T.O. and vice-president of Wycombe Trades Council, and a printer, who represents S.O.G.A.T. on Southall Trades Council.

When the white members are divided further into occupational categories, the executives appear to contain an over-representation of professionals (clergymen, teachers, social workers, lecturers, and lawyers), and an under-representation of businessmen.

TABLE 5.3
SOCIAL CLASS OF WHITE EXECUTIVE COMMITTEE MEMBERS
(according to the Registrar-General's scale)

| Committee | Social Class | | | |
	1 and 2 *Professional,* *executive, and* *managerial*	*3a* *Routine* *non-manual*	*3b* *Skilled* *manual*	*4 and 5* *Semi- and* *unskilled* *manual*
Birmingham	10‡	–	–	–
Bradford	4	–	–	–
Ealing	17*‡	2	1	–
Hackney	6‡	1	1§	–
Huddersfield	4	2§	–	–
Sheffield	9†	1§	–	–
Tower Hamlets	9	2§	1§	–
Wycombe	12‡	1	1	–
Total	71	9	4	–

* Includes one member not interviewed about whom information was obtained.
† Includes three councillors.
‡ Includes two councillors.
§ Includes one councillor.

Eighty-five per cent of all the white executive members fall into social classes 1 and 2. All but two of the fifteen white office-holders on the committees are in these two social classes. There are no white members doing semi-skilled or unskilled jobs. Of the remaining thirteen in the routine non-manual or skilled manual categories, five are councillors. (We shall see that the participation of councillors is not entirely voluntary and that many of them cannot be described as committed and active members of the community relations committees.)

TABLE 5.4
OCCUPATIONS OF WHITE EXECUTIVE COMMITTEE MEMBERS

	Total	Number of these who are retired
Social and health workers	12‡	1
Clergy	11	–
Teachers, lecturers	11†	1
Housewives*	8	–
Managers, administrators	8§	–
Clerks in public employment	8§	3
Lawyers	7	–
Company directors, manufacturers	5‡	–
Trade union officers	4†	–
Accountants	2†	–
Printers	2†	–
Electrical engineer	1†	–
Police Inspector	1	–
Sales representative	1†	1
Foreman bricklayer	1	–
Armed Forces	1†	1

* These were located according to their husbands' occupation in the social class table.
† Including one councillor.
‡ Including two councillors.
§ Including three councillors.

The under-representation of businessmen appears especially marked if one takes into consideration the fact that five out of the thirteen 'managers, administrators, and company directors, manufacturers' are councillors.

Table 5.5. showing the amount of education received by white executive committee members reinforces the fact that they are largely a middle-class professional group. The largest single category consists of University graduates (40 per cent of all the white executive members).

The discrepancy between the social status of committee members and the local population which they allegedly 'represent' is particularly glaring in the case of Tower Hamlets. The 1966

TABLE 5.5

EDUCATION OF WHITE EXECUTIVE COMMITTEE MEMBERS

	Up to 15	School 16–19	Further education	University degree
Birmingham	2	2	2	4
Bradford	1	–	–	3
Ealing	1	6	7	5
Hackney	2	–	1	5
Huddersfield	2	1	1	2
Sheffield	2	2	1	5
Tower Hamlets	3	2	2	5
Wycombe	2	5	3	4
Total	15	18	17	33

Census showed that professional, employer, and managerial groups amounted to less than 5 per cent of the total working population of Tower Hamlets, which in the view of the local Council of Social Service 'could be regarded as too small for a vigorous and dynamic community life based on good leadership and social skills'.[1] The high proportion of professional representatives on Tower Hamlets' committee is partly explained by the fact that five of the twelve white members do not live in the borough. These comprise two who had been born in the borough, had left the area but had returned to work there as social workers, one as a senior career adviser, the other as head of the Jewish Advisory Bureau, a branch of the local C.A.B. network. Two others of the five have never lived in the area but one, the police inspector and liaison officer for the division, works in the borough. The other is general secretary of the Council of Christians and Jews, which though having a West End headquarters had originally directed its activities to the East End in co-operation with the Council of Citizens of East London. The fifth, the T.G.W.U. officer, born and bred in the borough, had moved to Essex three years previously but retained family contacts in Tower Hamlets.

Table 5.6 emphasizes the way in which Tower Hamlets community relations committee and to a lesser extent Hackney are exceptional. In Tower Hamlets the two members of the executive committee who have lived in the borough all their lives

[1] F. W. Skinner (ed.), op. cit., p. 6 and p. 53, refers to the G.L.C. Housing Committee's concern about the almost complete disappearance of the middle class from East London.

are significantly both borough councillors who work outside the borough. The remaining five white members who have lived in the area five years or less all work in the area in socially-oriented work (in the Church, local authority employ, or settlement houses). In each case the change of place of work had resulted in a change of former place of residence. In three of these five cases anyway their work was unavoidably residential.

TABLE 5.6
YEARS SPENT IN DISTRICT‡ BY WHITE EXECUTIVE COMMITTEE
MEMBERS

	All life	20 plus	15–19	10–14	5–9	0–4	Does not live in district
Birmingham	4†	–	2†	–	2	2	–
Bradford	1	2	–	–	1	–	–
Ealing	4*	2	2	2	5	4	–
Hackney	2*	1†	–	–	1	2	2
Huddersfield	2†	2	–	–	–	2	–
Sheffield	4*	3	–	1*	2	–	–
Tower Hamlets	2*	–	–	–	1	4	5
Wycombe	2	2	4†	1	3	2	–
Total	21	12	8	4	15	16	7
Councillors in total	10	1	2	1	–	1	

* Including two councillors.
† Including one councillor.
‡ District is defined as area served by community relations committee (e.g. in case of Wycombe it includes the R.D.C.) except in the case of London boroughs where district is taken to include contiguous borough as well, as long as there does not appear to be marked contrast in styles of life, wealth, etc. of contiguous borough.

The same need to recruit white members from outside the local authority is also evident in Hackney. The then Mayor of Hackney (an ex-Labour councillor who was defeated in his Dalston Ward seat in the May 1968 local elections but was nevertheless elected Mayor by both parties' agreement) lives in a different part of London. So does the full-time secretary of the Immigrants Advisory Committee of the London Council of Social Service.

In the case of all the remaining community relations committees serving county boroughs and in the case of Wycombe, a committee serving a non-county borough and its surrounding district, greater diversity in social class of the local population ensures that sufficient recruits for the executive committee of the type sanctioned by the N.C.C.I./C.R.C., can be found. But the inevitable corollary is that in the majority of cases such white members live in areas of the towns or cities comfortably far from the pockets of urban decay and high concentrations of immigrants.

All the eighty-three white members interviewed except for three, belong to at least one other organization apart from the community relations committee. These three include surprisingly the chairman of the Wycombe committee, for whom the committee's constitution had to be adapted to enable him as an 'individual' member to become chairman.

The other organizations which white executive committee members belong to are a good indicator of the motivation and self-selection which operate for both organization representatives and individual members. Table 5.7 shows that their interests are predominantly channelled through associations which could broadly be termed as socially or politically 'aware', rather than purely recreational associations. However there are noticeable differences among the committees, which go quite far in explaining the different 'styles' of various committees. This cannot be explained in terms of the class composition of the committees which as we have seen does not vary so very significantly.

Table 5.7. includes *total* organization membership including organizations which members represent on the committee with the exception of church membership *per se* which has been excluded from this particular list even though religious institutions can be affiliated to a committee, as is the case in Ealing where a local Methodist church sends a representative. This list must therefore be consulted together with Table 5.2 otherwise religious influence on the committees will be underestimated, e.g. the Anglican Church in Birmingham is represented by the Bishop of Birmingham's Chaplain for community relations.

Certain features merit comment. Firstly the degree of 'churchiness' of the Wycombe and Ealing Committees' representation. This is particularly striking in the Wycombe case, because the organizations represented or belonged to are all religious but not specifically concerned with race relations as is the case with some of the organizations in Ealing. When asked how and why

Table 5.7
ORGANIZATION MEMBERSHIPS OF WHITE EXECUTIVE COMMITTEE
MEMBERS
(according to type of organization and number belonging)

Birmingham
ten white members

	Organization	Number belonging	Office held
Party	Labour party	3	
political	Conservative party	1	
Multiracial	Anti-Apartheid	2	
	M.C.F.	1	
	U.N.A.	1	
	Birmingham International Council	2	
Union	Trades Council	1	secretary
Business	Chamber of Commerce	1	
Community	Sparkbrook Association	1	executive
associations/	Council for Neighbour Groups	1	
Neighbour-	Handsworth Community Venture	1	
hood groups	Ladywood Community Centre	1	
	Balsall Heath Community Association	1	
Health/	Shelter	1	
Welfare	Homeless Bureau	1	
	Catholic Friendship Housing Association	1	full-time worker
	Furnished Rooms Tribunal	1	
	Industrial Tribunal For Redundancy	1	
	Birmingham C.S.S.	1	
	Birmingham Settlement Commission	1	
Sports	Golf Club	2	
	Rugby Club	1	
Cultural	Friends of Municipal Art Gallery	1	
Total		28	

Bradford
three white members*

	Organization	Number belonging	Office held
Unions	Bradford Trades Council	1	secretary
Welfare	Bradford Hospital Management Committee	1	
Cultural	Bradford Historical Society	1	
Multiracial	Yorkshire Committee for Community Relations	1	
Total		4	

* No additional information on this point was obtained from the Bishop of Bradford (chairman) who is undoubtedly involved in a range of local organization on account of his position.

TABLE 5.7 (*continued*)

Ealing
twenty white members

	Organization	*Number belonging*	*Office held*
Religious	Society of Friends	1	
	Acton Council of Churches Race Relations Committee	1	
	Acton/Ealing Council of Churches	3	
	Moral Welfare Association	1	
	Fellowship of Reconciliation	1	
	Catholic Institute for International Relations	1	
Party political	Liberal party	2	honorary secretary (ex-local candidate)
	Communist party	1	
	Labour party	4	
	London Co-op. party	1	
Multiracial	U.N.A.	4	one—honorary chairman
	Indian Youth Club	1	
	Ealing Overseas Student Association	2	
Unions	Trades Council	1	secretary
	National Graphical Association	1	
	A.T.T.I.	1	
	N.U.T.	1	
Professional associations	Institute of Certified Accountants	1	
	Health Visitors Association	1	
Pressure groups	National Council for Civil Liberties	2	one on executive
	Hounslow C.A.S.E.	1	
Social/	Round Table	1	president
Welfare	Family Aid Society, Southall	1	chairman
	Ealing Elderly People's Welfare Association	2	honorary secretary
	London Training Committee on Youth Work	1	
	Catholic Housing Association	1	
	Rotary	1	
Community association/	Ealing Civic Society	1	
Neighbourhood group	Southall Neighbour Community Association	1	
Cultural/ Sports	Questors Theatre Club	1	
Total		42	

TABLE 5.7 (*continued*)

Hackney
seven white members

	Organization	Number belonging	Office held
Party political	Labour party	4	
	Conservative party	1	
	Co-operative Society	2	
Multiracial	M.C.F.	1	
	Human Rights Year Committee Hackney	2	one—secretary
	J.C.W.I.	1	
	U.N.A.	1	
	Anti-Apartheid	1	
	Council of Christians and Jews	2	
	C.A.R.D.	2	
Unions	S.O.G.A.T.	1	
Pressure group	C.N.D. Stoke Newington	1	
Cultural	Hackney Debating Society	1	one—secretary
	Hackney Education Forum	1	
	Hackney Society	3	one—executive
Social/	Jewish Board of Deputies	1	
Welfare	Rotary	1	
Total		26	

Huddersfield
six white members

	Organization	Number belonging	Office held
Religious	Society of Friends	2	
Party political	Labour party	2	
Multiracial	Yorkshire C.R.C.	1	
	International Women's Society	1	
Unions	N.A.L.G.O.	1	
Social/ Welfare	Lions	1	
Professional	Assistant Mistresses Association	1	
Pressure groups	Oxfam Committee	1	
	Famine Relief Committee	1	
Welfare	Hospital Management Committee	1	
Others	Federation of University Women	1	
	Federation of Women's Organizations	1	
	International Women	1	
Total		15	

TABLE 5·7 (continued)
Sheffield
ten white members

Organization		Number belonging	Office held
Religious	Council of Churches	2	
	Free Church Council	1	
Party political	Labour party	3	
	Conservative party	1	
Unions	Municipal and General Workers	1	
	U.S.D.A.W.	1	
Business	Trades Council	2	one—secretary
	Junior Chamber of Commerce	1	
Health/ Welfare	Yorkshire Council of Social Service	1	
	Regional Hospital Board	1	
	National Health Executive Council	1	
	Disablement Employment Committee	1	
	Adventure Playground Association	1	deputy chairman
Neighbour-hood group	District Federation of Community Associations	1	secretary
Total		18	

Tower Hamlets
twelve white members

Organization		Number belonging	Office held
Party political	Labour party	4	
Multiracial	C.A.R.D.	1	
	Anti-Apartheid	1	
	Martin Luther King Foundation	1	
	Council for the Education of the Commonwealth	1	
	Council for Education in World Citizenship	1	
	Shepherds Bush Social Welfare Organization (W.I. Organization)	1	
	British Caribbean Association	1	
	British Nigerian Association	1	
	Council of Christians and Jews	1	
	C.C.E.L.	3	
	Quaker Race Relations Committee	2	
Pressure groups	Peace Pledge Union	1	
	C.N.D.	1	
Union	T.G.W.U.	1	
Social/ Welfare	Brady Clubs Organization	1	
	Tower Hamlets C.S.S.	4	
	School Management Care Committees	3	
Neighbour-hood group	Tower Hamlets Society	1	
Total		30	

TABLE 5·7 (*continued*)

Wycombe
fourteen white members

	Organization	Number belonging	Office held
Religious	Council of Churches	1	
	Society of Friends	1	
	British Biblical Society	1	
Party	Liberal party	1	president
political	Labour party	1	
	Communist party	1	secretary
Multiracial	Human Rights Year Committee	1	treasurer
	United Nations Association	1	
Unions	N.U.T.	1	
	N.F.B.T.O.	1	
	Trades Council	1	honorary vice-president
Professional	Local Law Society	1	
associations	National Register of Housewives	1	
Welfare	F.H.A. Management Committee	1	
	Red Cross	1	
	N.H. Executive Committee	1	
	National Childrens Home	1	Board secretary
Cultural	Local Historical Association	2	
Sports	Sports Organization	1	vice-president
Total		20	

they became involved in the community relations committee, four of the thirteen white members of Wycombe, and five of the nineteen in Ealing cited religious conviction. Ealing committee has a higher average number of memberships per person than High Wycombe. It includes people holding office in 'pressure' group organizations such as N.C.C.L. and proportionately more who are active members of political organizations (for example the two Liberal party members in Ealing had both been local candidates for their party), or unions than High Wycombe. One may reasonably assume that religious influences are counterbalanced by other factors in Ealing. Four of the nine immigrants on E.I.F.C. thought there were too many 'church people' on the English side. By contrast the 'secularity' of Hackney community relations committee is striking. Only one church-connected person is involved on the executive, the Rector of St. John's, Mare Street, the main parish church in the borough. He is by no means a nominal representative recruited to show the Anglican Church is

9

participating. He had been a founder member of the I.F.C. in Willesden where he had been rector for the previous seven years. On moving to Hackney he deliberately sought membership of the committee.

TABLE 5.8
RELIGION OF WHITE EXECUTIVE COMMITTEE MEMBERS

	Church of England	Roman Catholic	Jewish	Friends	Methodist	Other non-conformist	None	Not known
Birmingham	4	1	—	1	—	—	3	1
Bradford	2	1	—	—	—	—	1	—
Ealing	5	2	1	1	2	1	7	—
Hackney	1	—	2	—	—	—	5	—
Huddersfield	1	—	—	2	—	1	2	—
Sheffield	7	—	1	1	—	1	—	—
Tower Hamlets	4	3	1	2	1	—	1	—
Wycombe	4	—	—	1	3	—	6	—
Total	28	7	5	8	6	3	25	1

Another contrast in the interests of white members as reflected by their organizational affiliations is apparent when Sheffield community relations committee is compared with other committees. The organizations which members in Sheffield belong to can all be considered highly 'respectable' and 'established'. There is a noticeable absence of any other multiracial group or pressure group of any type. At the same time, an effort has been made to involve institutions like the Trades Council. This 'establishment' orientation has been a conscious policy adopted by the chairman of the committee, who considers it to be the prerequisite for the continued support of the City Council. To some extent Sheffield community relations committee resembles Birmingham, except that the former has the money and the ear of the Town Hall as compensation. The Birmingham committee can be considered as hardly being taken into account by the local authority.

As is to be expected white executive committee members display greater than average political commitment in terms of

TABLE 5.9
POLITICS OF WHITE EXECUTIVE MEMBERS

	Labour			Conservative			Liberal	Communist	None	Won't say
	White executive	Councillors elected	Councillors nominated	White executive	Councillors elected	Councillors nominated	White executive	White executive	White executive	White executive
Birmingham	4	–	1	2	–	1	–	–	1	1
Total 10										
Bradford	1	–	–	1	–	–	–	–	1	1
Total 4										
Ealing	10	–	–	1	–	3	2	1	4	–
Total 21										
including one councillor, and one other executive member not interviewed										
Hackney	5	–	2	–	–	2	–	–	–	–
Total 9										
including one councillor not interviewed										
Huddersfield	2	1	–	–	–	–	1	–	2	–
Total 6										
Sheffield	2	1	2	1	–	2	1	–	2	–
Total 11										
including one councillor not interviewed										
Tower Hamlets	5	2	–	1	–	–	1	–	3	–
Total 12										
Wycombe	3	1	–	2	–	1	3	1	3	–
Total 14										
Total 87	32	5	5	8	–	9	8	2	16	2

Note The above table includes information about four committee members who were not interviewed whose political affiliations are well known. Three of them are Conservative councillors.

party political support,[1] and this again not surprisingly, is left of centre.

From Table 5.9 it can be seen that about half of the white executive committee members, forty-two out of eighty-seven, belong to or support the Labour party. Of the seventeen Conservative party members or supporters, nine are councillors, nominated to the community relations committees by their borough councils. Typical of these is a Conservative councillor nominated on to the Wycombe executive committee as vice-president. When asked during the interview why he was involved in the community relations committee, he replied: 'It would be wrong to allege I involve myself for any other reason than the fact that I am the chairman of the Rural District Council.' Five of the Labour members are also councillors nominated rather than elected onto the executive, whose commitment is also limited to the fact that they represent wards of heavy immigrant concentration, such as Spitalfields in Tower Hamlets and Attercliffe in Sheffield, which was the original reason for their being sent as delegates by borough councils to the committees. However, whereas there are no Tory councillors who have actually been *elected* onto the eight executives (all had been nominated as a result of their borough council's automatic right to appoint representatives), there are in fact five white Labour councillors who sit on the committees as a result of election from the general council of the community relations committee (also one Indian Labour borough councillor).

Only sixteen of the eighty-seven white committee members claimed they did not belong to or support any political party. Even if councillors are disregarded, about three-quarters of the remaining white members are party members or supporters. Only three of the eighty-seven white members said they did not vote in the 1966 general election.

Fifty-two of the eighty-five white executive committee members who were prepared to say how they had voted in 1966,

[1] Various studies have shown the connexion between voluntary association membership and political activity. R. Freedman and M. Axelrod, 'Who Belong to What in a Great Metropolis', *Adult Leadership* (No. 2, November 1963), found that the higher the level of formal group participation claimed by Detroit residents, the more likely they were to state they had voted. For further discussion of this, see M. Maccoby, 'The Differential Political Activity of Participants in a Voluntary Association', *American Sociological Review* (Vol. 23, 1958), and G. Almond and S. Verba, *The Civic Culture* (Princeton, N.J., Princeton University Press, 1963), p. 309.

had voted Labour (60 per cent). Forty-two of the sixty-six non-councillor executive members (63 per cent) had voted Labour. Only twelve had voted Conservative (18 per cent).

There is quite a degree of variation among the different committees with respect to the political outlook of their members. What Hackney committee appears to lack in religious motivation is made up for in political conviction. All the English executive members either belong to or support a political party. In this respect its membership is unique. Whereas some committees have a definite left bias in the political attitudes of white members (Hackney, Ealing, Tower Hamlets), some show a more even spread of political attitudes. Birmingham committee is an example of this, as is to be expected of a committee specially 'selected' to put pressure on 'influentials'. Wycombe committee is a better example. Nearly one quarter of its members belong to or support the Conservative party (see Table 5.9). A further description of these three might help to illustrate the diversity in commitment and motivation. One of the three is the vice-president, the chairman of the Rural District Council referred to earlier. Another is Mrs. John Hall who has been co-opted on to the committee because she is the local Conservative M.P.'s wife. She gives as her only reason for involvement the fact that as an M.P.'s wife she is obliged to participate in all activities in the constituency. Since June 1961, John Hall had been pressing for greater control of immigration from the Commonwealth. In May 1968, at an open meeting at Frogmore, in Wycombe, he denied that Enoch Powell's recent speech was racialist. He later tabled an all-party Parliamentary motion calling for a temporary stop to the entry of all immigrants including dependents until a complete survey had been made of the social and economic effects of immigration. In July 1968, he voted against the Race Relations Bill in defiance of the wishes of the Leader of the Opposition and the Shadow Cabinet, on the grounds that such a bill would stir up latent prejudice among the white community and make the work of those in the field of race relations more difficult. The last of the three members singled out in High Wycombe is the widow of a civil servant who originally spent ten years in the Indian army. She cited her colonial experience and her interest in missionary work (she was a practising Methodist) as the reasons for her involvement in the community relations committee.

TABLE 5.10

WHITE EXECUTIVE COMMITTEE MEMBERS AND 1966 GENERAL ELECTION

	Labour			Conservative			Liberal	Communist	None	Won't say
	White executive	Councillors elected	Councillors nominated	White executive	Councillors elected	Councillors nominated	White executive	White executive	White executive	White executive
Birmingham Total 10	4	–	1	2	–	1	–	–	1	1
Bradford Total 4	1	–	–	2	–	–	–	–	–	1
Ealing Total 21	13	–	–	1	–	3	3	–	1	–
Hackney Total 9	5	–	2	–	–	2	–	–	–	–
Huddersfield Total 6	3	1	–	1	–	–	1	–	–	–
Sheffield Total 11	4	1	2	1	–	2	–	–	1	–
Tower Hamlets Total 12	7	2	–	2	–	–	–	1	–	–
Wycombe Total 14	5	1	–	3	–	1	4	–	–	–
Total 87	42	5	5	12*	–	9*	8	1	3	2

* These figures are based upon the assumption that the known Conservative party activists whom we did not interview voted in 1966.

It is interesting that of the fourteen white members on Wycombe executive, three mentioned their experiences in the army in India during and just after the war, as one of the reasons for their becoming interested in the community relations committee. Two others mentioned more recent experience of the Commonwealth. The chairman, for example, had been a tea planter in India and is married to a Parsee Indian. Similarly, the one Conservative member on the Bradford committee is a solicitor who served as a young man in the Indian army and who was a Conservative councillor in the early 1960s. He speaks some Urdu and with the help of a Ghurka clerk has built up a large Pakistani clientele. He presented himself as more or less unofficial liaison officer for Pakistanis since 1952. He had been on both the earlier Council of Churches and Council of Social Service Committees on immigration in Bradford and remains today the treasurer of the community relations committee. He is however the only white member on Bradford's executive who has had experience of living in the Commonwealth, whereas five of the fourteen Wycombe executive committee have, by far a greater proportion than on any other committee. Thirteen of the eighty-three white executive committee members interviewed have spent a substantial period of time in the Commonwealth. Hackney is the only committee which does not include anyone in this category. Eleven of the thirteen cited 'service overseas' as one of the reasons for their involvement in their local committee. The nature of the service overseas ranged from service in the Indian army (four), to, in one case, working in India before and after independence as Nehru's secretary. Two others were actually born in India, and of these one has been recently teaching at the University of Accra in Ghana. Two others had worked in Africa for over twenty years, one in the Church in Zambia and the other with her husband on mass education programmes in various countries. Two others had spent a short time travelling and working, one in India, the other in Kenya.

These illustrations have been offered to suggest that differences of style may exist among different committees. The white members of any one committee are not necessarily homogeneous in terms of social class, degree of commitment to the work of the committee or in their interpretation of what the committee should be doing. Nor will the characteristics of executive committee members of different committees necessarily be identical or even similar. Subsequent chapters will point out the particular variations which different committees have adopted in the interpretation of their role. The differences of degree and kind of party political adherence and organizational affiliation spelt out should help to explain further variations in attitudes to crucial issues such as government immigration policy.

TABLE 5.11

ATTITUDES OF WHITE EXECUTIVE COMMITTEE MEMBERS TOWARDS GOVERNMENT IMMIGRATION POLICY

	Dissatisfied on 'Left'	Satisfied	Dissatisfied on 'Right'	Don't know or won't say
Birmingham	4 (40%)	4	2	–
Bradford	3 (75%)	1	–	–
Ealing	13 (68%)	4	2 (Tory councillors)	–
Hackney	7 (88%)	1	–	–
Huddersfield	2 (33%)	3	–	1
Sheffield	2 (20%)	5	3 (including two councillors, 1 Labour, 1 Tory)	–
Tower Hamlets	8 (75%)	1	1 (Labour councillor)	2
Wycombe	8 (57%)	5	1 (Tory councillor)	–
Total	47 (57%)	24 (29%)	9 (11%)	3 (4%)

From Table 5.11 it can be seen that there was more intense dissatisfaction expressed by white executive members from the three London committees on the subject of immigration policy than from the other committees, with the exception of Bradford. We shall see that Bradford's white members' dissatisfaction differs qualitatively from that of the members of the London committees.

An examination of the attitudes of members to the Commonwealth Immigration Act of 1968 (restricting entry to Britain of Kenya Asians with British passports), further shows some of the variations in attitudes.

Although the majority of the white executive committee members on each committee claimed they disapproved of the 1968 Act (and, as we shall see, a majority of the immigrants on the committees, too), not all the committees expressed their concern to the N.C.C.I. Both Bradford and Sheffield community relations committee failed to register an objection, considering

TABLE 5.12
ATTITUDES OF WHITE EXECUTIVE COMMITTEE MEMBERS TOWARDS
1968 IMMIGRATION ACT

	Approve	Disapprove	Don't know
Birmingham	1	8 (80%)	1
Bradford	–	4 (100%)	–
Ealing	3 (including two Tory councillors)	14 (74%)	2
Hackney	1	7 (88%)	–
Huddersfield	1	5 (83%)	–
Sheffield	4 (including two councillors, 1 Tory, 1 Labour)	6 (60%)	–
Tower Hamlets	3 (including 1 Labour councillor)	9 (75%)	–
Wycombe	4 (including 1 Tory councillor)	10 (71%)	–
Total	17 (20%)	63 (76%)	3

this a matter for the National Committee, not a local committee concern. Significantly the C.R.O. in Bradford had been reported in the *Telegraph and Argus* as stating that Bradford had reached saturation point and justifying the passing of the 1968 Commonwealth Immigration Act. At the annual general meeting of the Bradford committee held a month after this statement, the executive refused to dissociate itself from the C.R.O.'s statement. Nevertheless, in reply to our question, the white executive committee members (who included the committee's leading figures, its chairman and treasurer) unanimously expressed disapproval of the legislation. Three out of four of them claimed they were generally dissatisfied with government immigration policy. The point is that although the executive expressed quite 'militant' views to us, they had taken no action to express their views more forcibly and their main spokesman, the C.R.O., had put forward the opposite opinion with no comeback from the members.

Sheffield's failure to register any complaint about the 1968 Commonwealth Immigration Act is more easily explicable. Although more white executive members claimed they disapproved than approved of the 1968 Act, the responses to the previous, more general question about immigration policy are a better indication of why Sheffield's committee took no action. The white executive contains the lowest proportion, of all the eight committees, of those who expressed dissatisfaction with government immigration policy, which they considered too restrictive, and a higher proportion than any other committee of those who considered existing immigration policy too *liberal*. The margin between those who disapproved and those who approved of the 1968 Act was also far smaller among the Sheffield white executive committee members, than on any other committee.

Members of the executives of the eight committees were also asked their attitude towards the Race Relations Act of 1968 (which extended the limited provisions of the 1965 Race Relations Act to discrimination in the fields of housing, employment, and credit facilities).

TABLE 5.13
ATTITUDES OF WHITE EXECUTIVE COMMITTEE MEMBERS TOWARDS 1968 RACE RELATIONS ACT

	Satisfactory	Inadequate	Unnecessary/ Undesirable	Don't know
Birmingham Total 10	6	1 (10%)	2	1
Bradford Total 4	2	2 (50%)	–	–
Ealing Total 19	8	6 (31%)	4 (including 2 Tory councillors)	1
Hackney Total 8	2	6 (75%)	–	–
Huddersfield Total 6	5	–	–	1
Sheffield Total 10	8	1 (10%) (councillor)	1 (councillor)	–
Tower Hamlets Total 12	4	6 (50%)	1	1
Wycombe Total 14	6	6 (43%) (1 councillor)	2	–
Total 83	41 (50%)	28 (34%)	10 (12%)	4 (4%)

The attitudes of the members reflected factors such as whether the committees had in fact discussed the contents of the Race Relations Act, and if so at what stage in the process of legislation, and with what purpose. The committees which had discussed it exhaustively in the early stages when it was not yet enacted included more white executive members who were aware of its inadequacies. The very fact they considered it the committee's function to examine the proposals, and criticize if necessary, or suggest alternatives, implied they recognized the provisions could be inadequate. Conversely, the fact that a high proportion of white executive members on a committee may have expressed dissatisfaction with the extent of the Act's power did not necessarily mean that the committee had actually done anything to intervene in the procedural stages of the legislation.

Hackney for example, whose white members expressed the greatest amount of dissatisfaction with the adequacy of the new provisions, had discussed the preliminary Street Report. In September 1967 it set up an *ad hoc* committee to study the Bill as soon as it was issued, and recommended an extension of the proposed powers of the Race Relations Board. Bradford committee on the other hand refused to discuss the Race Relations Bill when some members wanted to do so at their A.G.M. in April 1968, on the grounds that no useful purpose was served by discussing it when the likely changes were not yet settled! It does not ever appear to have rediscussed the Bill or the eventual Act, yet half of the white members considered the provisions of the Act inadequate but considered, no doubt, that it was not the committee's role to make recommendations.

Actions by the other six committees fall somewhere between these two extremes. Birmingham, Tower Hamlets, Ealing, and Wycombe executive committees all issued critiques of the Bill in the spring and summer of 1968. Tower Hamlets committee sent their amendment to the Home Office. The latter two committees notified their respective M.P.s of their views. Huddersfield committee held a public meeting about the Bill in June 1968 but there is no mention on the minutes of any amendments being proposed, and all the white executive committee members appeared quite satisfied with the 1968 provisions. Sheffield seems to have been the only other committee, apart from Hackney, which discussed the Street Report in March 1968 and they referred it to their employment subcommittee. Two executive committee members were sent to the meeting which the N.C.C.I. convened with the Home Secretary in the early stages of the Bill. There is no record of any suggested amendments by the committee. The minutes record that the C.R.O. held a meeting in the Attercliffe area to explain the Bill to Pakistanis in June 1968. No further action was taken. The overwhelming majority of the white executive committee members of Sheffield committee appeared quite satisfied with the Act in 1969.

Further light will be thrown on the significance of these tables when the attitudes of the immigrant members of the executives of the eight committees are similarly tabulated (Chapter 6). It will then be shown to what extent the attitudes of immigrant members resemble those of white members of their committee, whether there is a difference in priorities in the expression of disapproval by immigrant members of different committees as well as by immigrant and English members of the same committee.

CHAPTER 6

Immigrant Representation on the Committees

Before the social characteristics of the immigrant members on the eight executive committees are considered, we will examine the pattern of immigrant settlement and the nature of immigrant organizations. In 1961, 71 per cent of the four major coloured immigrant groups, Indians, Pakistanis, Jamaicans, and other Caribbeans, were living in the six major conurbations, London and West Midlands having 47 per cent and 14 per cent of the country's total. The regional pattern does not vary much from one ethnic group to another but the proportion of Pakistanis in the Yorkshire conurbations is relatively high. New immigrants between 1961–6 tended to make their home on the basis of the regional distribution of 1961, so that the distribution remains much the same.[1] A number of factors encourage co-operation and organization among immigrants from the same place of origin. There are also reasons why social interaction among immigrants from the same country should follow the same patterns of demarcation and cleavage as at home. In particular, settlement patterns among Asian immigrants follow linguistic regional divisions, and then more specifically village and kin groupings.[2] Asian immigrants come mainly from four distinct regions of India and Pakistan. The Indians from the Jullundur and Hoshiarpur districts of the Punjab, and from Central and South Gujerat, the Pakistanis from the Punjabi-speaking area of West Pakistan including the Mirpur district of Kashmir, and the Sylhet district of East Pakistan.[3] In

[1] Rose *et al.*, op. cit., pp. 100–3. In 1966, 59 per cent were living in London and the West Midlands. N. Deakin, B. Cohen, and J. McNeal, *Colour, Citizenship and British Society* (London, Panther, 1970).
[2] R. Desai, *Indian Immigrants in Britain* (London, Oxford University Press, for Institute of Race Relations, 1963).
[3] See Chapter 'The Sending Societies' in Rose *et al.*, op. cit., for full description.

the U.K., immigrant village-kin groups may spread over a number of towns. In different parts of the U.K., in terms of social interaction it is the village-kin group which unites immigrants into different linguistic regional communities. Immigrant associations are also contained within the linguistic regional group. There is no association which decisively crosses linguistic-regional barriers. The regional socio-cultural wholes which constitute isolable—social—systems in India are also the largest units found here.[1] There is no 'all-India' society. The Indian Association in Bradford and the Indian Society of Great Britain in Birmingham described by Desai were composed almost wholly of Gujeratis.[2] Similarly, the Indian Workers' Associations are almost universally Punjabi.

Reciprocal obligations, consensus in decision-making, and cohesion characterize Pakistani social and economic relations in Britain as in Pakistan. This takes place in a clearly-defined patrilineage group, the *baradari* or brotherhood comprising a number of extended families. Therefore, East Pakistanis live exclusively apart from West Pakistanis (Punjabis or Azad Kashmiris). Demographically the two Pakistani groups are different, the imbalance between the sexes being far greater among East Pakistanis than among West Pakistanis.[3] In Bradford, there is no sharing between West Pakistanis from different regions. Campbellpuris and Mirpuris generally avoid each other and houses are grouped according to area of origin.[4] The same cleavage is found in the existing political and social welfare organizations. The National Federation of Pakistani Associations founded in 1963 is largely dominated by East Pakistanis and has been subjected to savage attack in the Urdu West Pakistani *Asia Weekly*.[5] In Sparkbrook, Rex and Moore noted that the Pakistan Welfare Society comprised East Pakistan members only, despite its president's claim that it represented all Pakistanis in Birmingham and despite the fact that the majority of Sparkbrook Pakistanis were from Mirpur and Campbellpore.[6] Such formal voluntary associations appear of very secondary importance in comparison with primary village and kin loyalties and over-all

---

[1] Desai, op. cit., p. 18.   [2] Ibid., p. 98.
[3] Rose *et al.*, op. cit., p. 441.   [4] Ibid., p. 444.
[5] Ibid., p. 504. Also, *Asia Weekly* (10 February 1968).
[6] Rex and Moore, op. cit., p. 167.

membership numbers are only a very small proportion. The Pakistanis have up till now been rather reluctant to take political action or become involved in organizations concerned with their domestic predicament in England. They are more interested in organizations pre-eminently concerned with issues of home politics and frictions between East and West Pakistan.[1] This tendency appears to be exacerbated by the fact that among Pakistanis there has been very little mixing of the landless peasants and the educated immigrants.[2] This was noticed by Rex and Moore who described an educated graduate Pakistani who was very aware of his 'superiority' over the majority of 'ordinary' Pakistani immigrants. He had been approached by fellow Pakistanis to form a Campbellpore Association but declined, his intention being to integrate into British society and leave the Sparkbrook Pakistani community.[3]

There does not appear to be the same fissure between the small section of urban, educated Sikhs and the majority of Jat farmers in the more homogeneous Indian Punjabi migration.[4] This is advanced as a reason why Sikh communities have thrown up so many leaders and have been able to organize community services on such a scale. DeWitt John pointed out that the reputation of Sikh immigrant leaders within the immigrant communities in Britain depended largely on their relationship with the 'ordinary' immigrant.[5] Most leaders won their way to prominence with their *Ilaqua* group through activities in England, the leaders being often the first from the *Ilaqua* to settle in England.[6] Within the Punjabi community in Britain there is very little regionalism. The *Ilaqua*

---

[1] See Rose *et al.*, pp. 445–51, which points out that very few complaints, for example, have been received by the Race Relations Board from Pakistanis. Analysis of the correspondence columns of *Mashriq* and *Asia Weekly* (circulation 24,000 and 14,000, in 1967) revealed not a single letter of complaint about racial discrimination. This point about Pakistani apathy was made independently to us by an East Pakistani in Tower Hamlets community relations committee executive, who had just co-founded a new 'League of Overseas Pakistanis' whose objective was specifically to increase the awareness of fellow Pakistanis about race relations in Britain. Restrictions recently imposed on the entry of fiancés by the Home Office has possibly made Pakistanis more aware of the religious and cultural implications in recent trends in government immigration policy.

[2] Rose *et al.*, op. cit., p. 453.   [3] Rex and Moore, op. cit., pp. 122–3.

[4] G. S. Aurora, 'The New Frontiersmen', quoted in Rose *et al.*, op. cit., p. 453.

[5] DeWitt John, *The Indian Workers Association in Britain* (London, Oxford University Press, for Institute of Race Relations, 1969), p. 141.

[6] Ibid., p. 53.

groupings express kinship and friendship ties, not a sense of identification with a district of the Punjab.[1] DeWitt John also illustrates
the extent to which competition for office in the local I.W.A.
parallels the nature of the struggle for power in Punjabi villages.
Each *Parti* or loose alliance in village politics derives its support
from kinship ties, connexions other than political, such as economic dependence, friendship, obligations for favours.[2] Similarly,
I.W.A. alliances include groups primarily of close kin, though also
of cliques of activists, but as Aurora points out the traditional
criteria of social status are reversed in the diaspora. The most
important quality for an emigrant is knowledge of English,
followed by influence with employers. Membership of a high caste
is the least important of granted attributes.[3] Greater heterogeneity
seems to be developing among Punjabis in England. DeWitt John
notes that the number of men who are only 'social workers' (that
is, informally looking after the welfare of fellow kinsmen) and
I.W.A. politicians is decreasing. The role of the 'social worker' is
changing because more recent arrivals from the Punjab (admitted
under 'B' vouchers as skilled professionals) tend to be university
graduates. The need for help in simple matters has decreased but
the need for help in more complex transactions such as mortgage
problems has increased. This has encouraged some 'social workers'
to leave factory jobs and go into business as insurance agents or
shopkeepers. Fewer I.W.A. officers now work side by side with
their followers in factories.[4] We found an example of such a
tendency among the community relations committee members we
interviewed in Ealing. One of the present Sikh executive members
had been general secretary of Southall I.W.A. in the early 1960s
and had worked as a machine operator on coming to England in
1961. Recently he set up on his own as an estate agent, with very
presentable premises situated along the main Uxbridge Road.
He had also recently been elected a Labour councillor for
Northcote ward. DeWitt John also points out the increase in the
number of non-Jats as the Punjabi community grows, and the
concomitant appearance of formal associations appealing to caste
minorities, especially scheduled castes.[5] DeWitt John points out
that the newly-arrived graduates often do not enter I.W.A.

[1] Ibid., p. 119.   [2] John, op. cit., pp. 95 ff.
[3] Quoted in Rose *et al.*, op. cit., p. 455.   [4] John, op. cit., pp. 116–17.
[5] Ibid., p. 121.

politics because of the firm control of existing politicians and also because they feel the I.W.A. is not interested in their predicaments as professionals confronted by discrimination.[1] The fluidity of Punjabi politics and the schism in the Indian Communist parties after the Chinese invasion have created further division among the Sikh political *élite* in Britain. The apparent homogeneity of the Punjabi immigration can no longer be assumed.

It is possible to identify within the immigrant population from the Indian subcontinent both the social bases of certain forms of social solidarity and some very marked cleavages. One cannot so readily deal with the social structure of the West Indian migrants in Britain. Studies of West Indians in Britain have come to conflicting conclusion about the distinctiveness of West Indian culture. Some writers, notably Patterson[2] and Richmond,[3] have emphasized the differences between West Indian culture and British culture. Others, such as Rex and Moore,[4] have stressed the similarities. In many respects this conflict arises from the fact that the West Indies is a highly stratified society with a very English upper class, a middle class which aspires to a stereotyped and now rather dated English life-style, and a lower class which is forced by administrators and teachers to defer to the English cultural model but lacks the resources either to establish a coherent alternative of its own or to follow the middle-class model effectively.[5] Accordingly, the different interpretations of West Indian immigrant culture derive either from differences between samples studied or from the West Indian's ability to present alternative faces of his mixed cultural model. In much of their social life they show an ability to move between behaviour that is recognizedly English and behaviour that has its roots in what may be called a West Indian culture. We do not intend to delve any further into this difficult subject, in any case the definition of any complex culture raises major problems. We have referred to it in order to throw light on the general lack of large or effective West Indian

[1] Ibid., p. 122. Also Rose *et al.*, p. 406.
[2] S. Patterson, *Dark Strangers* (London, Oxford University Press, for Institute of Race Relations, 1963).
[3] Research in Bristol by A. Richmond and M. Lyon reported in Rose *et al.*, op. cit., p. 423.
[4] Rex and Moore, op. cit.
[5] M. G. Smith, *The Plural Society in the British West Indies* (Berkeley, University of California Press, 1965), and F. Henriques, *Family and Colour in Jamaica* (London, Eyre and Spottiswoode, 1953).

organizations in Britain. This lack can be partly attributed to the diversity of islands from which West Indians come: most of the West Indian organizations that do exist are based upon specific island groupings. But the nature of West Indian culture is perhaps a more important factor in the general absence of solidarity. The most educated migrants from the West Indies used to regard themselves as British and to have no wish to be associated with immigrant organizations. At the same time the less educated but nevertheless upward mobile migrants were also more interested in acceptance by the British than in solidarity with the class of people they looked down on in the West Indies, and from whom they probably differed in life-style and possibly skin colour. Where they became involved in organizations within their ethnic group, it was in non-political 'fraternities', so popular amongst the 'respectable' upper-working and middle class 'back home'.

As far as the large underprivileged group of West Indian migrants are concerned, coping with urban housing problems and with the long hours of work necessary for both men and women to maintain an acceptable standard of living has left little time or energy for participation in organizations. In this respect they are no different from most other underprivileged groups, as we have shown. They find their recreational facilities in the West Indian sects[1] or in social clubs run by middle-class people, both black and white, for profit. Indeed many social organizations have sprung up which initially appear to offer some basis for black solidarity but degenerate into exploitative drinking clubs. These survive only because they offer a place where the lower-class West Indian can relax with his friends away from unwelcoming whites in English pubs and clubs.

As the middle-class West Indians have come to recognize that they are not readily accepted in what they were taught to regard as their 'mother country', naturally some of them have sought to establish organizations to represent the point of view of West Indian migrants. In building up organizations that will cut across class barriers, they have to face not only the common problem of apathy but also the suspicion on the part of working-class West Indians—coming from a rigidly stratified society that still has to overcome the impact of slavery and colonialism—that

[1] M. J. C. Calley, *God's People* (London, Oxford University Press, for Institute of Race Relations, 1965).

the middle classes are only interested in them to exploit them. The result is an absence of significant West Indian organizations despite numerous attempts at setting them up.[1] At the time of writing though, new organizations are beginning to emerge amongst young black men in London which may prove more able to win the support of a generation whose connexions with the West Indies are slight and whose sense of grievance is very deep. These associations involve a new more inclusive and more radical approach to the organization of the black people in Britain.

The main purpose of these comments was to emphasize that there are considerable differences in the degree of cohesion of different immigrant groups and that considerable cultural, class, and ideological cleavages may exist within ethnic groups. Even where an Asian 'community' may appear as a close-knit network to the outsider there will probably be a hierarchy of different statuses. Commonwealth immigrants bring with them certain social divisions which persist despite the transformations produced by immigration and settlement in a new social structure. Other new divisive factors may be symptomatic of integration within a new social structure. Political allegiances derived from the country of origin affect relationships within the same ethnic group. An important issue as far as the community relations committees are concerned would therefore seem to be how the committees should attempt to represent this heterogeneity. An example of how community relations committees can be affected indirectly despite themselves has been given by DeWitt John. He suggests that competition within a Punjabi community for office in the Indian Workers' Association can affect Sikh immigrants' relationships with multiracial committees:

If a Punjabi politician wins an office or becomes a personal friend of the most influential whites on a sub-committee it is quite difficult for his rivals to work on that sub-committee. After all if the two men are personal rivals within their own committee, then it is difficult for one to accept a position of inferior status in a context where both men are treated as representatives of their own community and conduct themselves as such. Moreover, if the politician on the sub-committee often has occasion to recruit other immigrants to participate in social functions, playgroups or other such activities, his prestige within the immigrant community will rise. His rivals may see this as a threat to

[1] Rose *et al.*, op. cit., Chapter 25.

their positions and feel obliged to denigrate the committee or even attack it in public.[1]

More problematically, should community relations committees attempt to sound out and help to articulate all interests in immigrant communities if they appear relevant to the social situation of immigrants in this country? Or should the community relations committees reflect the power situations prevailing both in immigrant communities and between different immigrant communities and the white population?

These questions are obviously intimately related to the goals which community relations committees formulate. These as we have indicated are by no means clear. In practice, the issue does not assume importance because of the committees' lack of power which means they do not become an arena for competition between different immigrant groups. Programmes and projects organized by the community relations committees rarely affect the life chances and life-styles of the vast majority of coloured immigrants. Gaining control of a community relations committee becomes an irrelevancy because of the irrelevance of what it can do.

It remains significant that community relations committees have often not considered such implications. Their attempt to involve immigrant organizations is rather haphazard. The main concern is the number of immigrant organizations involved rather than the interests or values represented. Sometimes care is taken to specifically exclude certain interests. The following examples will illustrate what can happen when community relations committees align with or against a particular immigrant viewpoint.

We stressed in Chapter 2 the importance of the relationship between the structure of an organization, its goals, and its strategies. Many 'voluntary liaison committees' as they were called started with 'welfare objectives' (doing things for immigrants). Nottingham Consultative Committee was one of these. The following describes how some of the members tried to change its orientation by attempting to change its structure and on failing were obliged to withdraw from it.

After the 1958 disturbances in Nottingham, the Indian

---

[1] John, op. cit., pp. 125 ff.

Workers' Association and the Afro-Asian West Indian Union were invited to affiliate to the consultative committee. The West Indian group tried to politicize the committee and arrange for direct immigrant participation in the committee's affairs. Differences came to a head between 1961–2 during the discussions about the Commonwealth Immigrants Act. G. Powe, secretary of the Afro-Asian West Indian Union argued that the committee should openly oppose immigration controls. Eric Irons, the West Indian Educational Welfare Officer among Coloured People appointed in 1960 by the Nottingham Education Authority and considered the most influential West Indian by the consultative committee's white members, felt that 'the Committee should concentrate on work in Nottingham and the matter of restriction should be left to the politicians' (minutes, 10 April 1961). Although Powe won his point, his other suggestion that the committee meetings be opened to all interested coloured people who should be able to vote, was not conceded in essence. The consultative committee decided that others could attend as observers, not as voters. In 1963, Powe and his Afro-Asian West Indian colleagues resigned because they felt they could be more effective in building a politically conscious immigrant community from outside the consultative committee. They left partly as a result of the existing committee passing a new constitution which restricted participation to invited organizations.

Five years later, within what had become the official orthodox community relations movement, a similar sequence of events occurred in Bradford. There appears to have been disagreement from the time of the formation of the steering committee mandated to draft a constitution. The view of G. S. Sanghera, the chairman of the I.W.A., who represented the United Sikh Association on the steering committee and on the subsequently elected executive, was that the consultative council was dominated by a small group from the outset and that the council was unprepared to develop an equitable scheme for immigrant representation. In April 1968, Mr. Castell Hamilton of the Afro-West Indian Association, at the council's A.G.M., raised the matter of a speech reported in the local *Telegraph and Argus* in which the C.R.O. sought to justify the 1968 Commonwealth Immigration Act. The chairman's reply was that the C.R.O. had been expressing his own views and was not speaking for the council, and that despite the crisis in race relations caused by the 1968 Act, the consultative council would continue its work. This precipitated the resignation of Castell Hamilton (on behalf of the Afro-West Indian Association), and Sanghera of the United Sikh Association and the Multiracial Campaign Committee C.A.R.E. (Committee for Racial Equality, which had been founded in May 1966 to take action against racial discrimination where the consultative council failed to do so, but to work in over-all co-operation with the council). Their grounds for leaving were three-fold: the failure of the council to unequivocally dissociate itself from the C.R.O.'s statement, the failure of the council to make public their views on the Race Relations Bill, and the undemocratic way in which the A.G.M. had been conducted. The officers had been re-elected *en bloc* and there was doubt whether this sparsely attended A.G.M., with only twenty-two people present, had been adequately publicized. Attempts to get the support of the organizations who had left, notably an attempt to involve them in discussion on the possibility of setting up an immigrant centre, have been unsuccessful. A meeting called to discuss this proposal in January 1969 ended in mutual recriminations. Aggressive speeches from the floor were met by autocratic chairmanship and a constructive dialogue was impossible.

At the time of our research, therefore, there were examples of immigrant and other organizations ceasing to participate in community relations committees through disagreement with the dominant white group over the ideal structure and objects of the committee. Also, we found a converse example in Wycombe of immigrant organizations being discouraged from full participation in the committee by a long-established, predominantly-white executive committee which had been wedded to the same rather paternalistic approach since its inception in 1960. Eight of the present twenty-one executive members have been on the executive since 1960 and of these all are white except for one (the president of the Pakistan Cultural and Welfare Association). The secretary of the Commonwealth People's Association (an organization more or less confined to West Indians from St. Vincent living in Wycombe) complained during his interview that his organization, though founded in 1963, had not been invited by the committee to send a representative until 1965. He thought this was because the C.P.A. had been involved with the local Trades Council and

Young Socialists in trying to combat a colour bar operating in certain Buckinghamshire public houses, and had employed tactics of confrontation of which the committee disapproved because they caused too much publicity.

The elections at the A.G.M. in 1967 increased the number of immigrants on the Wycombe executive from four to eight (including a Pakistani treasurer who resigned during the year). An election was provoked largely by the fact that there were a number of new nominations from immigrants in the general council in response to an attempt by the chairman to renominate the retiring committee. Two of the seven white members who had been on the executive since its inception were in fact defeated in the election but reinstated through co-option. After the election one of the authors heard apprehension expressed by certain white members regarding the number of immigrants on the executive. There was certainly some reluctance on the part of white officers on W.D.I.C. to devolve responsibility on to immigrant members and the efficiency of the first immigrant elected treasurer in 1967 reinforced their fears. The officers had all been white until 1967 when a West Indian vice-chairman and a Pakistani treasurer were elected. However, a suggestion at a general meeting in 1968 (by the Trades Council delegate) for two co-chairmen, one immigrant and one white, was rejected on the grounds that immigrant members are 'insufficiently impartial'.

The logical extreme of exclusiveness operates in Birmingham where the community relations committee is appointed by the Mayor. In autumn 1968 after the fiasco with the Advisory Council, Birmingham's committee tried to broaden the immigrant representation on the nominated committee. One Sikh, one immigrant woman (the woman selected, a Pakistani, has since resigned through lack of time), and one working-class West Indian (a delegate from the T.G.W.U. to the Birmingham Trades Council) now sit on the B.C.R.C. because the committee considered it had previously been deficient in immigrant 'representation'. The immigrant members had up till then consisted of two doctors, one graduate teacher (a Pakistani), one Barbadian Methodist Chaplain for Overseas People, a representative from the Jamaican High Commission, and a West Indian bus driver.

A further factor which must be taken into account when analysing characteristics of immigrant participation is that just as

certain organizations and individuals have left committees after
adverse experiences, other immigrant organizations have refused
to participate on principle, thereby limiting the potential recruit-
ing-ground. I.W.A., Great Britain (which is now distinct and
separate from I.W.A. Southall, which does participate in Ealing
committee and in the N.C.C.I./C.R.C.), of which the Birmingham
branch is the most important, has never participated in community relations committees or the N.C.C.I./C.R.C., on principle,
considering them 'the product of a racialist document'[1] (the 1965
White Paper). It did however participate intermittently in the
West Midlands Commonwealth Welfare Council and is also
affiliated to Smethwick Council of Social Service.[2] During the
early 1960s it co-operated with the Coordinating Committee
against Racial Discrimination, a radical campaign committee set
up in 1961. Recently, the I.W.A. in Birmingham has engaged in
more public activity in response to the spate of racialist comments
emanating from a few City Hall spokesmen or from Tory national
politicians using the West Midlands as a platform. In March 1969,
1,000 members of the I.W.A. marched through Birmingham and
held a protest meeting against discrimination.[3] In 1968, it helped
to form the Black People's Alliance which had a mainly Birmingham base. DeWitt John also notes that militancy has not altogether kept the officers of I.W.A. Birmingham from co-operating
with officials of the N.C.C.I. They have referred to them cases of
discrimination. There is a great deal of informal contact and
co-operation on such matters, but also a concomitant fear felt by
I.W.A. leaders that this might lead to or be interpreted as
co-optation.[4]

In Huddersfield, the I.W.A. follows the I.W.A., Great
Britain, policy of not joining the community relations committee.
As an organization the I.W.A. there is not very strong and does
not compare for example even with Bradford I.W.A. The
president of Bradford I.W.A., Sanghera, followed the official
policy of boycott but kept in touch with the community relations
committee by participating in it wearing 'another hat', as the
representative of the United Sikh Association, until the debacle in

---

[1] *The Victims Speak* (I.W.A. Birmingham, 1965). See also John, op. cit., pp. 160–1,
and footnote p. 165.
[2] John, op. cit., p. 162.   [3] *Birmingham Post* (24 March 1969).
[4] John, op. cit., p. 163.

the spring of 1968. Also operating in Bradford is a branch of the Universal Coloured Peoples Association—advocating one variation of the Black Power philosophy—of which Abdullah Patel is the most vociferous spokesman. Not unexpectedly he has nothing but scorn for the Bradford community relations committee. What is more interesting is that he does in fact maintain a certain degree of communication with the committee if only in order to know what the 'devil is up to'. For example he was present at the meeting convened by the chairman, the Bishop, in January 1969, to discuss the possibility of setting up a social centre for immigrants in Bradford, although he certainly did not have a good word to say for the community relations committee while he was there.

In a similar way, at a national level, the West Indian Standing Conference expressed hostility towards the N.C.C.I. It withdrew from C.A.R.D. after two members of C.A.R.D. executive committee accepted to sit on the N.C.C.I., and stated that the 'V.L.C.s and numerous immigrant advisory councils while providing harmless outlets for well meaning people and jobs for the boys merely scratched the surface, and a much more serious attempt had to be made to contact organisations truly representing immigrants'.[1] On the local level, though, officers of W.I.S.C. have been involved in community relations committees. The C.R.O. in Tower Hamlets, Joe Hunte, is chairman of the W.I.S.C. One of the West Indian executive members of Hackney committee is on the W.I.S.C. executive. In Haringey the W.I.S.C. branch worked together with the recently-established community relations committee to try to persuade the Conservative Borough Council to alter its proposals for 'banding' and dispersing immigrant children among the various comprehensive schools in the borough.[2]

With all these reservations in mind, we can examine the nature of immigrant representation on the eight executive committees. On the face of it, 64 per cent, 35 out of 56 of the total number of immigrants on the executive committees, represent organizations (see Table 6.2). Obviously the whole question of what constitutes an immigrant organization comes to mind. The fissiparity of certain organizations has been documented.[3] At what point a group with loyalties based on kin, place of origin, cultural

---

[1] Rose *et al.*, op. cit., p. 509.   [2] *Race Today* (April, May, June 1969 issues).
[3] See for example John, op. cit., pp. 125 ff.

or political affinity becomes an 'organization' is hard to define, as Birmingham Advisory Council found to its cost.[1] When the Birmingham Advisory Council was inaugurated in February 1967 it included thirty-five immigrant organizations. By the autumn of 1968, seventy-three immigrant organizations belonged. In the month before the disastrous A.G.M. in October 1968, eleven new immigrant organizations applied for membership. Some of these organizations were undoubtedly created for the purpose of participating in the struggle for the chairmanship of the Advisory Council but it certainly raised the problem of what criteria should be employed for identifying a bona fide organization. The 'objective' criterion decided on by B.C.R.C. when it revised its constitution and created a 'community relations conference' in the place of the Advisory Council which it disowned, was a minimum membership of one hundred.

At the other extreme, leaders without organizations may be a product of the definition employed. The extent to which a self-appointed leader will be able to function will often depend more on the way in which the 'host community' on the community relations committee perceive him, than on his degree of acceptance by fellow immigrants. This applies to situations we found in community relations committees where immigrant members were known previously by the whites instrumental in the setting-up of the committee, and so were invited to participate. For example, in Birmingham, the one African on the committee, a South African coloured doctor who has lived in Birmingham since before the war, was personally well known to the chairman. They had been involved together in the Afro-American West Indian League of Coloured Peoples during the 1940s and in similar organizations set up to combat the discrimination experienced in England by coloured servicemen. He was invited by the present committee chairman to join B.C.R.C. partly for this reason, and he was meant to represent 'African interests' though he freely admitted during the interview that he was not in contact with any existing African organizations in the city.

In Hackney, several West Indians personally known to a social worker from the Immigrants Advisory Bureau of the London Council of Social Service were invited to participate in the

[1] 'Liaison Committees—Who Keeps Control of What?', *Institute of Race Relations Newsletter* (November–December 1968).

H.C.R.C. The West Indian information officer employed by the Town Hall since 1959, invited his G.P., a Barbadian doctor, to the 1965 steering committee which formed the present H.C.R.C. He, in turn, publicized the committee among his patients.

Thirty-five of the fifty-six immigrants on the eight executive committees represent organizations. These are tabulated in Table 6.1.

Table 6.1 is little help without some clarification of the size, function, and outlook of the organizations. Of those who represent organizations, the overwhelming majority come from organizations specifically for their own ethnic group. The one person noted as representing 'immigrants organizations' is a Pakistani who helps in the Immigrants Advisory Bureau now recognized as a local branch of the C.A.B., run by immigrants with a full-time Nigerian worker, for an immigrant clientele consisting mainly of East Pakistanis resident in the Spitalfields area. The four representing 'white dominated' organizations include a Barbadian Methodist Chaplain for Coloured People and a West Indian delegate from the Trades Council in Birmingham, a West Indian member of Southall Trades Council in Ealing, and a Pakistani representing the Workers Educational Centre, a part of Toynbee Hall specifically concerned with providing language tuition.

The fourteen West Indians representing West Indian organizations cover a fairly broad spectrum. They range from an officer from the Jamaican High Commission in Birmingham to a representative from the articulate North London West Indian Association affiliated to the West Indian Standing Conference in Hackney. Originally the Jamaican High Commission representative was the only West Indian on the Birmingham committee much to the chagrin of local W.I. organizations. The attitude of all the High Commissions, Indian, Pakistan, and West Indian, has been to discourage political association among immigrants.[1]

There are considerable difficulties involved in attempting to classify different immigrant organizations. Some West Indian organizations specifically reserve membership to immigrants from the same island. Others, although nominally more comprehensive, in practice tend to attract members from the same island. For example, the Commonwealth Peoples Association in Wycombe

[1] Desai, op. cit., p. 103, Rex and Moore, op. cit., p. 171, Rose *et al.*, op. cit., pp. 500-4.

TABLE 6.1
ORGANIZATIONS REPRESENTED BY IMMIGRANT MEMBERS

Organizations	Birmingham	Bradford	Ealing	Hackney	Huddersfield	Sheffield	Tower Hamlets	Wycombe	Total
West Indian	2	–	3	3	1	1	1	3	14
Indian	2	1	2	–	–	–	–	1	6
Pakistani	1	1	1	–	1	1	1	3	9
Immigrant	–	–	–	–	–	–	1	–	1
African	–	–	–	–	–	1	–	–	1
White-dominated	2	–	1	–	–	–	1	–	4
Local authorities	–	–	1	–	–	–	–	–	1
Total	7	2	8	3	2	3	4	7	36*

* This total includes one individual representing two organizations.

TABLE 6.2

WEST INDIAN ORGANIZATIONS ON EXECUTIVE COMMITTEES

	Island associations mainly concerned with West Indian politics and providing social and cultural facilities for compatriots in Britain	Number representing
Hackney	St. Kitts, Nevis Anguilla Association	1
Birmingham	Barbadian Association	1
	General Social and Cultural Organizations	
Sheffield	Sheffield West Indian Association	1
Ealing	Caribbean Overseas Association	2
Wycombe	Commonwealth Peoples Association	3
Hackney	Fraternities—mutual aid societies	2
	Organizations concerned more with social welfare and political needs	
Huddersfield	West Indian Welfare Association	1
Hackney	North London West Indian Association	1
Tower Hamlets	West Indian League	1
Ealing	Afro-Caribbean Association, Southall	1

consists largely of immigrants from St. Vincent, and the North London West Indian Association of Jamaicans and Barbadians. Although the latter and the St. Kitts and Nevis Anguilla Association both function in the Hackney area, there is little, if any, contact between them. The lack of contact between the Caribbean Overseas Association and the Afro-Caribbean Association, both functioning in Ealing, is the result of difference in declared goals. The C.O.A. is primarily a sports and social club. Its secretary thought that the Afro-Caribbean Association was too concerned with political issues such as Rhodesia and Enoch Powell, and insufficiently concerned with the social needs of West Indians in Ealing. The Caribbean Overseas Association is currently negotiating with Acton councillors for the provision of a social centre.

Reservations have been expressed at the beginning of this chapter about the meaning of 'Pakistani' or 'Indian Association', and the partial segments of the 'community' which such organizations embrace. Further difficulties are entailed when one tries to classify Asian immigrant organizations according to their functions, since it is almost impossible to separate the fulfilment of religious needs from the fulfilment of other social and cultural requirements. Similarity in names does not necessarily imply any resemblance in the functions. The Indian Social Club in Birmingham has a fairly exclusive membership, mainly of professionals, and is not Punjabi. Its namesake in Ealing exists as a pseudonymous cover for a particular Punjabi socialist faction in the wider arena of I.W.A. politics in Southall.

TABLE 6.3

PAKISTANI AND INDIAN ORGANIZATIONS ON EXECUTIVE COMMITTEES

Pakistani Organizations		Number
	Concerned with social welfare	
Wycombe	Pakistani Association	1
Wycombe	Pakistani Cultural and Welfare Association	1
Ealing	Pakistani Welfare Association	1
Bradford	Pakistani Welfare Association	1
Birmingham	National Federation of Pakistani Associations	1
	Religious needs	
Wycombe	Islamic Mission	1
Wycombe	Mosque Fund	1
Huddersfield	Huddersfield Mosque	1
Sheffield	Sheffield Muslim Association	1
	Political purposes	
Tower Hamlets	League of Overseas Pakistanis	1
Indian Organizations		
	Social and cultural	
Bradford	Indian Womens Association	1
Wycombe	Indian Association	1
Birmingham	Indian Social Club	1
Birmingham	Sikh International Brotherhood	1
	Political	
Ealing	I.W.A. Southall	1
Ealing	Indian Social Club	1

The variation in the extent of support that such organizations command can be well illustrated in comparing the I.W.A. Southall and the Indian Association of Wycombe. The former, currently operating among the most concentrated Punjabi community in the country, and the only I.W.A. to possess a centre and a cinema, claims a membership of 7,900 in 1969. The original representative from the Indian Association in Wycombe, who was elected on the executive in 1967, is still referred to as the representative for the Association by the rest of the executive even though the Association, founded in 1963, floundered and folded up after three meetings due to inadequate support. The Indian community in High Wycombe is the smallest of the three main immigrant communities in the area. During the period we were interviewing, this Indian representative tendered his resignation since he had obtained a new job entailing night shift work. When we completed our field-work a year later there was still no Indian on the committee.

This example highlights what must be one of the most crucial questions regarding immigrant participation in the committees, namely the extent to which immigrant executive committee members are 'representative' or typical of their communities. We have indicated why one should not expect immigrant executive committee members to be 'typical'. Our data regarding the social characteristics of the immigrant executive committee members of our eight committees emphasize this anticipated atypicality. Table 6.4 demonstrates the discrepancy between their social position and that of the overwhelming majority of Commonwealth immigrants who, as the 1966 Census showed, are mainly employed in manual work.

TABLE 6.4

SOCIAL CLASS OF IMMIGRANT EXECUTIVE COMMITTEE MEMBERS
(according to Registrar-General's scale)

	Executive members Social class				Office-holders	
	1 and 2 Professional, executive, and managerial	*3a Routine non-manual*	*3b Skilled manual*	*4 and 5 Semi-skilled unskilled manual*	*1 + 2*	*3-5*
Birmingham	3	1	—	2	1	—
Bradford	4	2	—	—	—	1
Ealing	4	1	3	1	—	1
Hackney	3	1	4	—	2	1
Huddersfield	2	1	—	1	1	1
Sheffield	3	—	—	2	—	—
Tower Hamlets	3	—	—	2	—	—
Wycombe	1	—	1	5	—	1
Total	23 46 per cent	6	8	13	4	5

The amount of education received reinforces this point further. Thirty-eight per cent of immigrant executive members are university graduates.

TABLE 6.5

EDUCATION OF IMMIGRANT EXECUTIVE COMMITTEE MEMBERS

	Up to 15	School 16–19	Further	University Degree
Birmingham	1	1	1	3
Bradford	–	1	–	5
Ealing	1	2	3	3
Hackney	2	3	2	1
Huddersfield	1	1	–	2
Sheffield	1	2	1	1
Tower Hamlets	3	–	–	2
Wycombe	2	3	–	2
Total	11	13	7	19* (38 per cent)

* 16 of these are Indians or Pakistanis.

Participation in a community relations committee pre-supposes a certain degree of adaptation and orientation towards the British social and institutional structure, since participation implies some commitment to remaining in this country on the part of the immigrant. Thus we would expect immigrants to participate at a particular stage in their life cycle, probably when the immigration of dependents is complete, rather than when they are single or temporarily alone and treating the ethnic 'colony' as a 'dormitory'. The formality of community relations committee meetings, with their adherence to 'constitutional' procedures, also requires a certain level of education and fluency in English. It is consequently not surprising that these factors are reflected in Tables 6.4 and 6.5.

Table 5.1 showed the proportion of members on each executive who are native white, West Indian, Indian, Pakistani or African. Table 6.6 summarizes the number of years spent in the district by immigrant executive committee members. In most cases this period is nearly equivalent to the total period spent in England.

The over-all pattern of years spent in the district by executive members of different ethnic groups reflects the broad chronological characteristics of the migration from their country of origin to Britain, i.e. the earlier migration from the West Indies in the 1950s followed by a later immigration from Asia. For example, H.C.R.C. has nine immigrant executive members, all West

TABLE 6.6

YEARS SPENT IN DISTRICT* BY IMMIGRANT EXECUTIVE COMMITTEE
MEMBERS

	20 plus	15–19	10–14	5–9	0–4	Does not live in district
Birmingham	1	2	1	1	–	1
Bradford	–	–	1	3	2	–
Ealing	–	–	–	7	2	–
Hackney	2	4	2	–	–	–
Huddersfield	–	–	1	2	1	–
Sheffield	–	2	1	–	2	–
Tower Hamlets	2	2	–	–	–	1
Wycombe	–	–	3	3	1	–
Total	5	10	9	16	8	2

* This is defined in the same way as in Table 5.6.

Indians, who have lived in the area for over ten years. Bradford committee's immigrant members, all Asians, have with one exception lived in the district for less than ten years. The length of time spent in the area by executive committee members also reflects the period during which it has been serving as a reception area. For example, in Tower Hamlets, the two executive committee members who have lived in the area for over twenty years are both ex-seamen from Sylhet in East Pakistan. The East End has had a dockland immigrant community dating from years before the large-scale influx from Commonwealth countries.[1]

There are clear differences in the degree of education and the occupations of the Asian executive committee members and the remainder, all but three of whom are West Indians. Thirty-eight per cent (19 out of 50) of the immigrants on the eight executive committees are graduates. Of these nineteen, sixteen are Indians or Pakistanis, i.e. sixteen of the total of twenty-five Indian and Pakistani executive committee members interviewed. Most of the Asians on the Bradford and Huddersfield committees are professional people who are relatively recent immigrants. The six Asians on Bradford committee comprise a doctor and his wife, a solicitor, a businessman, a teacher, and the wife of a university lecturer. The two Pakistanis in Huddersfield were both graduate teachers. This is about as untypical of the employment pattern of Pakistanis in the West Riding as it could be. The majority of

[1] Banton, op. cit.

Pakistanis in the West Riding are employed in semi- or unskilled shift work especially in the textile industry. The one Pakistan interviewed from the Birmingham C.R.C. is also a teacher whereas the Pakistanis in the West Midlands are the immigran group with the lowest over-all economic status. Over 55 per cen are in the unskilled manual worker category (compared to les than 8 per cent of the local English and Welsh population) working in particular in the metal manufacturing and meta goods industries.[1] The absence of Pakistani organizations con cerned with the political or social predicament of Pakistanis ir Britain has been referred to. It does not seem unreasonable tc suggest that in the majority of cases those Pakistanis involved ir the community relations committees through their own initiative are those with the greatest possible chance of absorption intc middle-class patterns of life in England. To cite another example one of the two Pakistanis interviewed on Sheffield committee is ir merchant banking. This tendency appears most marked where there are substantial settlements of Pakistanis, especially ir Bradford where a professional and entrepreneurial middle clas: has become clearly distinguishable in the past ten years.[2] It is no apparent in Wycombe where the community is much smaller anc less occupationally stratified, nor in Tower Hamlets where Pakistanis concentrated in the traditional reception area o Spitalfields[3] live in the most obsolescent part of the borough anc are employed in disproportionate numbers at low wage rates ir the clothing industry.[4] As in the case of white representation or the C.C.T.H., Pakistani immigrant representation has to be supplemented from those living outside the borough. The mair East Pakistani organization operating in Tower Hamlets, the Pakistan Welfare Association, is mainly concerned with matter: of individual welfare or with Pakistan's domestic problems. It: membership numbered around 3,000 at one stage. It now stand: at about 1,000 to 1,500, but it is quite self-sufficient and does no send a representative to the C.C.T.H. It did send one in the pas but when he left the area the links between the two appear tc have ceased.

We began by giving a list of the type of organization:

[1] Rose *et al.*, op. cit., p. 173.   [2] Ibid., p. 443.   [3] Leech, op. cit.
[4] Klim McPherson and Julia Gaitskell, *Immigrants and Employment: Two Cas Studies, East London and Croydon* (I.R.R. Special Series, 1969), p. 31.

officially represented by immigrant members. More important to consider, however, are the relative positions of the representatives in these organizations, as well as the extent of their, and individual 'members', other formal and informal contacts, if one is to gauge the degree to which they can be considered 'community leaders or spokesmen'. Organizational affiliation cannot be taken as a very reliable indicator but it is interesting that only nine out of fifty immigrant executive members interviewed did not belong to any immigrant organization, or any association which could be considered a multiracial campaign organization other than the community relations committee. Their distribution among the communities is as follows:

TABLE 6.7

IMMIGRANT EXECUTIVE COMMITTEE MEMBERS BELONGING TO NO OTHER IMMIGRANT ORGANIZATIONS

	Number	Origin	Immigrants interviewed
Birmingham	1	South African	6
Bradford	2	Indian/Pakistani	6
Ealing	1	Nigerian	9
Hackney	3	West Indian	8
Huddersfield	1	West Indian	4
Sheffield	–	—	5
Tower Hamlets	–	—	5
Wycombe	1	Indian	7

As is to be expected, in Hackney where the majority Commonwealth group is West Indian and there are only West Indians on the H.C.R.C., over a quarter of immigrant executive committee members have no formal affiliation to immigrant organizations. This is in contrast to the E.I.F.C. where the presence of a highly organized Punjabi group may act as an incentive to the vocal West Indian minority to articulate their views corporately. Certainly the Acton branch of the E.I.F.C. was formed partly because the Caribbean Overseas Association felt that too much emphasis was being placed on the problems of Southall Punjabis and insufficient attention paid to their own needs. Attempts were made by Southall I.W.A. in 1965 to get West Indians in their vicinity to organize themselves better so as to be more effectively represented on the E.I.F.C.

Bradford provides an interesting case because the two members without affiliations are both Asians. As will be remembered, Bradford C.R.C. had considerable difficulty in retaining the confidence of local immigrant organizations. The two referred to are recent immigrants (1966)—one a teacher from West Pakistan, the other a Punjabi businessman, both graduates. When asked how and why they became involved in the community relations committee, both mentioned specifically that the committee found it difficult to recruit immigrant support. In fact, the Punjabi businessman had been co-opted on to the education panel of B.C.C.C.C. by the headmaster of his son's school, Bradford Grammar School. When all the other Punjabi organizations withdrew from the council, he was elected to the executive to help fill the gap. At the time we interviewed him he had never attended a meeting, and was contemplating resignation. He had become aware of the reason why he had been 'needed', and introduced us to one of the Sikhs who had resigned from the executive. We have illustrated already how the informal network of acquaintance operates to get some members involved and this explains the case of the three West Indians in Hackney and the one South African in Birmingham (mentioned in the table) who belong to no organization yet sit on the executive committee.

The overwhelming majority of immigrant executive committee members do belong to immigrant organizations, and in many cases hold offices. Very few immigrant executive committee members belong to anything besides an immigrant organization. Also, there is a definite cleavage between the types of organization to which immigrant executive committee members belong and those in which English executive committee members participate. This of course varies from committee to committee but it appears to be most acutely expressed (as to be expected) in committees where the ethnic division within the committee coincides with the class division. Wycombe C.R.C. is a particular case in point. Almost all the white representatives are professional or managerial. Almost all the immigrants are in semi-skilled or unskilled jobs. Even the one white-collar worker is a publican, not a 'professional'. This is not to imply that there is a lack of ability or necessarily of education among the immigrants (since two of them were graduates but both in manual work). Their occupations and accompanying social status may have affected the white members' perception of them. Cleavages may be exacerbated further by the very apparent age difference of white and immigrant executive committee members in Wycombe. At least four of the fourteen white members are 60 years or over and seven are 50 years and over. The rest are well in middle age with the exception of two young men of 25 to 30 years who had only been on the committee for one to two years and did not stand for re-election in 1969. By contrast all the immigrants on the Wycombe executive committee are in their thirties or early forties.

Certain problems of communication between white and immigrant members of the Wycombe executive have occurred. A considerable amount of importance is attached by white members to orderly constitutional procedure which is understandably not appreciated as an end in itself by the immigrant membership.

When immigrant representation on the executive includes some who have broken into a middle-class pattern of life, there is a greater likelihood of their and the white executive committee members belonging in common to some other organization apart from the committee, or of immigrant members belonging to other multiracial campaign committees and so on. This extra experience and the greater number of contacts with people in the race relations field which may accrue, may also affect the general 'style' of the committee and the expertise it can call on. A committee with a considerable proportion of professional immigrants need not necessarily, however, have immigrant members with numerous organizational contacts. As we have seen in Bradford's case, there can be powerful reasons discouraging immigrant organization *élites* from participating. Where such constraints do not operate, the correlation between the number and type of other organizations belonged to and the social class of the immigrant concerned is striking. In Wycombe where all but one immigrant executive committee member are in manual jobs, none belongs to more than one organization other than the community relations committee and these organizations are all 'immigrant' organizations. In Tower Hamlets the five immigrant members of the executive have fourteen memberships of organizations between them. All belong to at least one, but two of the five account for ten of the memberships between them. Both are graduates who had come to England in the 1950s, one from

Dacca, East Pakistan, where he was a journalist, the other from Guyana via the U.S.A. The former is now a West End restaurateur, living in Streatham. He was interested in the East End because it contains the largest Sylheti Bengali community in London. The latter was employed by Kensington and Chelsea Health and Welfare Departments as a psychiatric social worker. Both participated originally in the N.C.C.I. before the 1968 fiasco, are currently members of the Greater London Conciliation Committee of the Race Relations Board, and chairman and treasurer respectively of the Joint Council for the Welfare of Immigrants. They are also chairman and vice-chairman of Kensington and Westminster committees respectively. The former was also founder president of the National Federation of Pakistani Associations. He is now sponsoring the League of Overseas Pakistanis which, it is hoped, will concentrate more on race relations in Britain.

In Sheffield, two of the five immigrants interviewed account for seven of the eleven organization memberships, and for all the memberships of the associations centred outside the immigrant communities. One is the Deaconess Madge Saunders who came from Jamaica in 1966 at the invitation of the Presbyterian Church to do welfare work among West Indian women. She is currently president of the West Indian Association, on the Sheffield Radio Council Committee, as well as being on the Board of Governors of a local secondary modern school, and on the committee of the Sheffield and District Housing Society, a multiracial housing association formed in the late 1950s by the Sheffield Council of Churches. The other is Mr. Doullah, a young single West Pakistani graduate, who came to England in 1963 and lived for a time in Hampstead, London. He is now working in merchant banking with a Pakistani bank, is secretary of the Sheffield Muslim Association, a lay member of the local Hospital Management Committee, and a member of the Samaritans.

The same point holds for Birmingham, though in this case members of the committee have been picked specifically because of their alleged contacts. Here, two of the six immigrants interviewed account for nine of the total nineteen memberships. One is Dr. Prem, an Indian doctor, who came to England before the war, served as a Labour councillor in Birmingham shortly after the war, and was instrumental in getting the Commonwealth

Welfare Council for the West Midlands formed in 1956.[1] He currently lives in Halesowen, in Worcestershire. He was also chairman of the children's panel on the N.C.C.I., and on the N.C.C.I. executive, is vice-chairman currently of the Birmingham committee and was vice-chairman of the Advisory Council before its demise. He belongs to the Indian Social Club (which mainly caters for professionals), the Socialist Medical Association, the 'priority area playgroups committee', the central committee of Indian organizations in the West Midlands, as well as being nominal honorary president of the community relations committees in West Bromwich and as far afield as Newham and Gloucester. The other is a young East Pakistani graduate teacher, who came to England in 1963, was involved in student politics in Pakistan, is currently chairman (although this has been disputed) of the National Federation of Pakistani Associations, a member of the Black People's Alliance, the Vietnam Solidarity Campaign, and the International Cultural Society.

The immigrant executive committee members to a very large extent constitute an *élite*, either by being office-holders in immigrant organizations, or by being recently-admitted Asian graduates who are better equipped for adaptation to English middle-class society, or both. It is difficult to generalize to what extent the existence of the committee is of relevance to immigrants beyond those sitting on the committees. This will depend on a number of factors: what the community relations committee as a local organization can offer, the extent of local immigrant organization, and the attitudes of immigrant organization leaders towards the local committee. It is difficult to gauge how many Commonwealth immigrants actually belong to 'immigrant organizations'. It might be hypothesized that specific religious or cultural needs, a sense of common identity, and the awareness of their difference from the white society would lead to a greater rate of organization than would be expected among the indigenous population of the same class. For example, Goldhamer found that whereas among Protestants and Catholics working-class persons belong to fewer associations than their white-collar equivalents, among the Jews the relationship was reversed. He suggests that many of the Jewish workers are foreign-born and join *Landsmanchaften*, etc. These associations no longer attract their children who are also less

[1] Prem, op. cit., p. 30.

TABLE 6.8
ORGANIZATION MEMBERSHIPS OF IMMIGRANT EXECUTIVE
COMMITTEE MEMBERS

Organization	No. who belong	No. who are/were officers of this organization
Birmingham (Five immigrant members)		
Jamaican Community Council	1	
Barbados Association	1	
West Indian Community Federation (Winson Green)	1	
Sikh Temple Committee	1	executive committee
Indian Social Club	1	founder president
Sikh International Brotherhood	1	
Central Committee of Indian Organizations in West Midlands	1	chairman
National Federation of Pakistani Associations	1	chairman
Black People's Alliance	1	
Birmingham Trades Council	1	
Transport and General Workers Union	1	
Mt. Pleasant Community Association	1	executive committee
Anderton Park Parents Association	1	chairman
Socialist Medical Association	1	
Priority Area Playgroup Committee	1	chairman
International Cultural Society	1	president
Vietnam Solidarity Campaign	1	
Newham/Gloucester/West Bromwich Community Relations Committees	1	honorary president
Cricket Club	1	
Bradford (Four immigrant members)		
Pakistani Society	2	1—president
Federation of Pakistani Associations	1	
Pakistani Association	1	
Pakistani Writers Guild	1	
Indian Womens Association	1	secretary
Standing Conference of Womens Organizations	1	
Ealing (Eight immigrant members)		
I.W.A. Southall	3	2—present general secretary and executive member
Sikh Cultural Society	1	ex-general secretary
Indian Social Club	2	1—present executive member
Ahmaddiya Muslim Community West Middlesex	1	public relations secretary
Pakistani Welfare Association	1	
Southall Afro-Caribbean Association	2	1—secretary
Caribbean Overseas Association	1	secretary
C.A.R.D. National Executive	1	vice-chairman
C.A.R.D. West Middlesex	1	chairman

TABLE 6.8 (*continued*)

Organization	No. who belong	No. who are/were officers of this organization
Ealing (continued)		
C.A.R.D. Acton	1	chairman
Joint Council for the Welfare of Immigrants	2	
Movement for Colonial Freedom	1	
Anti-Apartheid	1	
Trades Council	1	on executive
Hayes and Harlington Community Relations Committee	1	on advisory committee
Amalgamated Engineering Union	1	
Amalgamated Society of Woodworkers (local branch)	1	president
Communist party	1	
Labour party	1	
Hackney (Five immigrant members)		
North London West Indian Association	1	one of founder members
West Indian Standing Conference	1	executive membership officer
Association for Jamaican U.K. Residents	1	vice-chairman
St. Kitts, Nevis, Anguilla Association	1	president
Co-operative Credit Union	2	
Fraternities	3	1—chairman
Human Rights Year Committee Hackney	1	vice-chairman
Friends of Toc H	1	
London Transport Choral Society	1	
Huddersfield (Three immigrant members)		
West Indian Welfare Association	1	president
Pakistani Association	1	on executive
Mosque Committee	1	
Council of Churches	1	
Yorkshire C.R.C.	2	
Labour party	1	
Liberal party	1	
Sheffield (Five immigrant members)		
West Indian Association	2	1—president
West Indian Community Association	1	
Sheffield Muslim Association	1	secretary
Pakistan Welfare Association	1	
Nigerian Union	1	
Hospital Management Committee	1	
Samaritans	1	
Sheffield District and Housing Society	1	
Sheffield Radio Council Committee	1	
Board of Governors of local secondary modern school	1	

TABLE 6.8 (continued)

Organization	No. who belong	No. who are/were officers of this organization
Tower Hamlets (Five immigrant members)		
League of Overseas Pakistanis	1	founder member
Shilpi Shangsael (Bengali Cultural Association)	1	founder member
Afro Asian Society	1	
Immigrants Advisory Bureau	1	
West Indian League	1	on executive
Joint Council for the Welfare of Immigrants	2	2—current chairman and treasurer
Race Relations Conciliation Committee Greater London	2	
Westminster Community Relations Committee	1	chairman
Kensington and Chelsea Community Relations Committee	1	chairman
Equal Rights Committee	1	
Kensington Labour party	1	
Stepney C.N.D.	1	
Wycombe (Six immigrant members)		
Commonwealth Peoples Association	3	3—present chairman, ex-chairman, and present secretary
Pakistani Cultural and Welfare Association	1	present chairman—chairman for last eight years
Pakistani Association	1	welfare officer
Islamic Mission and Mosque Fund	1	secretary

inclined to join the typical social and athletic clubs of the native population.[1] Nevertheless, Rex and Moore found that the number of Pakistanis in their Sparkbrook sample who formally belonged to the existing associations was small.[2]

It is yet more difficult to try and estimate the extent to which the existence of a community relations committee is known in immigrant communities. Daniel Lawrence found that of a random sample of 122 male coloured immigrants drawn from the Nottingham Central Parliamentary constituency (in which the community relations office is situated), ninety-one (approximately

[1] M. Goldhamer, 'Some factors affecting participation in voluntary associations', (Ph.D., Chicago, 1943).
[2] Rex and Moore, op. cit., p. 167.

75 per cent) had not heard of the committee.[1] A further twenty-three (19 per cent) claimed to know of the committee but further questioning revealed that they knew literally nothing about it. Of the remaining eight who knew something of the committee, two were members of immigrant organizations and had in this capacity been associated with the committee. The twenty-two Pakistani respondents were the most ignorant of the three ethnic groups studied. Only one claimed to have heard of the committee and when questioned further was found to know nothing about it. Only three of the twenty-seven Indian and five of the seventy-two West Indian respondents knew anything about the committee.

Interesting in this connexion is a comment made by Rashmi Desai on the reasons for the failure of an Indian society in Birmingham in the early 1960s, compared with the success of a similar organization in Bradford.[2] Whereas the Bradford association's aims seemed intelligible to immigrants and met a felt need, the formal rigidity of the Birmingham association's constitution, its vague and generalized aims, and its concern with relations with the host society made it look remote to the immigrants, as it appeared concerned with the problems of the community, not the individual, and did nothing to secure the immediate participation of its members. It became easy prey to the schisms within the local community and was killed shortly after its inception by the opposition of another faction. Such an illustration may give some idea of the magnitude of the problems entailed in mobilizing immigrant involvement in multiracial committees.

Given that the community relations committees do recruit their immigrant members from an *élite*, which varies from committee to committee in its contacts and connexions with the immigrant communities, we can proceed to look at the views of immigrant members on politics and crucial issues such as immigration policy and legislation against discrimination. We will examine whether these views reflect the differences in the type of

---

[1] Daniel Lawrence (forthcoming Ph.D. thesis, University of Nottingham). Nottingham Central Parliamentary constituency contains the bulk of coloured people in Nottingham. The Meadows which has also a large coloured settlement lies in Nottingham South and there are substantial pockets of immigrants in Nottingham West. Thus while the sample cannot be claimed to be entirely representative of all coloured people in Nottingham there is no reason to think it is particularly unrepresentative.

[2] Desai, op. cit., pp. 90–3.

membership already observed in different community relations committees, and whether their attitudes differ from or reinforce those of the white members on their committee.

Most of the immigrants on the committees use their rights as citizens to vote. Only four out of the fifty interviewed had not voted in the 1966 general election. Of the remaining forty-six, forty-three voted Labour, two voted Conservative (both were members of the Birmingham C.R.C.), and one voted Liberal (see Table 5.10 for white members votes). Twenty-six out of fifty, just over half the immigrants, do not belong to or support any political party as such. The percentage for white members, excluding councillors, is only 24 per cent, sixteen out of sixty-six (see Table 5.9). The twenty-four immigrants who claim to belong to or to support a particular party are all left of centre, eighteen supporting the Labour party, four the Communist party, and two the Liberal party. None belong to or support the Conservative party.

TABLE 6.9
POLITICS OF IMMIGRANT EXECUTIVE COMMITTEE MEMBERS

	Labour	Conservative	Liberal	Communist	None	Total
Birmingham	2	–	–	–	4	6
Bradford	1	–	–	–	5	6
Ealing	2*	–	–	4	3	9
Hackney	5	–	1	–	2	8
Huddersfield	2	–	1	–	1	4
Sheffield	2	–	–	–	3	5
Tower Hamlets	1	–	–	–	4	5
Wycombe	3	–	–	–	4	7
Total	18	–	2	4	26	50

* One of the two supporting Labour on Ealing's committee has been a Labour councillor since 1968 for Northcote Ward.

Views on government immigration policy are given in Tables 6.10 and 6.11.

The proportion of immigrants and white members classifiable as dissatisfied on the left with government immigration policy is approximately equal and constitutes a majority in both cases: 57 per cent of the whites and 62 per cent of the immigrants. None of the immigrants fell into the 'don't know' category, or wished for more stringent control. Hackney is an interesting case of

TABLE 6.10

ATTITUDES OF IMMIGRANT EXECUTIVE COMMITTEE MEMBERS
TOWARDS GOVERNMENT IMMIGRATION POLICY

	Satisfied	Dissatisfied on Left	Dissatisfied on Right	Don't know	Total
Birmingham	1	5	–	–	6
Bradford	4	2	–	–	6
Ealing	1	8	–	–	9
Hackney	5	3	–	–	8
Huddersfield	2	2	–	–	4
Sheffield	2	3	–	–	5
Tower Hamlets	–	5	–	–	5
Wycombe	4	3	–	–	7
Total	19 (38%)	31 (62%)	–	–	–

difference within the committee. Tables 6.9 and 6.10 show that
five of the six who were satisfied with immigration policy are West
Indians. Seven of the ten who were dissatisfied 'on the left' are
white. It does not seem unreasonable to suggest that the West
Indians on the H.C.R.C. are less affected by the vicissitudes of
government decisions on dependants and fiancés. They came in
the 1950s or before and are drawn from a group whose immigration generally is virtually complete, i.e. most dependants are
already here. To the whites on the H.C.R.C. the issue is much
more one of principle. However, when asked their view on an
isolated issue of 'principle', the Commonwealth Immigration Act
1968, all but one of the West Indians on the H.C.R.C. expressed
disapproval of the legislation. This was also the case with the six
immigrants on the Bradford committee, more of whom had
expressed satisfaction than dissatisfaction with government
immigration policy. When asked their opinion of the 1968 Act they
all stated they disapproved of it.

West Indians have been subject to certainly as much racial
discrimination as Asians and the Race Relations Act 1968 is of
immediate relevance and importance to them. The majority of the
West Indians on H.C.R.C. considered the 1968 Act inadequate.

The proportions of white and immigrant members considering
the Race Relations Act 1968 to be satisfactory or inadequate
differ considerably. Thirty-six per cent of the immigrants considered it satisfactory. A majority, 58 per cent, considered it

TABLE 6.11
ATTITUDES OF IMMIGRANT EXECUTIVE COMMITTEE MEMBERS
TOWARDS COMMONWEALTH IMMIGRATION ACT 1968

	Approve	*Disapprove*	*Don't know*	*Total*
Birmingham	–	6	–	6
Bradford	–	6	–	6
Ealing	–	9	–	9
Hackney	1	7	–	8
Huddersfield	2 (both Pakistanis)	2	–	4
Sheffield	2	3	–	5
Tower Hamlets	–	5	–	5
Wycombe	1	6	–	7
Total	6 (12%)	44 (88%)	–	50

TABLE 6.12
ATTITUDES OF IMMIGRANT EXECUTIVE COMMITTEE MEMBERS
TOWARDS RACE RELATIONS ACT 1968

	Satisfactory	*Inadequate*	*Unnecessary/ Undesirable*	*Don't know*
Birmingham	2	4	–	–
Bradford	4	1	1	–
Ealing	2	7	–	–
Hackney	3	5	–	–
Huddersfield	1	3	–	–
Sheffield	–	5	–	–
Tower Hamlets	2	2	–	1
Wycombe	4	2	–	1
Total	18 (36%)	29 (58%)	1 (2%)	2 (4%)

inadequate. Fifty per cent of the whites considered the legislation
satisfactory. Only 34 per cent considered it inadequate. A substantial number of white members, 12 per cent (of whom nearly
half were councillors), considered the legislation either unnecessary or undesirable. In all cases except for Bradford and Wycombe
committees, more immigrant members thought the Race Relations
Act inadequate. Bradford is a striking example of the contrary,
especially as the white members of that committee are equally
divided and there is not a majority considering the Act satisfactory

as there is in Ealing, Birmingham, Huddersfield, and Sheffield. It will be remembered that the secession of the more militant immigrant members of the Bradford committee had partly been motivated by the committee's failure to discuss and make known their views on the then proposed Race Relations Bill. The immigrants who now remain on the committee are all in comfortable professional occupations and are owner-occupiers, therefore less likely to be as vulnerable to discrimination. Table 6.13 incorporating the responses on all three items (immigration policy, the 1968 Immigration Act, and the Race Relations Act) by committee members shows that the white members on Bradford committee appear more militant than the immigrant members.

Mention should also be made of the community relations committees members' own opinion of their 'representativeness'. The social position of both white and immigrant executive committee members has been discussed. This is summarized in Table 6.14.

We are considering a very 'select' group of people of whom 70 per cent fall into social classes 1 and 2. Most executive committee members were aware of the deficiencies in the membership. Only a minority on any committee thought the present executive committee membership to be satisfactory. The absence of white working-class participants was remarked on, and the need to involve both trade unionists and the 'ordinary man' was widely recognized. It was felt that the immigrant representatives consisted of the more articulate of some immigrant communities but that smaller minority ethnic groups were not participating in some areas. The 1966 Census shows that there are substantial numbers of Africans, Cypriots, and some Asians living in the borough of Hackney, yet only West Indians apparently play any role in the H.C.R.C. Tower Hamlets borough contains Somalis, Maltese, Gambians, and Greek Cypriots, communities which do not have any contact with the C.C.T.H.

In this chapter, and the one that preceded it, we have shown that the control of community relations committees is in the hands of a limited circle of people who cannot be said to be either a 'community élite' or typical members of the groups of people with which community relations committees apparently aim to work. Our next concern is to see whether the committees can develop activities that enable them to permeate beyond this group.

TABLE 6.13
ATTITUDES OF EXECUTIVE COMMITTEE MEMBERS TOWARDS GOVERNMENT IMMIGRATION/RACE RELATIONS POLICY
(using all three questions)

	Dissatisfied on Right / No dissatisfaction			Dissatisfied on Left on one issue			Dissatisfied on two issues			Dissatisfied on all three issues		
	Total	White	Immigrant	Total	White	Immigrant	Total	White	Immigrant	Total	White	Immigrant
Birmingham	3	3 (includes 1 Conservative councillor)	–	4	3	1	4	3	1	5	1	4
Bradford	–	–	–	4	1	3	4	1	3	2	2	–
Ealing	4	4 (2 Conservative councillor)	–	4	4	–	9	6	3	11	5	6
Hackney	2	1 (1 Conservative councillor)	1	3	–	3	4	1	3	7	6 (2 Labour councillors)	1

TABLE 6.13 (continued)

	Dissatisfied on Right/No dissatisfaction			Dissatisfied on Left on the issue		Dissatisfied on two issues		Dissatisfied on all three issues	
	Total	White	Immigrant	White	Immigrant	White	Immigrant	White	Immigrant
Huddersfield	2	1	1	3	4 Immigrant 1	2	2 Immigrant –	–	2 Immigrant 2
Sheffield	4	4 (2 Conservative councillors)	–	3	5 Immigrant 2	2	3 Immigrant 1 (1 Labour councillor)	–	3 Immigrant 3
Tower Hamlets	2	2 (1 councillor)	–	2 (1 councillor)	3 Immigrant 1	2	4 Immigrant 2	6	8 Immigrant 2
Wycombe	4	3 (1 Conservative councillor)	1	–	3 Immigrant 3	7 (1 Labour councillor)	8 Immigrant 1	4	6 Immigrant 2

TABLE 6.14
SOCIAL CLASS OF WHITE AND IMMIGRANT EXECUTIVE COMMITTEE
MEMBERS
(Registrar-General's social class scale)

	1–2	3a	3b	4–5	Total
Birmingham	13	1	–	2	16
Bradford	8	2	–	–	10
Ealing	21	3	4	1	29
Hackney	9	2	5	–	16
Huddersfield	6	3	–	1	10
Sheffield	12	1	–	2	15
Tower Hamlets	12	2	1	2	17
Wycombe	13	1	2	5	21
Total	94 70%	15	12	13	134

CHAPTER 7

Objectives and Achievements

In this chapter we will examine the objectives or goals of community relations committees and the activities which contribute towards these goals. We have already shown that the community relations movement developed in a rather haphazard way, and that only recently, under heavy fire from their critics, has the N.C.C.I./C.R.C. begun to develop a more sophisticated formulation of goals for the 'movement' it leads. Hitherto the only guide-line for local committees has been provided by the 1965 White Paper which laid down fairly clear suggestions as to the form committees should take and included some ideas on the 'functions' of committees, but was very vague on some of the issues that were to become particularly contentious in the next few years.

The N.C.C.I. provided a model constitution for local committees based upon the guide-lines laid down in the White Paper. This constitution contained some suggestions for the 'objects' of local committees which most of the committees have accepted. These objects are splendidly general and one suspects that most committees were happy to adopt them more or less as they stood to leave time to get down to what seemed at the time the more practical problems of defining membership, composition of the executive, procedure for elections, and so on. Committees were set up, therefore, with their roles still largely undefined. There were obvious advantages in this approach to the formulation of the objectives of local committees. As the N.C.C.I. was only too ready to point out, a strong line from the government or N.C.C.I. would have stifled voluntary initiative, and there were advantages to be gained from diversity and flexibility in a movement that was trying to do something new to English society. There are, however, two aspects to vagueness about objectives. It is argued that such vagueness leaves room for experiment, development, and the

exercise of new initiatives. Vagueness can also indicate a rudder-
less situation, in which external forces or present activities are
allowed to overshadow purpose. Donnison has talked of the 'three
types of indeterminacy, discretion, vagueness, and unexplicitness,
which necessarily characterize the objectives of social services and
pervade their development'. He states: 'Discretion, vagueness,
and unexplicitness are only tolerable and useful if their limits are
reasonably clear and their implications restricted in scope.
Objectives which are too precisely defined tend to be restrictive
if cautious, or disruptive if radical. But objectives which are too
vague tend to destroy a sense of purpose and provide no foundation upon which to establish proper standards of performance.'[1]
Accordingly, for the community relations committees, the problem
is to achieve what Gross has called the 'clarity-vagueness
balance'.[2]

There are factors operating upon community relations committees which make it difficult for them to 'tip the balance' in the
direction of clarity, and in particular to develop really positive
conceptions of their roles.

If there is any concept which can be said to have been used
to describe the goals of community relations committees, it is the
concept of 'integration'. This was defined as the goal for public
policies on race relations by Roy Jenkins, at a meeting of voluntary
liaison committees in May 1966. Jenkins defined integration 'not
as a flattening process of assimilation but as equal opportunity,
accompanied by cultural diversity, in an atmosphere of mutual
tolerance'.[3]

Jenkins' definition has been widely quoted. The authors of
Colour and Citizenship see it as expressing a positive approach to
race relations by contrast with the aimless and negative attitude
characterizing government policy until Jenkins' term of office at
the Home Office.[4] Yet, if it defined the goal of government policy,
it only defined what Perrow has called its 'official goal'. Perrow
argues:

---

[1] D. V. Donnison, V. Chapman, *et al.*, *Social Policy and Administration* (London, Allen
& Unwin, 1965), pp. 240–1.
[2] B. M. Gross, *Organisations and their Managing* (New York, Free Press, 1968), p. 290.
[3] N.C.C.I., 'Address given by the Home Secretary the Rt. Hon. Roy Jenkins, M.P.,
on the 23 May 1966 at the Commonwealth Institute, to a meeting of Voluntary
Liaison Committees' (London, N.C.C.I.), p. 3.
[4] Rose *et al.*, op. cit., p. 514.

Official goals are purposely vague and general and do not indicate two major factors which influence organizational behaviour: the host of decisions that must be made among alternative ways of achieving official goals and the priority of multiple goals, and the many unofficial goals pursued by groups within the organisation. The concept of 'operative goals' will be used to cover these aspects. Operative goals designate the ends sought through the actual operating policies of the organization; they tell us what the organization actually is trying to do, regardless of what the official goals say are the aims.[1]

This point is made with specific relation to 'integration' by John:

> The trouble with the word *integration* is that it is difficult to translate into practical terms. Does integration mean that immigrant children would not learn Punjabi in schools? Does it mean an end to arranged marriage or to the immigrants' concern with Indian politics? Does it mean that Britons have to accept Punjabi lodgers in their homes?[2]

The problem here is not merely a practical one of deciding which policies fit the objective 'integration'. Even with Jenkins' rejection of assimilation, the concept still involves the notion of two or more sides adjusting to each other, and the idea of adjustment by those sides without the possibility of spelling out how much that adjustment should be. Within the scope of the ideal it is still possible for the 'host' society to demand a very low degree of cultural diversity, and for 'immigrants' to expect equality while making few cultural concessions. In as much as 'equal opportunity' is a crucial aspect of the concept, there is considerable disagreement as to whether this should involve merely equal access in a legal sense, or a more positive form of equality in which social and cultural disadvantages in achieving competitive success are overcome.

Eisenstadt argues 'that it is impossible for any large scale immigration to have so little effect on the absorbing country as to make no change at all in its institutional contours'.[3] What is more, he implies that the impact of immigration on the receiving country will be minimized if either the maximum possible assimilation of immigrants occurs, or the immigrants have a

---

[1] C. Perrow, 'The Analysis of Goals in Complex Organizations', *American Sociological Review* (Vol. 26, 1961), p. 855.

[2] John, op. cit., p. 37.

[3] S. N. Eisenstadt, *The Absorption of Immigrants* (London, Routledge & Kegan Paul, 1954), p. 16.

minimal impact upon the country's status system. In other words, if immigrants do not achieve or aspire to equality. This means that 'integration', defined in positive terms, will have a disruptive impact upon the host society, and that the effective pursual of integration as a goal will provoke resistance.

The community relations approach to this problem is based upon two assumptions: that there are two communities, or sub-communities, the 'hosts' and the 'immigrants'; and that they can be brought together to recognize that they have common interests. Thus eventually a unified common community will be created.

The roots of this approach to race relations lie in Myrdal's argument that discrimination against the Negroes is at variance with American values.[1] Accordingly a consensual approach to American race relations was built up in which emphasis was put upon exploiting this overriding value commitment and persuading powerful people to become involved in a co-operative effort to improve intergroup relations. The bible for this particular approach has been Dean and Rosen's *Manual of Intergroup Relations*,[2] a book which seems to have influenced the formulation of the N.C.C.I.'s recommendations to community relations committees in this country. Such an approach obviously fits with the continual assertions of politicians about the basic fair-mindedness of British people. An approach of this kind was suggested in the N.C.C.I.'s notes of guidance on the formation of local committees. A similar note was struck in the first report of the Community Relations Commission: 'The attitude of the host community and the need for the host community from its side to come to terms with the minority elements in its midst are of crucial importance.'[3]

We have referred to the tendency for a much greater emphasis to be laid upon the organizational issue of who should participate than upon the question of the 'purpose' of the development of community relations committees. In decreeing that there should be this full partnership of 'host' and 'immigrant' communities, the White Paper, the N.C.C.I., and the C.R.C. are ensuring that the latter issue will be a difficult, if not impossible, one to tackle effectively. We argue this because of the sociological naivety of the underlying assumptions.

[1] G. Myrdal, *An American Dilemma* (New York, Harper, 1944).
[2] Dean and Rosen, op. cit.   [3] *Report for 1968–9*, para. 8.

The general case against this sort of approach is well stated by Rex and Moore in a critique of the orthodox vocabulary of race relations, with its use of such terms as integration, accommodation, and assimilation:

Such vocabularies assume a host/immigrant framework in which the culture and values of the host society are taken to be contradictory and static and in which the immigrant is seen as altering his own patterns of behaviour until they finally conform to those of the host society. The frame of reference is a cultural one and culture is seen as an independent variable which may change regardless of man's position in the structure of social action and relations, and regardless of the degree to which he possesses property and power.[1]

Community relations committees are supposed to be engaged on welding two 'communities' into one. In practice, neither side in this supposed two-sided relationship is itself a unity which may be dignified by the name of 'community', and it must be expected that there will be fairly fundamental conflicts of interest between elements on either side. In the words of Morris and Rein, 'community organization theory is utopian in that it sees a community as essentially unstratified and not representative of various and conflicting subgroups. The inherent good nature of man should enable him to act in good faith for the good of the total community when certain good impulses are liberated in him. Conflicts in vested interest as integral facets of the relationship between man and his environment are largely omitted in this view.'[2] They suggest that community organization theory assumes that the community will behave in a 'rational' manner in seeking to correct inadequacies in its own structure, once these are pointed out.

In practice, if community relations committees succeed in bringing into their ranks representatives of all the various interests on both sides of this theoretically two-sided relationship, it seems reasonable to predict that the formulation of policies which alter

---

[1] Rex and Moore, op. cit., pp. 13–14.

[2] R. Morris and M. Rein, 'Emergent Patterns in Community Planning', an extract from their *Social Work Practice, 1963*, reprinted in Frieden and Morris (eds.), *Urban Planning and Social Policy*, p. 26. For other examples of the kind of theory they are criticizing see M. Ross, *Community Organization: Theory and Principles* (New York, Harper, 1955) and R. Lippitt, J. Watson, and B. Westley, *The Dynamics of Planned Change* (New York, Harcourt, Brace and World, 1958).

the structure of the existing relationships will be a process which will either prove impossible or will break up the coalition.[1]

It is much more likely, however, that it would prove very difficult to form such a coalition in the first place, and that a multiracial committee of this kind would fail to get the representatives of important interest groups, particularly those in the 'host community' who have something to defend, to become effectively involved in its work.[2] The data we collected on the characteristics of the members of the eight committees we studied confirm this view. To a greater or lesser extent all eight committees could in no way be said to contain a cross-section of all groups, or all powerful groups, in the 'host community'.

It may be thought that this fact might simplify the goal-setting problem. In the sense that cohesion around certain objectives can be achieved within the committee, this is true, but community relations committees will be in the situation which Burton Clark has described as having 'precarious values' in which they can be easily diverted from their commitments.[3] Clark suggests three situations in which values tend to be precarious: 'when they are undefined'; when the positions of 'functionaries', people responsible for translating the values into action, are 'not fully legitimated'; and when 'they are unacceptable to a host population'. Community relations committees face the intellectual problems we have outlined above in defining their goals. Many of their members, quite apart from the immigrants, are 'outsiders', middle-class intellectuals with political convictions that place them on the left; and a commitment to racial integration is a value 'unacceptable' to large sections of the population. We may expect to find, as Clark did in his study of adult education in California,[4] that community relations committees are highly susceptible to diversion into activities which are not central to the achievement of their original stated objectives.

Two very clear American examples of this process were the curbing of Mobilization for Youth by its sponsors,[5] and the crisis

[1] McKee, op. cit.

[2] L. Killian and C. Grigg, *Racial Crisis in America* (Englewood Cliffs, N.J., Prentice Hall, 1964).

[3] B. R. Clark, 'Organizational Adaption and Precarious Values', *American Sociological Review* (Vol. 21, 1956), pp. 327–36.

[4] B. R. Clark, *Adult Education in Transition* (Berkeley, University of California Press, 1956).   [5] Moynihan, op. cit., p. 124.

which occurred in New Haven over a legal advisory service when it tried to identify with a particular cause rather than represent the whole 'community'.[1]

Only one of the eight community relations committees we studied had made any significant attempt to spell out its aims and objectives. This was the Birmingham committee, which we have already noted as markedly different from the other seven. Birmingham's committee has no responsibility to a larger council and no voluntary membership to demand activities. It has therefore been able to sit back and attempt to assess its situation in an uninterrupted way.

The role of the Birmingham committee was spelt out by the C.R.O., in a document accepted by the committee, in the following terms:

After some thought I am persuaded that the central core of our work lies in carrying out the following roles:

1. To evaluate the social and community problems of the City paying particular attention to their influence for good or ill on race relations in the City.
(An example of this would be the analysis of the needs of the inner ring areas that the Chairman prepared for our meeting with the City's M.P.s.)

2. To persuade by appropriate means the various power structures in the community to take action upon our analysis of the situation so as to improve community and race relations.
(An example of this would be the actual discussion with the M.P.s or the representations that were made by the Committee to the Education Department and to the Housing Management Department.)
(No's. 1 and 2 could be described as the major 'political' responsibilities of the Committee.)

3. To be constantly in touch with significant opinion within the immigrant community relating to their needs and wishes in order to be able to interpret their needs to the community as a whole.

4. To assist by all means possible the host community to think through the significance of the changes that have taken place in the 'racial balance' of the City's population and to help the community to become sufficiently sensitive to these changes.
(These last two responsibilities could be described as social education.)

[1] P. Marris and M. Rein, *Dilemmas of Social Reform* (London, Routledge & Kegan Paul, 1967), pp. 171–5.

It is interesting that this discussion gives primacy to a political pressure group role, a role which many committees seem to have sought to avoid. The political situation of local committees in relation to local authorities will be examined in Chapter 8. As may be expected, the Birmingham committee found it difficult to put their conception of their role into practice in an effective way.

The members and officers of the other seven committees have tried to develop a coherent policy for their committees. But the Birmingham committee appeared to be the only one which had taken formal steps to try to crystallize its views on its objectives.

In attempting to formulate a general theory of organizations Parsons uses 'primacy of orientation to the attainment of a specific goal . . . as the defining characteristic of an organization which distinguishes it from other types of social systems'.[1] But we are faced with examining what are undoubtedly organizations, many of whose members are quite unclear about their goals except in the very general terms discussed above. Where some members do have fairly clear conceptions about goals, there is by no means consensus upon the subject within any single organization.

Of course, the 'structure functionalist' theorist will dismiss this reduction of Parsons' proposition to a discussion of the goal conceptions of individuals by suggesting that it will still be possible to discover the *organization's* goals. To do this we must either make a judgement which Albrow has shown to involve bias by 'siding with one party or the other in saying what the objective ought to be',[2] or try to judge the goals of community relations committees from what they actually do. While we are not unprepared to present what we think community relations committees ought to do, we are trying here to discover what they actually do. If we judge their goals from their activities, we are left with the conclusion that their disparate activities are linked by no coherent philosophy other than a general concern for the welfare of immigrants, in the widest possible sense.

Marris and Rein deal very well with this confusing process by which community action programmes are developed:

[1] T. Parsons, 'A Sociological Approach to the Theory of Organizations', *Administrative Science Quarterly* (Vol. 1, 1956), p. 66.

[2] M. C. Albrow, 'The Study of Organizations—Objectivity or Bias', in J. Gould (ed.), *Penguin Social Sciences Survey* (Harmondsworth, Penguin, 1968), p. 155.

Any practical organization will naturally develop by such a pragmatic fusion of means and ends. An initial purpose leads to a preliminary framework of action, that framework suggests other purposes which it might fulfil, the further organization of action takes these new purposes into account—and so on, until a working structure is evolved which has its own momentum. Once the organization begins to function, it tends to be as preoccupied with finding a use for its resources as with adapting resources to a pre-determined purpose. But as practice diverges from theory, and the internal demands of the organization's structure impose their own logic, the coherence of the whole enterprise is endangered. . . .

This interplay between the exploitation of means and the realization of ends can be seen continually in the organizations created by the Ford Foundation and the President's Committee. Sensitive soundings of influential groups by Foundation staff and Federal departments preceded any precise statement of purpose: the programme proposals which followed were, characteristically, criticized for lack of clear aims; the final proposals were a compromise, in which expediency was rationalized by very generalized goals. This was largely a process of political accommodation, by which people of varying aims and resources sought a common purpose compatible with a realizable instrument of institutional co-ordination. But it was also a process of intellectual exploration, as ideas were redefined to give them form.

Once the projects began to put their programmes into effect, their actions were more than ever shaped by the means to hand. They were under pressure to produce results, and reluctant, at the outset, to run too great a risk of failure: so they accomplished first the programmes which came easiest—a summer camp, vacation jobs for high school students, training courses for well qualified applicants, holiday tasks for college volunteers—rather than those which mattered most. Sometimes they even appropriated to their sponsorship activities already in being. And in developing their plans, they went after new money, rather than new ideas. The organizations soon acquired an interest in their own survival, growth and influence which upset their original agenda.[1]

This picture of the haphazard development of activities under the influence of the need to do things that were easy and non-controversial, and their legitimation by reference to 'very generalized goals', corresponds closely with the picture one receives of the activities of most of the community relations committees.

Marris and Rein, op. cit., pp. 33–4.

The factors which may contribute to the restriction of activities to certain fields have been the subject of Chapters 5 and 6 and will be further discussed in Chapter 8. Our concern here is to make it clear that the comments made by Marris and Rein are applicable to the community relations committees we studied and help to determine the lack of a consistent pattern in the committee activities.

Members of the executive committees of the eight community relations committees were asked what they considered to be the main achievements of their committee. The answers were very diverse. Very few people were prepared to say that their committee had achieved nothing. This is not very surprising as we were interviewing active participants in the organizations. But most committees contained a number of people who found it difficult to speak with any great enthusiasm about their achievements. Many were well aware of the puny accomplishments of their organization. In quite a number of cases, people claimed no more for their committee than that it 'stands for something', or that it 'helps to reassure immigrants that someone is aware of their problems'. A large number of the achievements mentioned were those of the C.R.O. and of other full-time staff. The more candid of our respondents were prepared to concede that the committee as such had done very little. Finally, a question about the short-comings of their committee drew forth a large number of comments. Most involved either a certain scepticism about the whole enterprise or a desire to carry out the existing range of activities more effectively.

The only 'achievement' mentioned by members of all eight committees was the role of their C.R.O. as a caseworker and source of advice for immigrants. This was mentioned by fifty people out of 133. This is a very interesting finding since community relations committees are extremely ambivalent about the caseworker function. After some of the very early attempts by local authorities to provide special social workers for immigrants, there was a marked reaction against the idea that immigrants should be provided with special services of this kind on the ground that this might mean their exclusion from normal services. C.R.O.s have specifically sought to avoid a situation arising in which as soon as an immigrant sets foot in a Town Hall he is promptly rerouted to the community relations office.

This particular point was covered in the 1965 White Paper:

> Voluntary liaison committees can also usefully help immigrants with personal welfare problems but an important principle to be borne in mind is that the object should be to help immigrants to use the ordinary facilities of social service provided for the whole community. It would be a mistake to build up any permanent form of special service for immigrants which would encourage and perpetuate separatism.[1]

In practice community relations officers find it very difficult to draw a neat distinction between cases in this way, for a number of reasons. The relationship between community relations committee and local authority is a delicate one. In many instances local authorities have been prepared to accept the case for a community relations committee on the assumption that it will make it easier for them to deal with immigrants. They expect to be able to call in the community relations officer when they find it difficult to handle coloured people. At the same time the C.R.O. will be interested in achieving a working relationship with local authority departments. He may well hope that giving assistance with social work in this way will help to establish relationships that will subsequently enable him to raise policy issues.

There is a second point to be made about pressure from the local authority to engage in welfare work. That is that one response to this pressure is to insist that additional staff are required to take on casework responsibilities. Three of the committees we studied acquired additional staff in this way. Although there are a number of other, perhaps better, reasons why casework responsibilities are taken on, it is understandable that committees and C.R.O.s may respond, above all, to a desire to develop their organization without paying much attention to the resulting 'goal displacement'.[2]

The Sheffield committee has developed in this way as a welfare organization, accepting a fairly large local authority grant to do work that, in Bradford for example, is performed by special liaison officers inside the local authority departments. The need for this kind of development is due to the presence of immigrants who do not speak English and who possess a markedly different

---

[1] 1965 White Paper, para. 70.
[2] The concept is Merton's: *Social Theory and Social Structure* (Glencoe, Ill., Free Press, 1957), p. 199.

culture. It is only to be expected that community relations officers will be needed to help with social casework under these circumstances, particularly when they share the language and culture of one of the immigrant groups. In such a situation the line of least resistance is to provide help to the local authority. In the short run the needs of people demand that help is provided. This very easily becomes a function of the organization. The business of persuading the local authority to take on special staff, and urging them to train and perhaps helping to train English staff to meet such problems, is a long-run solution that can easily be forgotten in meeting the needs of the moment.

The tendency for C.R.O.s to become involved in casework is also furthered by the expectations of immigrants. People who face difficulties in dealing with unfamiliar English local authority agencies may come to expect the C.R.O. to provide help. Once again, as with demands for help from the local authority, the C.R.O. is going to be reluctant to turn people away when he is eager in general to establish strong contacts with the immigrant population in his area. People are going to give their support to an organization that can do something for them, they are going to expect a concrete response to their own pressing problems and may not be impressed by abstract arguments in favour of supporting the community relations committee. In this way, social work may be vital for establishing rapport, for meeting people, and for finding out their needs.

Immigrants, like everyone else, may suffer from the fragmentation of the social services, from the lack of any agency which will treat them as wholes. Again the C.R.O. may find himself subject to demands to take the total interest in an individual that no one else will. Equally, there are loopholes in the social services. The C.R.O. may find that his services are required when no one else can do anything. Again, here, the circumstances of people different from the people the social services are used to dealing with, may reveal loopholes. In this category we must include one form of casework which has become a speciality for community relations officers: the provision of help and advice to people who are trying to find their way through the increasingly intricate tangle of immigration laws.

Help with immigration problems would seem to be a form of casework which community relations committees are well equipped to provide. Nevertheless some committees are so concerned to avoid becoming casework agencies, and also so reluctant to tangle with the difficult political and legal issues connected with immigration control, that they are not prepared to tackle this kind of work. For example, in Birmingham, the C.R.O. requested his committee's permission to fight the case of an illegitimate West Indian dependant child refused admission to the country. Members of the committee opposed this on the grounds that he should not be doing casework and suggested that the matter be referred to the C.R.C. or to International Social Service. A year or so earlier the committee had rejected the C.R.O.'s suggestion that they should support the voluntary Joint Council for the Welfare of Immigrants, whose main concern is immigration problems. Since the Birmingham committee has attempted some forms of casework, one can only suspect that their ambivalence is related to the particularly controversial nature of immigration cases. These cases can, if they are fully accepted, form a large part of a C.R.O.'s casework load as the figures from Wolverhampton on page 178 show.

C.R.O.s also become involved in social work when an agency showing prejudice or ignorance has prevented immigrants from getting a fair deal. The C.R.O. will normally seek to get the agency to revise its policy towards the aggrieved individual, but to do so may involve a considerable measure of casework in itself. Most social workers expect to have to devote a certain amount of time to 'fighting' other agencies.

This leads us to a special kind of casework which C.R.O.s engage in, attempting to overcome various kinds of discrimination. Before the 1968 Race Relations Act the only way of tackling discrimination in housing, employment, and services was through informal channels. Community relations committees could have had an important role to perform in opening up and exploiting such channels. For example, several committees claim a considerable measure of success in opening up opportunities for white-collar employment. Since the 1968 Act, committees have been a little less sure of their role in relation to discrimination. One of the committees we studied, Wycombe, instructed its C.R.O. not to concern himself with cases of discrimination. People who alleged discrimination should be passed on to the Race Relations Board. The Community Relations Commission in its paper on the duties of C.R.O.s lists as one duty: 'To conciliate disputes which lie outside the provisions of the Race Relations Act (1968) but in which community relations may be affected.' It is clear that it is undesirable that C.R.O.s should engage in unsuccessful conciliation and then pass a rather stale case on to the Race Relations Board, but the actual situations which face C.R.O.s may not make it easy for them to decide to leave the cases alone. The individual complaining about discrimination wants a job, house or service, not to score a point in law. He may hope that immediate informal intervention will achieve something. The C.R.O. will therefore be under considerable pressure to try to do something. Also, discrimination is a complex phenomenon which cannot be tackled by the law alone. So, while the Commission's concept of the duties of C.R.O.s does not include the combating of specific discrimination, it does include 'to promote and assist in programmes of public education and cooperative endeavour for positive and harmonious relationships within the community'. This, to our reading, includes trying to see that discrimination does not occur. With such a general concern it is difficult to turn one's back on individual cases, and it may be argued that it is only by finding out about individual cases that one acquires any general knowledge of the incidence of such problems. On this point Ann Dummett has argued cogently: 'The Race Relations Board, whose legal powers are very limited indeed, is dependent on a considerable degree of public support if it is to work well. Failing this public support, it requires at least the active voluntary cooperation of a conscientious minority, in bringing instances of racial discrimination to light, and in providing the information to prove a case . . .'[1] a role which community relations committees, amongst others, can play.

Another matter generally involving discrimination in which the Race Relations Board is more or less powerless is the industrial dispute which involves, or is complicated by, interracial conflict. A number of C R.O.s have been involved in issues of this kind, and it is hard to accept that community relations committees do not have a role to play there. However, the Department of Employment and Productivity has recently produced a paper stressing the role of their own conciliation officers. The Community

---

[1] A. Dummett, 'What To Do', *Race Today* (Vol. 1, No. 3, July 1969), pp. 72–5.

Relations Commission has advised C.R.O.s to avoid becoming directly involved in industrial disputes. In Bradford the C.R.O. claimed some success in conciliating in disputes. In Birmingham, committee members expressed concern about their impotence in the face of some serious disputes in their area. One cannot but harbour the suspicion that once again the C.R.C. is advocating ducking away from controversial issues. The problem for them here is, once again, that what may be needed is not so much conciliation as assistance to the weaker party, immigrant workers, in securing real attention to their point of view.

In discussing casework on matters of discrimination we have moved a long way from the pressures for casework coming from the local authority, which figured first in our list of pressures upon the C.R.O. If the community relations committee is successful in establishing itself as an organization concerned about the well-being of immigrants, if it secures the trust and respect of the various groups and organizations around it, it is bound to subject its staff to this kind of multiple pressure to provide services to individuals. Community relations councils are the only organizations in the field with a general concern about race relations (we exclude the Race Relations Board as its concern is circumscribed by the law). It is not surprising that an enormous range of individual issues and problems will be brought to their staff. The people who bring these problems cannot be rebuffed by reference to some sophisticated formulation of the functions of C.R.O.s drawn up by the Community Relations Commission. The following statement from the annual report of Wolverhampton Council for Community Relations provides a good summary of the kinds of casework undertaken:

6. *Casework*

We accept in principle that we are not a casework agency but the necessity of the situation has imposed upon us the functions of a transferral casework agency in many cases. There are moreover a number of situations for which no established agency as yet exists and we have felt it incumbent upon us to do what was required in the interest of providing a climate in which it would be possible to advance more harmonious relationships.

The following is a distribution of the casework for the year.

1.	Relatives from home	97
2.	Conciliation work including neighbouring disputes, noisy parties etc.	73
3.	Travel, passports and other documents	53
4.	Housing, accommodation	42
5.	Employment, dismissals etc.	37
6.	Family, matrimonial	34
7.	Police, legal aid courts	31
8.	National assistance claims/sick benefits	29
9.	Child-care problems	16
10.	Educational problems	16
11.	Repatriation	9
12.	Miscellaneous	18
		——
		455
		——

We remain convinced that if many situations are faced in the early stages long before they become aggravated by other pressures, the chances of success are increased.

The work has grown until now we have an average of seven callers each day. Many of these can be dealt with on the initial visit and no further record is kept. Of those needing some sort of continuation work we have had 455 cases during the year. Sixty-three were active when the year closed.

One special form of casework which everyone acknowledges is very much within the field of C.R.O.s is 'conciliation' where there is no question of racial discrimination in the legal sense. Useful work has been done by C.R.O.s and by volunteers from the committees in disputes between neighbours. One activity of this kind has been developed in Hackney, since July 1968, when a deputation of white people visited Stoke Newington police station threatening to take action of their own against West Indian parties. A West Indian member of the executive of the Hackney committee has been empowered to act as a mediator and accompany the police in their investigations of alleged disturbances. Some members of the Hackney committee were apprehensive that this might mean siding with the police against the West Indian community, but the West Indian involved is an independent-minded man who commands the confidence of a wide cross-section of people.

However, the doubts expressed about this activity explain

why, despite the fact that conciliation has always been seen as a valuable function for community relations committees, it does not form a large part of the work of local committees. The situation committees find themselves in, and the serious nature of the issues involved, make it very difficult to maintain an independent position in a conciliation role. Furthermore, such problems rarely reach the community relations committee until they have reached a fairly intractable stage. Most people never get to the stage of involving a third party in disputes with a neighbour.

More central to the objectives of community relations committees is the endeavour to prevent discrimination and inter-racial disputes by community education, in the widest possible sense. This is an objective for local committees which the Community Relations Commission is emphasizing more and more. Yet local committees have considerable difficulty in translating such an objective into concrete action. Our concern here is to explore what is involved in education of the native white population that leads to the claim that this kind of activity is a crucial weapon against prejudice and discrimination.

The education activities of community relations committees take many forms. At the most general level the C.R.C. maintains that the committees themselves provide opportunities for mutual education. This is one of their reasons for the complex structure which we have described elsewhere. In the words of the 1965 White Paper: 'A voluntary liaison committee can provide a forum in which people of different racial origins can meet to discuss their difficulties and learn to understand each other's background and traditions and where the structure of British society can be explained to immigrants.'[1]

While it is true that the committees, and particularly their subcommittees, provide means for the discussion of issues which divide people, in practice it is difficult to combine the use of a committee as an effective sponsor of activities, with its use as a forum where people of diverse points of view can meet. As we have shown when we examined the social characteristics of the members of executive committees, the people who become involved in the activities of the committees are highly self-selected and are in general fairly sympathetic already to the immigrant point of view.

[1] 1965 White Paper, para. 69.

Amongst the committees we studied, Sheffield makes particular efforts to ensure that their subcommittees provide opportunities for immigrants to meet local authority officials, central government officers, and representatives of management. Sheffield has in this case a particular advantage, legitimation through the backing of the local authority.

The other committees have found it exceedingly difficult to acquire the participation of many of the people whom they would like to expose to the immigrant point of view. They have found it particularly difficult to get industrialists and businessmen to take any real interest in employment subcommittees.

In general terms, the organization provides but limited scope for mutual education. The next level at which education activities are carried on is through meetings and conferences. The general councils provide some scope here though many of them become bogged down by routine business matters. Some community relations committees have organized public meetings for the discussion of particular issues. Huddersfield organized a 'brains trust' on race relations, Tower Hamlets, a community forum, and Birmingham had the disastrous Advisory Council described earlier. Public education on some of the issues and problems was at least part of the purpose of these various ventures.

Conferences are a particular speciality of the Community Relations Commission. It and its predecessor have organized many such ventures at national, regional, and local levels. One particular device to tackle discrimination in employment which has been widely used is the 'employment conference', bringing together immigrants, employers, and trade unionists to discuss the issues. The need for action in the field of employment cannot be overstated. The P.E.P. Report conclusively documented the incidence of discrimination in employment which appeared to affect most severely the better qualified coloured immigrant.[1] The largest number of complaints received by the Race Relations Board concern employment.[2] The Board is well aware of the limitations of its powers in this field. The mere existence of legislation against discrimination is not sufficient to reverse the spiral which leads to under-achievement by coloured immigrants.

[1] Quoted in Daniel, op. cit., p. 81.
[2] Report of the Race Relations Board for 1968–9 (London, H.M.S.O., 1969), p. 9, para. 34, and Appendix IV.

The Report states:

'The small number of complaints against firms in which immigrants are not employed or are only employed in low status jobs suggests that immigrants are continuing to play safe by confining themselves to areas in which there is little risk of discrimination or to areas in which large numbers of immigrants are already employed. This could indicate ignorance of their rights under the Act or if an awareness does exist a general mistrust of or lack of confidence in the Act. There is a danger here of a vicious circle developing. If immigrants continue to confine themselves to comparatively safe job areas through lack of confidence or through inertia there is risk of a large number of complaints continuing to be rejected.'[1]

The Report continues: 'Experience here and in the U.S.A. has shown that the mere adoption of a non-discriminatory policy is no guarantee that the policy will be achieved. Confidence must be developed among immigrants and indeed among British coloured workers that new job areas and opportunities are being made available to them. Firms which since the Act have adopted non-discriminatory policies should at least make their sources of recruitment aware of the fact and if necessary develop contacts with immigrants for the same purpose. . . . Within a firm policy is unlikely to be implemented unless it is fully communicated to all concerned with the employment of others and steps taken by senior management to ensure that the policy is carried out. The problem presented by firms which have taken no steps to conform with the Act or who are still following a policy of unlawful discrimination are unlikely to be surmounted unless immigrants themselves are prepared to pioneer new areas of employment opportunities and to use the Act where resistance to their employment is encountered.'[2]

At a national level the C.R.C. has made some effort to contact and influence the important organizations in the field of employment. Consultations have been held with the C.B.I., T.U.C., the Institute of Personnel Management, the D.E.P., the Industrial Society as well as with individual unions and professional associations.[3] Here, we are concerned with the activities of the local committees and the opportunities available for a local

---

[1] *Report for 1968–9*, p. 13, para. 58.   [2] Ibid., p. 61, para. 59.
[3] *Report of the Community Relations Commission 1968–9*, pp. 31–4.

organization to bring about change in its immediate 'constituency' area. The policy of the Commission at the local level is to promote consultations between local employers, trade unions, and minority groups, often, as had been mentioned, in the form of employment conferences. The Commission seems to have implicit faith in the efficiency of such machinery:

Local community relations councils have been encouraged to work through specialist employment sub-committees and 21 of these have so far been formed. Their aim is to obtain the confidence of industry and thereby to involve the local business community in their work, and in this, employers and trade unions have been seen to have a common interest. By bringing in representatives of line and personnel management training, the trade unions, the Chambers of Commerce and the Trade Councils, and by utilising their commitment and knowledge, progress has begun to be made towards the establishment of equal opportunity in employment.[1]

The Commission's faith in the efficacy of conferences seems näive. Sheffield, Ealing, and Huddersfield community relations committees have organized such ventures. Hackney, on the other hand, was forced to cancel such a conference at the last moment when it was realized that attendance was going to be very small. Jak Baksi, the community relations officer, Hackney, admitted to the Parliamentary Select Committee on Race Relations: 'On employment we (i.e. the H.C.R.C.) have made very little progress. This is largely due . . . to a lack of interest on the part of employers, Trade Unions and Chambers of Commerce and other parties involved.'[2] Conferences are superficially impressive events but they are costly and it is questionable whether many people other than the already committed attend. Tower Hamlets committee, for example, tried to get local firms and industries to participate in their first 'community forum' but only one business sent a representative.

Some of the committees' work in employment is admittedly done behind the scenes and its results are difficult to evaluate. However, our analysis of the participants in the eight committees studied (Chapter 5) points to the lack of large employers or senior management on the executives or subcommittees. Similarly, not all committees have contact with trade unions, or members

---

[1] Ibid., p. 34, para. 100.
[2] P.S.C., Evidence taken at Hackney (1–2 April 1969), para. 3143.

'representing' trade unions or trades councils may not be those with responsibility for the formulation of policy.

The limitations on an individual committee trying to take initiative on its own is exemplified by Hackney's attempt to influence local businessmen by informal methods. The C.R.O. tried to persuade the personnel manager of a local firm, which was one of the largest employers in the borough, and twice-running winner of the Queen's award for industry, to modify the colour bar which was operating before the 1968 Race Relations Act came into force. An initial agreement was reached to employ a small number of coloured immigrants as an experiment, but this does not appear to have been repeated.[1]

To deal with specific issues some community relations committees have sought to ensure that the people they really want to influence are invited to defend their position and policies before a group of immigrants. Sheffield has done this with the town's M.P.s, Ealing with people responsible for housing policy, and Hackney and Tower Hamlets with the police.

The police have been quite prepared to subject themselves to these confrontations. Hackney organized a meeting at which a Deputy Chief Superintendent, a civil liberties lawyer, and Jeff Crawford, secretary of the West Indian Standing Conference (a well-known critic of the police) debated before an audience of two hundred. Crawford, while generally castigating the attitudes of the British police force towards Commonwealth immigrants, did however pay tribute to the efforts of Chief Superintendent Brown, the chief liaison officer of the Metropolitan G division covering Hackney.[2] Members of the H.C.R.C. felt that this, together with more informal meetings with the police, had led to improved police attitudes in their area.

By contrast the police inspector serving on the Tower Hamlets committee told us that he thought that the seminars organized by that committee at which immigrants met young police recruits, if anything increased the resentments of the policemen because the sessions turned into all-out attacks on the police force.

It is appropriate to digress a little here to look at the relations between local committees and the police in more detail. In January 1964 agreement was reached between the Metropolitan

---

[1] P.S.C. (1–2 April 1969), para. 3150.
[2] *Hackney Gazette* (1 November 1968). See also P.S.C., p. 1011, para. 3218.

Police and the Home Office that local officers should become members of what were then V.L.C.s and that training should be given to police recruits on the backgrounds of immigrants. A memorandum was issued to all Chief Officers by the Home Office in July 1967 entitled 'The Police and the Coloured Community'. By 1969 the Metropolitan Police had about 100 liaison officers, twenty-five of whom sat on community relations committees. Over thirty police forces outside the Metropolitan area have appointed liaison officers numbering about 100. Altogether, according to the results of an N.C.C.I. questionnaire, thirty-seven local community relations committees had at least one police representative, generally of inspector rank or above, and ten had more than one in 1968. In nine cases the representative was also the designate police liaison officer.[1]

In our group of eight committees, Hackney, Tower Hamlets, and Birmingham had police officers on their executives at the time we did our research. Ealing committee had a police officer on their executive until their 1968 A.G.M. but did not invite one to join their new executive. This was discussed at a general meeting which we attended. The executive's decision was defended on the grounds that the presence of the police officer inhibited immigrants from bringing before the committee information about police malpractices. This statement caused some disagreement and the executive agreed to re-examine the matter. Subsequently they decided to invite the police once again to send someone to meetings.

The general case against having police on an executive rests partly on the argument just quoted, partly upon the theory that the police have a *generally* inhibiting effect upon discussion, and partly upon the fact that the police are only concerned with a small part of the community relations committee's business. Consequently a number of committees have police officers amongst their members who generally sit silent unless police matters are raised.

It appears to us that the way complaints against the police are dealt with is a more central issue than that of whether police should sit on community relations committees or not. At a time when concern is increasing about the unsatisfactory nature of the formal complaints procedure under the Police Act 1964, there is

[1] Rose *et al.*, op. cit., pp. 359 ff.

no evidence that the opportunities provided for informal consultation between police and immigrants through community relations committees have made any real difference. In Tower Hamlets for example, the Inspector who sits as police representative on the C.C.T.H. is the 'liaison officer' at Commercial Street Police Station responsible for investigating complaints brought by coloured people against the police. He maintained that in the eighteen months previous to the time we interviewed him (May 1969), he had received only three complaints from Commonwealth immigrants, all from West Indians. He maintained that none of these could be substantiated. This is a borough where the major ethnic group is Pakistani. The police station is situated in Spitalfields, in the heart of the Pakistani settlement. The fact that no complaint has ever been brought by a Pakistani in this period when assaults were already being made locally on Pakistanis and were to worsen in 1970,[1] with allegations being made of inadequate police protection, suggests that either Pakistanis are unaware of the complaints machinery or more probably have no faith in it. That the liaison officer sits on the C.C.T.H. executive does not appear to us to have had much effect on local race relations one way or another.

We have referred to the confrontations arranged in Hackney and Tower Hamlets between the immigrant community and police officers. This approach enables the community relations committees to avoid taking sides themselves. Similarly the conciliation work in Hackney (see p. 178) involves an attempt by the committee to play a positive role in improving race relations without involving itself in conflict. Some members of the different committees, however, feel that the committees should not sit on the fence in this way but should make very clear a commitment on behalf of immigrants and against the police.

All the C.R.O.s and some active committee members undertake a large number of speaking engagements. These are obviously intended to contribute to public education. The efficacy of such activities will be discussed in conjunction with other 'educational' methods. Again here we find that particular attempts have been made to identify target groups, such as the police or the local Chamber of Commerce.

[1] *Guardian* (20 April 1970).

Other informal contacts between C.R.O.s and local decision-makers may be described as 'educational' in nature. Indeed one suspects that when it stresses the educational role of the local committees, the Community Relations Commission is seeing this as the main form of 'pressure group' activity for virtually powerless organizations, on the assumption that many influential people are liberal-minded and will alter their policies when they learn the 'facts'. Several of the executive members we interviewed saw this kind of behind-the-scenes activity as amongst the achievements of their committee. Normally such activity involves attempting to influence local authority decision-making, a facet of community relations committee activity we will examine in Chapter 8.

Several of the committees issue news-letters in which they attempt to a greater or lesser extent to educate the public. They consist primarily of useful information and reports of activities but propaganda of a more obvious kind is slipped in too. They tend to go mainly to the 'converted', the members and supporters of the committees. Ealing has tried to go further by distributing leaflets. Some of their members were dubious about this and most other committees would probably not be prepared to consider involving their organization in as overt a form of public education.

There is also uncertainty about the use to be made of the commercial Press for public education purposes. Executive committee members were questioned about their attitudes to publishing views on local and national issues in the Press. A very high proportion considered that views on national issues should be published at least sometimes. On local issues however rather more

TABLE 7.1

ATTITUDES OF EXECUTIVE COMMITTEE MEMBERS TOWARDS PRESS STATEMENTS

| | On local issues | | On national issues | |
	Totally opposed	Not totally opposed	Totally opposed	Not totally opposed
Birmingham	2	14	1	15
Bradford	6	4	0	10
Ealing	2	26	0	28
Hackney	3	13	0	16
Huddersfield	5	5	3	7
Sheffield	11	4	6	9
Tower Hamlets	2	15	1	16
Wycombe	4	17	3	18

committee members were in favour of maintaining silence. Half or more of the members of each of the three Yorkshire committees were opposed to putting out Press statements. In the other five committees there were fairly large majorities in favour of speaking out on some occasions.

These figures are, of course, reflections of the actual policies adopted by the committees: these attitudes have determined policies, and they have been influenced by policies that have been adopted. As far as national issues are concerned, if the 1968 Immigration Act did not tip most committees off the fence as far as engaging in public controversy is concerned, then Enoch Powell did.

On local policies, only Ealing and Birmingham have really tried to put across criticisms in the local Press. Ealing attacked aspects of the policy of dispersing immigrant schoolchildren, and some health and housing policies. Birmingham released to the Press their evidence to the Cullingworth committee on the allocation of council houses which was critical of present policies in their city. The very high opposition to criticism of local policies in Sheffield must be seen in the light of the close relationship between committee and local authority.

We have only been able to distinguish effectively between members totally opposed to publicity and others. We found a wide range of attitudes on this question, with a certain number of committee members in favour of a highly outspoken approach to issues of controversy. However, most people were unprepared to go as far as that. The great problem for community relations committees is to decide on the right tactics on this point. The 1965 White Paper seems to assume that committees can stay out of public controversy, they are expected to be 'non-political', yet it expects them to be involved in public education. Powellism has helped to reveal that these two injunctions are in many respects incompatible.

It is all very well to try to work out effective tactics on public controversy, but Press publicity cannot be easily controlled. The difficulties that have faced the Ealing committee in a situation in which other people are determined to seek publicity are discussed in Chapter 8 (the whole question of publicity will be examined further there). The Ealing C.R.O. is under continual pressure from the Press, and his speeches to local organizations are often reported. Some of the other C.R.O.s have been able to speak freely on many occasions without the Press paying any attention. What may be deemed controversial in one area may be totally ignored in another.

Few C.R.O.s have paid careful attention to their relations with the Press. Notable exceptions seem to be the C.R.O.s in Manchester and Wolverhampton. So, few can be said to have the question of Press publicity carefully under control. C.R.O.s tend to get grabbed by their local reporters when they want a story, rather than seek a working relationship with their local papers. Some committees, including Wycombe in our sample, have sought to control relations between their C.R.O. and the Press. In the case of Wycombe this was a result of a statement by the C.R.O. which the committee considered indiscreet. The effect of curbing him makes it difficult to build up a working relationship with the Press. Anyone who has had any dealings with reporters will know that to have to say: 'I'll refer your question to my committee', will drive the Press elsewhere for their stories.

Another kind of public education programme is the Accord campaign. This originated in Camden and was taken up by other committees including, in our sample, Hackney. Accord stands for action campaign to outlaw racial discrimination. The Accord programme Hackney devised included a church campaign (the local churches were asked to set aside one Sunday as Accord day), a schools campaign, and an endeavour to get local libraries to organize international weeks. Badges representing the Accord symbol were distributed and after the Mayor gave the lead by displaying Accord posters at the Town Hall, local traders were asked to display the Accord symbol, followed by a more explicit poster proclaiming 'Fight against racialism'. All this involved trying to capture public imagination to support an educational campaign by a sloganistic approach. The campaign seems to have petered out fairly rapidly. In due course Hackney members became concerned about the fact that they had created a new subcommittee for the Accord campaign, whose activities cut across those of its already existing education subcommittee.

This concludes our list of direct educational methods. All these approaches to education in race relations suffer from the same problem: whether direct approaches in this field have any effect. Social psychologists can give us little guidance on the gains to be made by these forms of education. Such evidence as we have suggests that much that is designed to educate bounces off those who are ill-disposed to immigrants, or may, worse still, simply entrench their attitudes by antagonizing them or forcing them to argue back.[1] We do know that the deeply prejudiced are largely uninfluenced by direct attack on their prejudices. We do not know how to distinguish between the deeply prejudiced and those who may be susceptible to influence.

Furthermore, a great deal of the arguments and information put out by community relations committees only reach the 'converted'. In a society where people are bombarded by advertisements, propaganda, and education from all sides, they are inevitably highly selective about the things to which they pay attention.

For these reasons, there are good grounds for doubt about the effectiveness of many of the educational activities of community relations committees. Many committee members were deeply sceptical about the educational activities of their organization, and few mentioned public education as amongst the achievements of their committee. Rather more interest was shown in approaches which involve primarily encouraging co-operation between blacks and whites. Four kinds of activity here merit our attention: activities designed to stimulate interaction amongst the young; the provision of facilities on an explicitly multiracial basis; the encouragement of collective action to solve common problems; and multiracial social activities.

Multiracial activities for the young are sponsored by committees partly with the explicit desire to create mutual tolerance through common activities, and partly in order to provide facilities needed by both immigrant and non-immigrant children in underprivileged areas. This dual purpose may be a source of difficulties to committees when they are faced with the phenomenon Americans describe as 'tipping',[2] when the white people

---

[1] C. I. Hoyland et al., *Communication and Persuasion* (New Haven, Yale University Press, 1961), and C. H. Stember, *Education and Attitude Change* (New York, Institute of Human Relations Press, 1961).

[2] M. Grodzins, *The Metropolitan Area as a Racial Problem* (Pittsburg, University of Pittsburg Press, 1958), p. 6; E. P. Wolf, 'The Tipping-Point in Racially Changing Neighbourhoods', *Journal of the American Institute of Planners* (XXIX, August 1963), pp. 217–22, reprinted in Frieden and Morris, op. cit., pp. 148–55; M. Meyerson and E. C. Banfield, *Politics, Planning and the Public Interest* (Glencoe, Ill., Free Press, 1955), p. 135.

remaining in a locality stop using the multiracial facilities provided. Then, committees are forced to decide whether it is essential to maintain multiracial activities or whether they have a commitment to provide needed facilities for immigrants which overrides other considerations.

As the Hunt Committee has shown,[1] this problem is particularly relevant to the provision of youth clubs. Some committees, including Sheffield in our sample, have put first the need to provide youth club facilities for immigrants, and have been prepared to do so without worrying about the fact that white youths are unlikely to use such clubs. Many other committees, on the other hand, have joined with the local authority youth service to try to attract immigrants to existing clubs or to create explicitly multiracial clubs. This is a task they have found to be very difficult, particularly where they are faced by immigrant groups of Asian origin.

It is probably true to say that the younger the children, the less difficult this particular problem is. Committees have been able to build successful multiracial activities based upon the populations of multiracial schools. Huddersfield and Tower Hamlets have built up a programme of summer holiday activities for multiracial groups in this way. These projects were both financed by Gulbenkian Foundation grants provided by the N.C.C.I. The Huddersfield project was run with the help of students from York University. In Tower Hamlets the United Nations Association recruited volunteers from fourteen countries.

For the younger children, too, some committees have been able to draw multiracial groups to the more informal facilities provided by adventure playgrounds. Committees in Lambeth and Southampton have scored successes of this kind. At this level, again, the encouragement of social interaction on a multiracial basis does not really apply, as children are drawn to these activities in their informal groups, which may or may not be multiracial, formed in the schools and in the streets.

Another activity which involves the provision of a facility, with its contribution to integration as a secondary but not necessarily essential purpose, is the multiracial playgroup. Next to casework the provision of playgroups is the most widespread

[1] *Immigrants and the Youth Service* (London, H.M.S.O., Department of Education and Science, 1967).

concrete achievement of community relations committees. Five of the eight committees we studied provide playgroups, as do most of the other committees about which we collected information. The committees in Bedford, Coventry, Manchester, Newham, and Wolverhampton have received special grants from the Gulbenkian Foundation towards playgroups. Thus, community relations committees have played an important part in extending some of the benefits of the hitherto largely middle-class, pre-school playgroup movement, to less privileged areas.

In general, playgroups do not face the tipping problem. On the contrary, in some areas, difficulty has been experienced in getting sufficient immigrant children to the groups. This is because many immigrant mothers need specific child-minding or day nursery facilities to enable them to go to work, not the half-day 'fringe benefits' provided by playgroups. This is why many committees have subsidized playgroups to provide them free or at very cheap rates. In Wycombe a group charging $17\frac{1}{2}$p a morning in order to meet its running costs has found it very difficult to get many immigrant children. Grants from local charities have been secured to enable some children to attend free.

As far as playgroups are concerned they may bring together a multiracial group of mothers, who may then come to recognize common interests and common problems. Many committees hope that this involvement in playgroups will in time provide the basis for other activities for mothers.

Another example of the provision of facilities on a multiracial basis is the multiracial housing association. One of the eight committees we studied has set up such an association, the Wycombe committee. This was organized in 1962 and has since become entirely independent of the committee. Its growth has been disappointingly slow, it has only acquired five houses. It functions as a source of interim accommodation for the housing authority. Its tenants are nominated by the local authority, and it houses them on a temporary basis prior, normally, to rehousing by the authority.

Another of the eight committees, Bradford, is currently involved in assisting with the establishment of a housing association, backed by an anonymous donation of £50,000 which is being administered by Shelter. Other committees have set up housing associations, notable examples being in Camden, Manchester, and

Oxford. The Camden association is particularly adventurous as it has engaged in projects involving new buildings.

Housing associations seem unlikely, at present, to face the 'tipping' problem as the people they house are too desperately in need of accommodation. Their contribution to the solution of the housing problem has naturally been minute. It is easy to be sarcastic about their scale, but their achievements are real enough to those who have been helped.

It is too early to judge at this stage what contribution they make to interracial tolerance. American studies have found that interracial contact in public housing experiments have had a positive effect on attitudes. The improvements in attitudes are often limited to the immediate contact situation itself, yet basic racist stereotypes are often affected too.[1] The scale of the provision of multiracial housing by the community relations committees cannot be compared with the American experiments. Bettleheim and Janowitz have put even the latter in perspective by commenting:

These studies invariably show that the experiences of living in inter-racial housing can be conducive to reducing hostile attitudes. But these studies deal with limited and specific housing projects where the pattern of social control is such that outside community pressures could be eliminated. Because of shortages of housing, or because of existing administrative authority, managers of such housing projects could enforce some system of quotas and thereby prevent mixed housing units from becoming all negro. These results must be matched with the day to day experiences when whole neighbourhoods undergo changes in ethnic or racial composition.[2]

Many people, inside and outside the community relations movement, consider that to make a better approach to the creation of interracial harmony than the direct provision of integrated facilities to underprivileged areas by an outside body, is the stimulation of collective action on a multiracial basis in those areas to provide, or to pressurize for, better facilities. Most of the community relations officers and some of their committee members are committed to the development of activities along these lines,

[1] Morton Deutsch and M. Collins, *Inter-racial Housing* (Minneapolis, University of Minnesota Press, 1951). D. M. Wilner, R. Walkley and S. Cook, *Human Relations in Inter-racial Housing* (Minneapolis, University of Minnesota Press, 1955).

[2] B. Bettleheim and M. Janowitz, *Social Change and Prejudice* (Glencoe, Ill., Free Press, 1964), pp. 78–86.

but as yet very little has been actually achieved. One of the most important developments of this kind is the Sparkbrook Association in Birmingham. The Birmingham committee is certainly a supporter of this association, but it lacks the resources or influence to give it any real positive help. On the other hand it recognizes it can play a part by sponsoring similar developments elsewhere in the city, and has been doing so in Handsworth. The Sheffield committee has developed a rather different approach, setting up a subcommittee in the Attercliffe area to provide a basis for community activities there. At the time of our research this functioned largely as a base for social activities and as a participant in the various schemes to meet the needs of Pakistani women and children.[1] For most committees, social and cultural events represent the most achieved so far in terms of participation on a multiracial basis.

It is easy to glibly suggest that community development should be an important field of activity for community relations committees. It has become fashionable to pay lip-service to the community development ideal. In practice, there are considerable difficulties in establishing community organizations on a multiracial basis in underprivileged areas. Also, community relations committees are organized in ways that make it difficult for them to become the sponsors of such organizations.

We have given some indication in Chapter 3 of the difficulties entailed. We have pointed out in Chapter 4 that with most committees, the emphasis upon the participation of borough-wide organizations means that most white members will be middle-class people living outside what would be the target areas for 'community development'. In the last resort, of course, seeking to develop these areas must involve making demands for the alteration of local authority policies or the redistribution of local resources. Chapter 8 on the relations between the committees and the local authorities examines the difficulties entailed in operationalizing this particular conception of the committees' role.

The last of the kinds of activities which community relations committees see as contributing to ameliorating race relations is social activities. At best social activities can provide the foundations upon which other things can be built, they can provide the

---

[1] S. A. Rasul, 'A Neighbourhood Project in Sheffield', *Race Today* (Vol. 1, No. 8, December 1969), pp. 238–40.

most natural kind of interaction between people. At worst they can become the most condescending kind of events at which well-meaning 'liberal' people try to be nice to the 'foreigners'. Committees find it fairly easy to put on social events that will be popular with members of both white and black communities, but these may merely parallel activities organized commercially elsewhere. A good modern dance will attract a large number of young people from both West Indian and native communities, but similar events are likely to go on regularly anyway. There is nothing forced about these occasions, but do people interact on an interracial basis at them? Perhaps the best argument for community relations committees continuing to sponsor such events is that they may make money and publicize the committee in a favourable way.

Perhaps the most successful kind of social event is the one which attempts to inculcate an understanding of other cultures, yet does not sacrifice popularity in the attempt. The most exciting achievements along these lines from our eight committees come from Hackney. Here social activities have been directed by a dynamic West Indian who is a P.R.O. by profession. An international variety concert attracted an audience of 800. At the time of our study, a most ambitious borough-wide talent contest was being planned, publicized on a vast scale with the distribution of 15,000 brochures.

The efforts of the other committees at providing international entertainments have met with varying degrees of success. Their success is difficult for the outsider to evaluate, in fact most insiders were reluctant to make great claims for such activities. It is difficult to know whether they do often turn out to be forced and condescending occasions, and difficult to know whether people other than the already committed attend such events.

Six of the eight committees we studied arranged social and cultural events fairly regularly. The committees in Birmingham and Bradford have largely ignored this kind of activity. While Hackney is most notable for the scale of its social activities, Sheffield has probably been the most active. During 1968 the Sheffield committee was involved in the following events:

International Evening, St. Mary's Community Centre   January
Help with UNA International Supper and Dance   March
Help to secure Commonwealth entries at Sheffield

Open Exhibition of Models and Handicrafts	April
International Show, Granville College	June
Coach tours of the city and surrounding countryside	Summer
Outing to Blackpool	October
Family social in Attercliffe	October
International Food Bazaar	November

This list gives some idea of the kinds of activities sponsored by an industrious social committee.

It is pertinent at this stage to question the committees' assumption that 'multiracial' activities are of value. Presumably they assume the result to be decrease in prejudice, although the intention is also undoubtedly the provision of services where these are deficient. In a summary of the findings of a wide range of studies conducted in the U.S.A. by sociologists and social psychologists, Pettigrew has shown that it is in the contacts between individuals of equivalent social status, in an atmosphere free from competition and stress that the chief hope of reducing the incidence of prejudice lies.[1] Black immigrants to this country have suffered a history of colonial domination and are compelled to live in the most deprived urban areas. Equality of status and an atmosphere free from competition and stress are crucial prerequisites for the reduction of prejudice, but these are not characteristics of the social situation in a typical inner city area. Deakin and Cohen have argued from this and for other reasons for an encouragement of voluntary residential dispersal of immigrants and have commented 'that the identification in the minds of the white majority between colour, poor housing conditions and a squalid environment is constantly reinforced as long as concentration in the inner city persists and even increases'.[2] We would use this also as an argument for the infusion of far greater amounts of money under the urban programme for the rehabilitation of the inner city areas for the benefit of all the deprived, regardless of colour. However, given the very apparent indicators of stress in inner city areas, provision of 'multiracial activities' for their own sake cannot be expected to reduce prejudice if it contributes little to the improvement of services in the area or the promotion of some positive

[1] T. F. Pettigrew, 'Racially Separate or Together?', *Journal of Social Issues* (Vol. XXV, No. 1, 1969).

[2] N. Deakin and B. Cohen, 'Dispersal and Choice, Towards a Strategy for Ethnic Minorities in Britain', *Environment and Planning* (Vol. 2, 1970), p. 198.

structural change in the social and economic conditions of black immigrants and the local white population. Logically, multiracial 'social' activities of the type described above should come last in the list of priorities for community relations committees. Yet, since social events are easily arranged, cost little, and are *uncontroversial* in nature, not threatening the *status quo* in any way, it is not surprising to find that six out of the eight committees we studied arranged social and cultural events frequently.

Many committees have found it easier to direct their educational efforts towards the most uncontroversial needs of the newer members of the immigrant population than towards the needs of a multiracial or underprivileged community. The presence of non-English-speaking immigrants in most areas has provided opportunities for the most straightforward kind of educational effort, the teaching of English. The most effective work of this kind has been undertaken in close association with local authorities. Once again, we find that much has been achieved in Sheffield. A good example of joint effort there is the language classes for Pakistani women described in the committee's report for 1968–9:

Miss Butt, our Welfare Officer, has helped the Local Education Authority in establishing a language class for Pakistani women at Darnall. The class meets two evenings a week and an arrangement has been made for a playgroup for the children who accompany mothers to the class. The Sheffield Pre-School Play Association and the Girl Guides have provided volunteers to take care of this playgroup.

Sheffield also provides language teaching for children based upon the Asian Youth Club the committee has set up in Attercliffe, and individual help is given to Asian children by volunteers from Sheffield University. While the local authority has been ready to support this kind of voluntary initiative, it has been rather slow to organize effective language teaching in its schools.

Another committee which has done a great deal in this field is Tower Hamlets. Initially language teaching has been based on Toynbee Hall, but it is now increasingly decentralized with volunteers visiting women and children in their own homes. The committees in Bradford, Wycombe, Ealing, and Huddersfield have also played a part in developing home tutor schemes under which students from local colleges visit immigrants in their homes.

In Ealing and Huddersfield, these teaching efforts have been supplemented by summer projects, with which the community relations committees have been associated. In Ealing, the project was organized by Community Service Volunteers. It included outings and various activities as well as teaching. Older children, mostly Asian, but including some white teen-agers helped with the teaching of the younger ones.

Success has not come so easily to other ventures concerned with educational provision for black children in primary and secondary schools. All the eight committees have set up education subcommittees which recognize that West Indians face certain educational problems but find it difficult to formulate policies to try to meet these problems. Michael Young and Patrick McGeeney have studied the difficulties encountered by Cypriots and West Indians.[1] In the particular school they studied in North London, far more immigrant than white parents had lived in the neighbourhood for less than two years, immigrant parents were more difficult to contact, and their knowledge of school matters was less. West Indian parents could not appreciate functions of play and seemed mystified by the laxness of discipline. Greek Cypriot parents criticized co-educational education on the grounds that it encouraged permissiveness. However, almost the same proportion of immigrant parents as other parents responded to the Headmaster's invitation to visit the school and meet their child's teacher as part of a programme to encourage the links between home and school. The authors conclude:

Some of the examples we have just given show how much failure in communication there is between home and school and how worthwhile it would be to try and improve it so that immigrant children could alongside the native born make full use of educational opportunities.[2]

Significant, then, is the comment of Alderman Masters, chairman of Hackney community relations committee, in evidence to the Parliamentary Select Committee on Race Relations:

We as a CRC would have liked to have got much more into the schools to deal with the problem before the children leave school to prepare

---

[1] Michael Young and Patrick McGeeney, *Learning Begins at Home* (London, Routledge & Kegan Paul, 1968), pp. 68–86. Also, since we completed our fieldwork, the Ealing committee has initiated a study of these particular issues.

[2] Young and McGeeney, op. cit., p. 86.

them for many of the problems. . . . We feel we have not been able to get in as much as we would like. There is a tendency for the education people to regard us as interfering outsiders.[1]

In general community relations committees have steered clear of fundamental issues affecting the educational chances of black children. The possible adverse effects on the performance of immigrant schoolchildren of white teachers' low expectations of them, have not been examined nor has the disproportionately high number of West Indian children wrongly allocated to E.S.N. schools.[2]

In the field of housing, 'fair housing groups' have been proposed to cope with discrimination. The 'fair housing group' idea comes from the United States and it owes its dissemination amongst community relations committees to the fact that the Gulbenkian Foundation provided money for the N.C.C.I. to finance them. Only three committees received such grants, Manchester, Nottingham, and Sheffield. One of the other committees we studied, Ealing, applied for a grant but was not awarded one. It decided to go ahead without funds. The committees in Hackney and Tower Hamlets joined a consortium of North and East London committees to apply for a grant. When this application was turned down no further action was taken.

The Sheffield committee have not set up a 'fair housing group' but have appointed a 'fair housing officer' for a three-year experimental project. They had some difficulty in finding a suitable person and the project did not start until December 1968, with a grant of £6,750. The officer has opened two housing advice centres, manned for short periods during the week, and is conducting a large-scale sample survey of the housing conditions and needs of immigrants. This is very similar to projects undertaken in Nottingham and Manchester, nearly a year earlier.

[1] *Evidence to the Select Committee on Race Relations*, p. 1055, para. 3340. See also p. 1013 where the public relations officer of the Antigua National Association, giving evidence, stressed the need for better information for West Indian parents about the English educational system.

[2] A confidential report was produced by I.L.E.A. concerning the number of West Indian children classified as E.S.N. in 1967, and the doubts felt by heads of E.S.N. schools about the suitability of classifying these children as E.S.N. In 1967, 28·4 per cent of children in E.S.N. schools in I.L.E.A. were of immigrant origin: of these, 75 per cent were of West Indian origin. Head teachers felt that 28 per cent of their immigrant children were wrongly placed compared with 7 per cent of their non-immigrant children.

The expression 'fair housing group' makes it sound as if something rather extraordinary is being done when clearly it is not. The Ealing 'fair housing group', though operating on a purely voluntary basis, set up an advisory service one evening a week in Southall. At the time of our interviews, they were planning to undertake a survey. After seven months of the advice service they analysed the thirty-three inquiries received. They had had calls at about the rate of one a week. All the inquiries were within the scope of the Citizens' Advice Bureau.

The surveys financed by the Gulbenkian Foundation may produce findings of importance for policy-making in immigrant areas. For example, Manchester's fair housing group has produced a memorandum (considered by the Town Hall at the time of writing) about the redevelopment of Moss Side, arguing for a rephasing of the clearance process which would reduce the degree of dispersion of the local population and enable a greater proportion of families to be rehoused in the immediate area.[1]

Surveys are a fashionable form of activity for voluntary groups just at the moment. For example, Huddersfield have a permanent research subcommittee which has completed a study of the work experiences of immigrant school leavers. Generally, it is difficult for an amateur group to do more than provide a little additional factual evidence to supplement already available information. It is better therefore to use the resources of community relations committees to help larger-scale efforts organized by research organizations, as Tower Hamlets seems to have done in the case of a study of employment undertaken for the Institute of Race Relations. This is not to say of course that community relations committees need wait passively for social scientists to take an interest in their areas. They should be prepared to draw the attention of social scientists to the issues and problems which they perceive.

However many surveys are carried out and however competent or conclusive their findings, the most important concern of the community relations committee must be to secure their use to effect change. But community relations committees often appear to be too powerless to ensure this. An exercise conducted by the Birmingham C.R.C. may be a useful illustration of this point.[1] In

---

[1] L. Kushnick, 'Participation, Redevelopment and Moss Side', *Race Today* (February 1970).

January 1968 the committee made a short survey of policies of the city's estate agents. A one in nine random sample was taken from which twenty-two firms were obtained. Seven of these were not relevant to the investigation but ten of the remaining fifteen firms immediately accepted the condition of discrimination required by the bogus 'vendors' who approached them. The results of the survey thus reinforced findings about discrimination which reports such as the P.E.P. Report had highlighted earlier. However, the only use to which these findings appear to have been put was to have the results recorded in the committee minutes. We could find no evidence that B.C.R.C. followed up the survey once the 1968 Race Relations Act, which prohibited discrimination by estate agents, came into force.

Altogether the efforts made by the community relations committees to influence the housing situation of Commonwealth immigrants have been very slight. The formation of housing associations has been on a minute scale, and concerned as much with fostering multiracial tolerance as solving acute housing need. It has been well established that immigrants experience severe disabilities in the housing market.[2] The particular difficulties they experience are partly the product of racial discrimination by public and private agencies, and partly the result of low incomes which prevent them from escaping privately-rented furnished accommodation, where they are forced to pay high rents for very little.[3] Immigrants, and particularly West Indians, form a disproportionately high number of those in this insecure sector of the housing market.[4] They represent a disproportionately high number of the homeless in the inner London boroughs.[5]

Some of the community relations committees have paid little attention to this problem. Others are aware of it but are unable to formulate policies to try to tackle it. In general, these housing problems, shortage, inadequacy, and insecurity, are of a kind which community relations committees can do nothing effective about apart from pointing to their existence.

[1] An example of the limitations of the strategy of 'rational analysis', one of three possible sources of legitimacy for social planners.
[2] Rex and Moore, op. cit., Burney, op. cit., and *Evidence to the Parliamentary Select Committee on Race Relations*, 1971 (forthcoming).
[3] Notting Hill Housing Service interim report, 1968.
[4] Rose *et al.*, op. cit., p. 137.
[5] J. Greve *et al.*, *Homelessness in London* (London, Chatto & Windus, 1971).

A summary of the activities mentioned by committee members will give some idea of the importance attached to them. Table 7.2 lists the activities mentioned by more than a quarter of the members of each committee.

This table does not represent a summary of the achievements of the committees. It is a summary of the main achievements *perceived as such* by members. It represents, in some respects, their image of the committee, their view of what was worth doing as much as their view of what was well done. To attempt to use this data to suggest anything very significant about differences in committee policies would be inappropriate, unless to point out that Birmingham's committee is a kind of establishment pressure group, and not much else, or that all the other committees, bar Ealing, have played down the pressure group role, and that all except Birmingham acknowledge *direct* attention to the welfare of individual immigrants as amongst their main concerns. (Only two Birmingham members mentioned casework. The C.R.O. does a great deal, but he sought to de-emphasize this role. As we saw, his committee were unwilling to let him become too heavily involved in this kind of work.)

In this chapter we started with a general discussion of the problems entailed in formulating objectives for community relations committees. We showed that only Birmingham of the eight committees we studied had attempted to provide a formal statement of its position on this problem, and had in the process decided to give primacy to a pressure group role. In our discussion of the relations between the committees and the local authorities we will find that only one other committee, Ealing, has really sought to pay much attention to this sort of role, and that Birmingham's commitment to such a role has more reality at the theoretical than at the practical level.

The other six committees have made no real attempts to define their roles. Accordingly we are left to judge their objectives by the wide ranging pattern of activities we have described in this chapter. Most of these activities involved either welfare-oriented assistance to immigrants or the education of the 'host' community at a very rudimentary level. The low resources possessed by the committees ensure that they do not effectively come up against some of the more fundamental dilemmas associated with the concepts of 'community' and 'integration', but if their work

TABLE 7.2
ACTIVITIES OF COMMUNITY RELATIONS COMMITTEES (MENTIONED BY ONE QUARTER OR MORE MEMBERS)

	Birmingham	Bradford	Ealing	Hackney	Huddersfield	Sheffield	Tower Hamlets	Wycombe
Pressure group activity	X		X					
Casework		X	X	X	X	X	X	
General mutual education		X	X				X	
Playgroups			X				X	X
Social events				X	X	X		X
Improvement of immigrant/police relations				X				
Language teaching					X			X
Research					X	X		
Employment conferences						X		
Youth clubs						X		

expands, as it surely will to some extent, it is reasonable to predict that they will find that the present forms of organization and patterns of activity have taken root to such an extent that they will find it difficult to move beyond them.

We did not succeed in getting more than a very few of the people we interviewed to give us a clear formulation of what they saw as the objectives of their movement. As we predicted, the achievement of narrowly defined, largely non-controversial, practical goals have been given precedence over any attempts to formulate more fundamental objectives.

Community relations committees partly through their own choice, partly through the constraints of their position, tend to act as agencies of social control rather than social change. We have left out of this chapter one kind of activity more concerned with challenge to the *status quo*—the critical scrutiny of local authority policies. This type of activity together with the whole question of the pressure against their adoption of a radical stance will be the subject of the following chapter.

CHAPTER 8

Relations with Local Authorities

The 1965 White Paper set out 'the full backing of the local authorities' as essential for the success of local committees.[1] This was reinforced by a requirement that before a grant could be given to a committee by the National Committee for Commonwealth Immigrants, its local authority should be prepared to provide a matching grant. While the conditions under which the Community Relations Commission can provide a grant to a local committe or council are less rigidly defined by the Government, the Commission has continued to insist that the full co-operation of local authorities is essential. Our purpose in this chapter is to examine what this co-operation amounts to, and to consider whether such co-operation is wholly advantageous to local committees. For, while the Commission has been urging that little can be achieved by a local committee without an effective relationship with its local authority, critics of the Commission have suggested that such a relationship will have serious drawbacks.[2] It has been suggested, for example, that to achieve the full support of its local authority a community relations committee will almost certainly have to restrict its activities and its public statements to such an extent that it will be unable to retain the confidence of immigrants. This is, of course, a view of the local level which accords with the attack that has been made at the national level on the relationship between N.C.C.I./C.R.C. and the Government. One important test of the validity of this view will be provided by examining the circumstances under which friction has occurred between some local committees and their local authorities, and whether the committees which enjoy good relations with their town or city councils have, in any way, restricted their activities.

---

[1] 1965 White Paper, para. 66.
[2] See references to the criticism from Nandy and Michael Dummett made in Chapter 1. Also Ann Dummett, op. cit.

In a number of towns local authorities were involved in community relations councils right from the outset. Indeed, many local authorities were responsible for setting up such bodies. Prior to 1965, as has been shown, many committees were set up by local authorities on their own initiative. After the 1965 White Paper, Maurice Foley and Nadine Peppard toured the country urging local authorities to take such action. Some responded immediately, others were a little slower to move. Some in the latter group may have been persuaded by the fear that without such organizations they might find it more difficult to get the Government to listen sympathetically when they lobbied it for more resources to meet the 'problems' presented by 'immigrants'. In other cases, the N.C.C.I. increased the pressure on local authorities by encouraging voluntary groups to lobby or even to set up community relations councils without local authority support in the hope that thereby the authority's attitude could eventually be changed.

Rarely, therefore, after 1965 did local voluntary committees emerge without either local authority support or N.C.C.I. encouragement in lieu of an unwilling borough council. Of the eight committees we studied four were set up by local authorities after the 1965 White Paper. Three of the other four had origins lying before 1965. The other one was set up on the initiative of a local authority-sponsored International Co-operation Year Committee and with mayoral assistance. Of the three committees with older roots, Ealing International Friendship Committee was set up after Ealing Borough Council agreed to support a borough-wide version of the old Southall International Friendship Committee. Wycombe and District Integration Committee had been set up by the Mayor in 1960 (though it took this committee until 1967 to get the local authority to give it financial support). This leaves only one of the eight committees emerging to its modern form without any local authority involvement, the Council of Citizens of Tower Hamlets, set up by a very much older voluntary organization, the Council of Citizens of East London, in December 1965.

Because of the ambiguous and often behind-the-scenes nature of what preceded the setting up of many community relations committees, it is not possible to present any precise data on all the other local committees. The data given above give a fairly typical picture of the origins of most organizations of their kind. It is probably true to say that more than half the committees in the country owe their origins to the initiatives of local authorities. Quite apart from the promptings of Maurice Foley and the N.C.C.I., many local authorities experienced pressures from local organizations and individuals. For example, as far as the four committees mentioned above as set up by their local authorities were concerned, three were preceded by voluntary committees run by local church bodies which pressed for the setting up of voluntary liaison committees after the 1965 White Paper. Only in Hackney does there seem to have been no voluntary pressure, though Hackney had had a committee of councillors, the Commonwealth Citizens Consultative Committee, and a local authority-employed 'liaison officer' since 1959.

This shows just how complex the origins of many committees are. From our point of view, four of the committees studied, though not entirely without antecedents, owed their creation very largely to a local authority, while the other four had some 'life' of their own when they acquired local authority support. Ealing because it emerged from Southall I.F.C., Tower Hamlets because it was the creation of a long-standing anti-fascist organization, Wycombe because it had struggled along without any real local authority support since 1960, and Huddersfield because it emerged from a fairly lively International Co-operation Year Committee.

The contrast between these four committees and the other four can be further brought out. None of the four local authority-sponsored committees did more than select their staff in the period between their inaugural meeting and the appointment of their liaison officer or community relations officer. They were set up to acquire an N.C.C.I. grant to employ an officer, they did not see it as incumbent upon them to do any voluntary work until that officer arrived. Such a start obviously made it hard for the C.R.O.s to get voluntary activity going.

Wycombe, though rather moribund by the time its C.R.O. was appointed, had been in existence for seven years and had set up a housing association in 1962. Southall, too, had been in existence since 1963 and had sought to do useful work long before it had dared to hope that it might get a grant to pay for a full-time officer. Tower Hamlets had an official from the outset but it was building on the earlier work of the Council of Citizens of East London and had the support of an important autonomous body,

Toynbee Hall. Moreover, it initially paid for its own official. Huddersfield spent a year building up voluntary activities before it was able to appoint its voluntary secretary to the paid post of C.R.O.

It might be expected that this distinction between the two groups of four committees would also be reflected in their constitutional arrangements, with the local authority-sponsored committees subject to more formal controls than the others. This is partly but not entirely true. Birmingham and Sheffield stand out as two committees with close formal links with their town councils. Birmingham differs from the other seven committees by the fact that it does not possess a council of organization and individual members but is merely a group of Birmingham citizens selected by the Lord Mayor. This committee contains two city councillors, its chairman is an ex-councillor and sometime Lord Mayor, but the total local authority control over its composition is its salient aspect. Its secretary is its C.R.O. and its treasurer is the City Treasurer, though the latter appears to play no direct part in its deliberations.

Sheffield, on the other hand, has a general council composed of the representatives of local organizations. On this council there are ten local authority representatives, some councillors, and some officials nominated by various City Council departments. On Sheffield's seventeen-person executive committee there are five City Council members. Four are direct nominees of the local authority, required by the constitution, the fifth is the chairman, though there is no constitutional requirement that this office should be held by a local authority representative. In addition, the secretary of the Sheffield committee for community relations is the Town Clerk and the treasurer the City Treasurer, though again the constitution merely says that the general council shall elect these officers and does not bind them to elect local authority officials. Normally the Town Clerk's duties at meetings of council and executive are performed by the Assistant Town Clerk, and the City Treasurer rarely attends meetings. However, Sheffield City Council representatives play a significant role in the control of Sheffield C.C.R.

The constitutional provisions for local authority representation in the other two local authority-sponsored organizations correspond much more closely with those adopted by the other four committees studied. All six conform fairly closely to the 'model constitution' drawn up by the N.C.C.I. All six organizations provide for local authority membership of their full council or committee. Two of the six have constitutions requiring local authority representation on their executive (Ealing requires three such representatives on its executive. Hackney has four councillors on its executive, plus the Town Clerk and Housing Manager eligible to attend as observers). All but one of the remaining four committees have elected local authority members to their executives, though they are not required to do so. Huddersfield's chairman is an alderman who became involved because he was, as Mayor, chairman of the International Co-operation Year Committee. Tower Hamlets has elected two Labour councillors to its executive (all but three councillors in their borough are Labour, the remaining three are Communists). High Wycombe has one Labour councillor on its executive (though the Conservatives dominate the Borough Council). One of its vice-presidents, the Conservative chairman of Wycombe R.D.C., sometimes attends meetings. Finally, Bradford, strangely one of the local authority-sponsored committees, is the sole committee of the eight we studied which has no local authority representatives on its executive.

Formally, then, all eight committees have links with local authorities, but the strength of these links vary markedly. Formal representation of the local authority may or may not have a great deal of impact upon a community relations committee. This will depend upon who the representatives are, how they see their role, and how involved they are in the affairs of the community relations committee. Selznick sees the process of involvement of elements in the power structure outside an organization within that organization's own control structure as entailing two kinds of 'co-optation', 'formal' and 'informal'.[1] Formal co-optation helps to confer legitimacy upon an organization without effectively sharing power. Informal co-optation involves concessions to external power. After informal co-optation 'the character of the co-opted elements will necessarily shape the modes of action available to the group which has won adoption at the price of commitment to outside elements'.[2] Selznick's theory suggests two

[1] P. Selznick, *TVA and the Grass Roots* (Berkeley, University of California Press, 1949), p. 13.   [2] Ibid., p. 16.

alternatives which we may apply to the inclusion of local authority representatives in a community relations council. This inclusion may be merely 'formal'—a window-dressing operation—or it may represent the acceptance of curbs upon the freedom of action of the council. Selznick's analysis rests almost entirely upon a negative conception of power-sharing. It may be that informal co-optation will bring gains for an organization by providing it with powerful allies. Or any disadvantages in the way of limitations on freedom of action will be counterbalanced by the increased opportunities that may be provided in other directions by such powerful allies. Community relations councils are weak organizations, with small government grants, and a low potential for acquiring voluntary funds. In relation to their local authorities, they see themselves as faced by Hobson's choice. To co-opt may be to surrender power to the local authority. Not to co-opt or to co-opt formally may be to relinquish their only chance to acquire a powerful ally.

One further point must be made. Community relations councils are not only concerned about the pressures that may be put upon them by local authorities, they are also very concerned about the influence they may have upon local authority policies. The inclusion of local authority representatives in their ranks creates not merely the possibility of being influenced but also the possibility of influencing. Thus, to a certain extent, community relations committees are obliged to adopt what we have earlier described as a strategy of 'co-operative rationality'. One important reason why community relations councils are unlikely to disregard this point is that local authorities do not need to be represented at all within their membership in order to be influential: they have the financial whip-hand.

This last point is most important, for, as far as four of the eight committees are concerned, there is very little to say about local authority representation. In Birmingham, the fact that two committee members are city councillors is of no importance for the local authority control of a committee it nominates itself. In Bradford, even though local authority representatives do not sit on the executive committee, the community relations committee nevertheless regards the scrutiny of local authority policies as outside its terms of reference. In Ealing, the relationship between community relations council and local authority has been a very tense one, but the local authority representatives have not played a significant role in carrying the Borough Council's viewpoint into the deliberations of the community relations council. The conflict that has existed here has been between E.I.F.C. and the Borough Council, operating as distinct and separate organizations.

It is of interest to outline the position regarding local authority representation in Ealing in a little more detail. When Labour controlled Ealing Borough Council, up to May 1968, there were three local authority representatives on E.I.F.C. executive: the leader of the Labour group, the chairman of the Immigrants Committee of the Council (Labour), and a Conservative. These three councillors hardly ever attended E.I.F.C. executive meetings. When the Conservatives gained control of the Borough Council in a landslide victory in 1968, three Conservatives were appointed to the executive: the leader of the Group, his deputy (then prospective Parliamentary candidate for Southall), and another. Once again a high power group, but once again they proved to be virtual non-attenders. Then, in the course of the wrangle between E.I.F.C. and the Council, which put the whole future of E.I.F.C. in jeopardy, the Conservatives proposed to withdraw the local authority representation of six E.I.F.C. council members and three executive members. E.I.F.C. opposed this threat to its status and eventually the Tory leaders agreed to drop this proposal. But they decided that the local authority representatives on E.I.F.C.'s council and executive should 'serve in a personal capacity only', and the individuals nominated were rather 'minor' members of the council.

Since councillors have never been active in E.I.F.C., with one exception (the Indian Labour councillor Gill who had been on E.I.F.C. executive before his election to the council, who is an elected member of the executive, and only a local authority member of the council), who has little power as a new member of the very small opposition group, this change may be seen as only an attempt to undermine any tendency of E.I.F.C. to gain 'legitimacy' from the nominal presence of council representatives. It may be argued that if Ealing Community Relations Committee (the renamed E.I.F.C.) can win the support of some of the back-bench councillors, in the long run this backing may be of more use than the formal, but in practice almost meaningless, existence of senior local authority members on the executive committee.

The fourth committee about which there is little to say on the subject of local authority representation is Wycombe. Today, the only Wycombe councillor who takes any real interest in the community relations council is a member of the very small Labour group, who is both new to the local authority and relatively new to Wycombe. He is an impressive speaker and has experience of local government in Birmingham so he may carry some weight as an individual on the Borough Council. In as much as he does he is more appropriately considered Wycombe Integration Committee's representative on the Borough Council than vice versa. The chairman of the Rural District Council also takes some interest in the committee, but his council's contact with the committee is very slight and its financial contribution at the time of our research was £5 per annum towards the C.R.O.'s travelling to deal with 'cases' in the Rural District. Later this was increased to £25.

On two more of the eight committees the impact of the local authority representatives also seems to be fairly slight. In Tower Hamlets, there are two councillors on the executive of the community relations council. They are the only members of the executive who have lived all their life in the area, and stand in marked contrast to the other white members of the executive, all of whom either live outside Tower Hamlets or have moved there within the last five or six years as settlement wardens or clergy. The two councillors can be said to be the sole representatives on the executive of the borough's native white population. It is not surprising, therefore, that their involvement in the organization is rather slight. The prevailing attitude of Tower Hamlets Borough Council to C.C.T.H. is one of suspicion. On the other side there has been some criticism of the Borough Council within the ranks of the community relations council. One cannot really say that the councillor members have had any impact, either way, upon relations between the two bodies.

In Huddersfield, the chairman of the community relations council is a Labour alderman who became involved in the council after being Mayor in International Co-operation Year. He is the sole town council member on H.I.L.C. executive, which is perhaps unfortunate as the council has a large Conservative majority. He remains an influential and respected member of the Borough Council, has been allowed to retain the office of chairman of the welfare committee which he has held for many years, but his position in a minority group has obvious disadvantages for H.I.L.C. Since we studied the Huddersfield committee there seems to have been some attempts by local Conservatives to raise the temperature of the discussion of racial issues so that it may be that this handicap has become more apparent.

This problem of a close identification with the Labour party also applies to the two committees which have involved borough council members fully in their work. Both Hackney and Sheffield have senior members of the Labour group on their local authorities as chairmen of their community relations committees, and both have played a major part in the development of their organizations. In Hackney, the Borough Council was 100 per cent Labour until the elections of 1968 gave the Conservatives a small majority. It is not surprising that H.C.R.C. has been closely associated with the Labour councillors who became involved in it when the Borough Council's Commonwealth Citizens Consultative Committee was wound up. It is equally not surprising that some Conservatives in Hackney were prepared to use the record of some Labour councillors on race relations to try to win racialist support for themselves. One Conservative councillor described the chairman of H.C.R.C. and another councillor as 'the sort of men who are prepared to let all and sundry come to this country regardless of whether they have a home or job to come to'.[1]

The consequence of the change in power is that instead of having four Labour councillors on its executive, H.C.R.C. has two Labour and two Conservative councillors. While the Labour members remain active in H.C.R.C., the two Conservatives have so far shown little interest in the organization. Despite the change in the balance of power it has proved possible to prevent H.C.R.C. becoming a political 'football'. There are a number of reasons for this. First, the Conservatives came to power with no experience of local government, consequently they have been prepared to lean a great deal on the Labour elder statesmen. They did not fill the aldermanic bench with their own nominees, and they allowed the Labour party to nominate an ex-councillor as Mayor for the year 1968–9. Second, many Conservative councillors were unprepared

---

[1] Speech by Councillor George Jones at a Borough Council meeting, reported in *Hackney Gazette* (9 June 1968).

to endorse the racialist views of some of their colleagues. Many of them gave their support to the Mayor's commitment to the ideals of human rights year. The Mayor, who is also a member of H.C.R.C. executive, seems to have given a strong anti-racialist lead. Third, H.C.R.C. has acted with caution in the political field, When a West Indian member of its executive was reported in a local paper as saying that Tory councils had got into power in Hackney and other London boroughs because of Powellism, the chairman and C.R.O. of H.C.R.C. wrote to say that this was the member's personal view and in no way represented H.C.R.C.'s views 'which on the contrary would like to see the issue of race relations removed from the area of local politics and work towards achieving greater racial harmony on a non-political basis'.[1] On other occasions, too, H.C.R.C.'s chairman has made it clear that he is keen to involve Tories in the work of the organization.

If their position is measured in terms of financial support from the Borough Council, it may be argued that the arrival of the Tories in the Town Hall has benefitted H.C.R.C. As far as the role of their own councillor members are concerned this may be because the Labour members, who previously seem to have been concerned to restrain H.C.R.C.'s demands on the local rates, are now working positively for H.C.R.C. on the Borough Council instead of being primarily the Borough Council's agents in the ranks of H.C.R.C.

As we have seen, Sheffield's community relations committee is structured in such a way that one may expect the local authority viewpoint to be expressed effectively within its ranks. Its chairman is a Labour alderman who has been deeply involved in the work of the organization since the beginning. His party has been in power all the time, apart from the council year 1968–9. He is deputy leader of the Labour group and, at the time of our study, chairman of the city's finance committee. He has four council member colleagues on the executive of S.C.C.R., two Labour and two Conservative.

Another important local authority figure within the ranks of S.C.C.R. is the Assistant Town Clerk, who acts as secretary to the committee and executive, and who has taken a warm interest in the progress of S.C.C.R. since its inception. There can be no

---

[1] *Stoke Newington Observer* (13 November 1968).

doubt that these important local government figures have played
a major role in securing grants amounting to £6,500 per annum
for S.C.C.R.

Against this record of local authority support it should be
pointed out that most of the money is spent on providing case-
workers, who might otherwise be found within the local authority's
own departments. And the chairman of S.C.C.R. has been
unwilling to support the examination of local authority policies
by S.C.C.R. Up to the present the local authority has kept
S.C.C.R. firmly within terms of reference largely set by itself.
There are signs that both staff and some committee members are
uneasy about this relationship. In fact, in 1969, the C.R.O. stated
to the Press: 'A firm declaration of policy towards immigrants by
Sheffield City Council would go a long way to relieving their fear
about the treatment they receive in the city.'[1] It is not clear what
provoked this outburst from the C.R.O., but it seems to provide
evidence of underlying anxieties on his part despite his committee's
close relationship with the local authority.

We have suggested, then, that in only two of the eight
committees does the presence of local authority representatives as
active members of the organization have a significant impact. In
one case, Hackney, this involvement is probably quite vital for
the organization since the Borough Council provides one of the
main sources of white representatives in a borough which lacks
active voluntary organizations. In Sheffield, on the other hand,
there is a rich institutional life. The local authority involvement
is not so vital in this respect and the community relations council
has to accept a measure of local authority control in return for
substantial funds.

This neglect of local committees is not necessarily linked with
the absence of effective local authority representatives on the
community relations council. Whether an organization gets
effective council representatives amongst its ranks is obviously
affected by the personnel available, and by the willingness of
committees to woo the councillors. Furthermore, a committee
may acquire a good relationship with the local authority through
direct approaches, particularly to officers, as much as through its
local authority representatives. Several of the committees we
studied had most of their dealings with the local authority through

[1] *Sheffield Star* (12 May 1969).

direct contacts or through contacts between C.R.O. and officials rather than through their councillor members. We must now explore this aspect of relations between committees and local authorities.

In terms of the concepts developed by Selznick, only in one case, Sheffield, is there any indication that the co-optation of local authority members, represents 'sharing of power'. In all the other cases, co-optation helps to confer legitimacy to the committee and provides links that may assist the community relations council to influence local authority policies. This does not mean that local authorities do not exercise power over community relations committees, merely that power is not really exercised through the representatives of the authorities who are nominated to the committees.

Clearly one measure of the health of the relationship between local authority and community relations council is provided by the size of grant paid by the local authority. Table 8.1 summarizes the data on this point from the eight committees, together with data from Camden, the most generously supported of all the community relations committees. The product of a penny rate, and the number of immigrants from the 'new Commonwealth'[1]

TABLE 8.1
LOCAL AUTHORITY GRANTS TO COMMUNITY RELATIONS
COMMITTEES 1968–9

		Product of 1d rate in the borough	Estimated 'immigrants' in the borough 1966
Birmingham	Accommodation, secretary, and casework assistant	£ 211,850	49,870
Bradford	£1,250 and accommodation	41,934	13,170
Ealing	£4,100 and accommodation	96,000	16,770
Hackney	£2,500 and accommodation	57,300	23,630
Huddersfield	£125, secretary, and accommodation	16,965	5,600
Sheffield	£7,500	97,105	6,830
Tower Hamlets	£2,250	57,800	11,040
Wycombe	£250, accommodation, and stationery	15,860	2,840
Camden	£11,000	134,800	15,780

[1] *Sample Census 1966, Commonwealth Immigrant Tables* (London, H.M.S.O.). 'New Commonwealth' includes all Commonwealth countries except Australia, New Zealand, and Canada. Only people *born* in the 'New Commonwealth' are enumerated as 'immigrants', therefore the 'coloured' population of these boroughs is obviously much higher than this.

the 1966 Census estimates each authority to have are also provided. They give a clear indication of the puny nature of the sums
involved. One must however in all fairness point out that it has
been the community relations movement's misfortune to seek local
authority support at a time when the Government was seeking
to curb the growth of local expenditure.

Amongst the eight committees, only Birmingham, Ealing, and
Sheffield together with Hackney, which received an addition to
their grant after our field-work was done, are able to employ
more than a C.R.O. and secretary. These committees have received additional help in order to be able to provide additional
casework services, a function which may be regarded as the local
authority's responsibility anyway.

At the other extreme, Wycombe are only able to employ a
part-time secretary on their meagre grant. They share this plight
with thirteen of the twenty-three other local committees whose
C.R.O.s returned our questionnaire. They all either have only
a part-time secretary or have to rely upon a local authority or
council of social service secretarial pool.

Of the four committees who receive larger than normal
grants, the Birmingham Committee can hardly be said to have a
'generous' local authority by any standards when one examines
the product of its penny rate. It does not have much potential for
impact upon this city of over a million people and over 50,000
immigrants. Of the other three committees, while two enjoy good
relations with their local authorities (Sheffield and Hackney),
strangely enough the third has become involved in far more
extensive conflict with its Borough Council than any other
committee.

In order to explain how a situation arose in which the
Conservative-controlled Ealing Borough Council proposed measures that would severely curb the activities of E.I.F.C., it is
necessary to recall some of the past history of politics and race in
this troubled area set out in Chapter 2. Before 1965, what is now
the London Borough of Ealing consisted of three Middlesex
boroughs, Acton, Ealing, and Southall. Immigration became a
political issue in Southall in the early 1960s when agitation began
to build up against the growing concentration of immigrants from
India in parts of the borough. Southall Borough Council was
Labour-controlled but the leading Labour council members were

at best equivocal on race issues. Some of them were positively hostile to immigrants, as subsequent events were to demonstrate. Extremists continually sought to embarrass Southall Council. The British National party campaigned actively in the area and in 1963 anti-immigrant elements joined forces in Southall Residents Association. Southall Conservative party, which stood an outside chance of gaining the Parliamentary seat, sought to derive maximum advantage from this situation, and in 1964 the Conservative candidate set out to share the anti-immigrant vote with the British National party.[1]

Southall International Friendship Committee was formed in 1963 on the initiative of Southall Trades Council, specifically to try to check the growth of racialism. It sought to be non-political but many of its leading members were well towards the left of the political spectrum, and it was only able to acquire fairly nominal support from Southall Borough Council, unlike the neighbouring Willesden I.F.C., on which it was modelled, which had its Borough Council as its main sponsor. Southall Borough Council gave the I.F.C. a grant of £50 and permission to use the Town Hall for meetings, but refused to allow the Town Hall address to be used for mail. The Mayor became president but this was a purely nominal office of the kind which Mayors accept in a wide range of voluntary organizations. One of the Labour councillors became chairman of Southall I.F.C. This was in a personal capacity and not as a council representative, and he was made to suffer for his commitment when for the Ealing Borough Council elections he was relegated from the safe Labour ward he had represented on Southall Borough Council to fight instead in a Tory stronghold.

As the first elections for the new enlarged Ealing Borough Council approached, the Conservatives naturally tried to expose the Labour party's ambivalence on the race issue, and to frighten the Ealing electorate about the Southall 'wing' of the Labour party. The following quotation from a speech made in April 1964 by the man who was to become the Conservative leader on the Borough Council gives something of the flavour of this attack and helps to explain the subsequent difficulties faced by Ealing I.F.C. in working with a Conservative council:

[1] Deakin (ed.), op. cit., pp. 31–53. Also Foot, op. cit., pp. 210–17.

We have always felt that the Labour Council in Southall has been too easy with the Indians on the question of overcrowding.

Anyone who has watched the contortions of the Labour Party in Southall as they have angled, twisted and turned in order to secure both the support of the Indians and at the same time keep the support of their white supporters must have a nasty taste in their mouths.

One is left wondering what compromise or agreement has been concluded in the murky corners of Southall.

Can the inhabitants of Acton and Ealing, let alone of Southall, trust the Labour Party to defend our standards of public health and sanitation when they are willing to come to electoral pacts with people who do not respect these standards.

Electoral advantage seems more important to the Labour Party than public health.[1]

It was certainly true that at this time Labour was bidding for the electoral support of the powerful Indian Workers' Association while also trying to appease the Southall Residents Association. In 1964, the Conservatives made no real attempt to win Indian support. In later elections they were to take over the Labour role of trying to face both ways while the local Labour party, influenced by its new M.P., Sidney Bidwell, at long last took a firm anti-racialist line.

Labour won control of Ealing Borough Council, and soon after an issue arose which helped to clear the air on race relations as far as Ealing Borough Labour group was concerned. In June 1965, the new borough had to decide on the rules to be adopted for the allocation of council houses. The Housing Committee proposed that the residence qualifications for placement on the housing list should be five years in Greater London and at least one year in Ealing, a rule similar to the one adopted by most other London boroughs. At a meeting of the Labour group, some of the councillors led by two stalwarts of Southall Labour party, objected to these proposals. In a bid to pacify this opposition the group agreed to increase the number of 'points' awarded for long residence in the borough, but this did not satisfy some of the rebels. So, when, at the Council meeting, the Conservative leader moved an amendment to impose a fifteen-year residential qualification on persons not born in Britain, five of the Labour members

---

[1] Report of a speech by Councillor (later Alderman) Hetherington, to a meeting of Walpole Branch Young Conservatives, *Middlesex County Times* (18 April 1964).

supported it. These five rebels had the Labour whip withdrawn and four of them were subsequently expelled from the party for failing to give an undertaking to abide by group decisions in future. Two of the rebels stood as independent candidates in the 1968 local elections, with support from Southall Residents Association, and succeeded in retaining their seats.

Southall I.F.C. was transformed into Ealing I.F.C. in the spring of 1966, with full local authority support. The Borough Council provided an office in the Town Hall and a full-time secretary. In March 1968, it also enabled E.I.F.C. to employ an assistant community relations officer. Thus, although, as pointed out earlier, the Labour councillors on E.I.F.C. council and executive did not take much interest in the work of the organization, the attitude of the Borough Council while it was Labour-controlled was generally supportive.

In the spring of 1968, E.I.F.C. brought out two reports which were critical of Ealing Borough Council policies. Their education subcommittee published a discussion of the policy of dispersing immigrant children in which it advocated that this policy should be eventually dropped. As first steps in this direction they advocated that dispersal should be made either voluntary or based upon language disability, rather than upon race and colour.[1] This was a moderately worded document, in fact it was so carefully balanced that some of the national papers which reported its publication presented it as arguing *for* rather than against dispersal. It received a generally friendly reception.

E.I.F.C.'s housing subcommittee also produced a report in March 1968.[2] This followed an E.I.F.C. meeting at which the chairman of the Borough's Health Committee had defended the policy adopted by his committee on overcrowding. E.I.F.C.'s report was very critical of the Borough Council on this issue, alleging that the Council was applying a much more rigid overcrowding standard than other London boroughs and was only really enforcing this standard on Indian households. The report was also critical of the council housing allocation system under which persons are required to have lived five years in London

[1] Report of the Education Committee of Ealing International Friendship Council, 'The Education of the Immigrant Child in the London Borough of Ealing' (mimeographed, 1968).

[2] Ealing International Friendship Council, 'Memorandum: Overcrowding and Housing Policy' (mimeographed, 1968).

and to have been one year on the waiting list before their applications are considered. They may be still handicapped by the weight
given to long residence in the area under the points system. The
report pointed out that immigrants would obviously fare very
badly under this system. The report was strongly worded and was
resented by the Labour leaders of the Council. It was greeted by
the *Middlesex County Times* with the headlines 'Council Accused of
Colour Prejudice',[1] and the opponents of E.I.F.C. continue to
condemn it for the report. Several E.I.F.C. members thought
that the report was injudiciously worded, though they pointed out
that no attempt has ever been made to refute the allegations
in it.

E.I.F.C. was certainly not afraid to hit the headlines. In
early 1968, they made a firm public stand against Powell and
against the Immigration Act which restricted the entry of Kenya
Asians. The C.R.O., the Publicity Officer, and individual
members of the committee attacked the racialism of Southall
Residents Association and their allies.

In May 1968 the Conservatives won a large majority on the
Borough Council. That summer, after a general discussion with
E.I.F.C., they agreed to continue the local authority's support and
to nominate councillors to E.I.F.C. council and executive. In
November 1968, they began to have second thoughts about this
arrangement and asked E.I.F.C. to meet Borough Council representatives to discuss it. There was some delay in arranging this
meeting, which did not take place until January 1969. In the
interim the Press got wind of the situation. The *Evening Standard*
secured an interview with the Conservative leader in which he
attacked E.I.F.C. for expressing political viewpoints,[2] such as
calling Southall Residents Association racialist, and suggested that
the local authority might withdraw much of E.I.F.C.'s support.
The attack was countered by a local Labour M.P.[3] and by the
Labour leader on the Borough Council, who nevertheless suggested that some of the E.I.F.C. officers 'may go a bit
overboard'.[4]

When the meeting eventually took place the Borough

---

[1] *Middlesex County Times* (29 March 1968).
[2] Interview of Alderman Hetherington, *Evening Standard* (27 November 1968).
[3] Interview of W. Molloy, M.P., *Acton Gazette* (5 December 1968).
[4] Interview of Councillor K. Acock, *Acton Gazette* (19 December 1968).

Council's Co-ordinating Committee (the all-Conservative 'Cabinet' of the Council) made the following proposals to E.I.F.C.:

that it should move its office from the Town Hall and find its own premises. The Borough Council would increase its grant to make this possible.

that the new Assistant C.R.O. should be employed by E.I.F.C. and not by the Borough Council as his predecessor had been.

that direct Borough representation on E.I.F.C. council and executive should cease.

E.I.F.C. naturally found the second condition acceptable but was unhappy about the other two proposals. There was, however, some relief that the Borough Council had not taken the excessively tough line predicted. They sent a conciliatory letter to the Council expressing the desirability of councillor representation and an office in the Town Hall. To their surprise, as they obviously were in a very weak bargaining position, the Council agreed to meet them half-way on these points, offering them an office in a new Council block a few hundred yards away from the Town Hall, a grant sufficient for them to employ their own assistant C.R.O. and office secretary, and some Borough Council nominees 'to serve in a personal capacity only'.

In the light of their publicly expressed hostility to E.I.F.C., it is hard to explain why the Ealing Conservatives let E.I.F.C. off so lightly. In the interviews the Tory leaders granted us they were very keen to present themselves as 'reasonable' men. Moreover, while seeking to extract the maximum political capital from an attack on E.I.F.C., the leader of the group had no need to stoop to vindictive measures against them. Significantly, too, in the 1968 local election, an Indian Labour candidate in one of the wards in Southall had been opposed by an Indian Tory candidate. The latter did better than the other Tories in the ward, and was compensated for his failure to win by appointment as an alderman. So it appears that the Tories are now taking some interest in wooing the Indian vote, and perhaps this restrained them from taking too tough a line against E.I.F.C. Such an interpretation is particularly plausible in view of the fact that the deputy leader of the Conservative group is prospective Parliamentary candidate in Southall. The Tories seem to want to play consensus politics in Southall, they were trying to push E.I.F.C. into a similar position.

This last observation introduces what is perhaps the most important of several general conclusions we can draw from E.I.F.C.'s disturbed history. While it is true that, far more than any other of the eight community relations councils we studied, E.I.F.C. has been a political organization, it can be argued that the situation in which it was created and has lived since has been one in which it could hardly keep out of politics. It is often urged that community relations councils should try to keep race out of politics. But being non-political is of course an euphemism for refraining from challenging the *status quo*. However even if one accepts the popularly used restricted definition of being non-political, refraining from becoming involved in conventional party political controversy, it is clear that in a situation like that in Ealing in which the political parties and pressure groups like the S.R.A. are determined to treat race as a political issue, such a course of action is not feasible for a community relations committee. Southall I.F.C. was created to counter Southall Residents Association. It was natural that it attracted 'political' people from the left. The commitment of many of these people to E.I.F.C. has been kept alive by the way in which S.R.A., B.N.P., and, in a more subtle way, the Conservative party, have maintained race as a live issue in local politics.

Only one other of our eight committees was in a town in which there had been widespread exploitation of the race issue in politics, the Birmingham committee. But it has already been made clear that this is very much an establishment committee closely linked to the Town Hall. It has therefore not been in the forefront of political battles. It has suffered in another way, being written off as an organization of no consequence by most of the immigrant organizations in the city. By contrast, Southall I.W.A. is one of the few Indian Workers' Associations to have anything to do with its local community relations council. Ealing's community relations council has remained an organization which, whatever its failings, has not betrayed its immigrant members.

One community relations council, not in our group of eight, which has experienced a turbulent history, and can be said to have been similarly deeply involved in local politics for apparently much the same reasons, is Wolverhampton. While one council which has been both relatively successful and outspoken on race relations, but which has not been embroiled in controversy, is

Camden, which has been blessed by a political context in which responsible leadership has been given on all sides.

Many other community relations councils are on the edge of situations which may tend in due course to embroil them in politics. While in Camden a Tory Councillor has assumed the chairmanship of the community relations council and maintained the stand against racialism taken up by his predecessor, in neighbouring Brent the community relations council is an object of suspicion to the Tory councillors as a Labour party 'baby'. These gentlemen were sufficiently concerned about the relationship between borough and community relations council to pass a Council resolution repudiating the anti-Powell stand taken by the latter body.

The coincidence of the rise of Powellism with the capture of most local authorities by the Conservatives has obviously tended to inject the seeds of controversy into community relations council/ local authority relations. This has happened even where the community relations council has never regarded the scrutiny of local authority policies as within its scope. Such is the case, for example, in Bradford. In many areas right-wing extremists are raising their voices to condemn community relations councils as pro-immigrant organizations. In most cases, as we found in Hackney, Huddersfield, Sheffield, and Bradford, these people are at present merely minor irritants, but they are awakening anxieties on the part of community relations council members. In some respects, if they put an end to the kind of complacent statements we heard, particularly in Bradford, suggesting that racialism, discrimination, and the inequitable treatment of immigrants by local authorities reported elsewhere in the country just do not apply in 'our town', they may lead to some community relations committees seeing their situations in a truer light.

The main conclusion we have drawn from the Ealing 'affair' is that the community relations council could hardly stay outside politics. But the Conservative councillors we interviewed clearly thought that E.I.F.C. had brought retribution upon themselves by getting into politics. Their view involved two interlinked arguments that are worth further examination in relation to all the community relations councils we studied. They argued that:

1. E.I.F.C. had been unduly provocative by continually embroiling itself in public controversy.

2. E.I.F.C. has no need to act as a pro-immigrant pressure group and lead attacks on local authority policies.

We will examine how all eight committees approach these two sensitive issues, and whether community relations councils can operate effectively without making themselves in some measure vulnerable to attack on points of this kind.

The first point of criticism of E.I.F.C. was that it was too prone to get involved in public controversy, that it could have done much of its work equally successfully, perhaps even more successfully, without much of the publicity it acquired as a crusading anti-racialist organization. Whether or not to become embroiled in controversy, whether or not to attack Powell, whether or not to attack Government immigration policy are issues which exercise all the committees we studied.

On the national level, 1968–9 proved crucial. The Kenya Asians issue was a final indicator of the N.C.C.I.'s weakness. Powell's various outbursts also provoked counterblasts from many quarters. Substantial majorities in all eight committees condemned the Government's action over the Kenya Asians. It goes without saying that Powell found next to no support in their ranks. The case for translating indignation into protest was made partly in terms of a belief in community relations councils as public educators on matters of race relations, though few had much confidence in this crude form of public education. The other, more important, argument for protest was that the retention of the confidence of immigrants in community relations councils required actions of this kind.

The case against protest made by many members was that such action achieves little and may alienate potential allies, which brings us back to the local authorities. Some members maintained that protest on national events could be left to the Community Relations Commission. Local committees should only lend their support when there was a local angle to a national story (support for Powell by a local M.P. etc.). One politically sophisticated member of Hackney committee suggested that collective protests should be avoided, but that committees should encourage individual officers or members to issue statements or letters to the Press.

All the committees except Sheffield and Bradford discussed the 1968 Immigration Act and conveyed their opposition to it to the N.C.C.I. However, the six committees got varying local Press coverage. It is difficult to say whether the fact that the anti-racialism of Ealing committee became so very apparent while the attitudes of the other five committees which issued protests received little attention in their localities has anything to do with the force with which they were expressed, or is merely a function of the extent to which the local papers were prepared to give prominence to their point of view. We formed the impression that the three London committees probably put over their points of view fairly powerfully, while Birmingham was largely prepared to leave the C.R.O. to deal with the issue through his involvement in the National Association of Community Relations Officers, and Wycombe and Huddersfield's protests were rather muted.

Wycombe committee was particularly divided over the tactics of protest. A consequence of this was that an anti-Powell demonstration in Wycombe caused trouble within the committee. Wycombe's C.R.O. supported the demonstration, which was organized by local left-wingers and supported by the community relations committee in Oxford. The chairman and some of the white members of the executive deplored this identification of the community relations committee with a public demonstration, and sought to ensure that the C.R.O. did not take such action in future. The chairman also wrote to a local paper disassociating the committee from the demonstration and claiming that Wycombe immigrants were not involved in it. This action alienated four of the seven immigrant members of the committee who specifically referred to the incident during our interviews, six months after the event, and saw it as an attempt to placate the local Conservative M.P., John Hall.

It seems to us that the trouble caused by this incident in Wycombe is symptomatic of a situation in which the committee has failed to achieve any cohesion around a coherent programme of action. In this respect the Wycombe incident is not unlike the row which developed in Bradford over a similar issue. By contrast the Sheffield committee has largely ignored national events without provoking internal conflict so far.

One of the main hypotheses upon which this research was based was that the committees would find themselves on a knife edge between maintaining the quiet acceptance of the *status quo* which would satisfy the local authorities, and asserting a strong

16

anti-racialist line which would satisfy many immigrants and their supporters. We have quoted the history of the Ealing committee at some length to show how bad relations developed between that fairly radical committee and a Conservative local authority. The troubles within the Wycombe and Bradford committees are examples of the other kind of difficulty, the alienation of immigrant members by avoiding taking a really clear public stand against racialism.

Yet there is a tactical case against outspoken anti-racialism. We can support our 'knife-edge' thesis with examples from only three of the eight committees, together with perhaps the 'establishment' committee in Birmingham which faced considerable hostility from within the 'Advisory Committee' and which has not had much success in winning the confidence of its local authority. Of the other four committees, one, Sheffield, has made its position as an establishment committee with local authority support very clear, and has avoided becoming involved in protest. That it has adopted this role without conflict with its immigrant members may be due to the fact that it has been very successful within its own fairly narrowly defined, predominantly welfare, sphere, and it has carefully selected most of its immigrant participants so as to avoid including 'militants'.

In Tower Hamlets and Hackney, skilled leadership seems so far to have prevented extreme difficulties. Both committees have been more concerned to assert their radicalism in conflict with the N.C.C.I./C.R.C. than within their own boroughs. Huddersfield has been able to make quiet if slow progress in a town where, on the whole, conflict over race has been kept at a low key. There are signs, however, that National Front and Powellite activity are on the increase. In due course the community relations committee might find itself in a political atmosphere not unlike that in Ealing.

The second of the points made about E.I.F.C. dealt with the situation in which Ealing has become engaged in public controversy about local policies. Whether or not this kind of issue is a source of trouble in a locality will, naturally, depend upon whether local authority policies are positively anti-immigrant or neglectful of the needs of immigrants, as well as upon the relationship between local community relations committee and local authority. Therefore, there is not really anything to say about

Huddersfield on this point. Not because it has particularly good relationship with its local authority, we have seen that Huddersfield Borough Council does not take much interest in H.I.L.C., but because Huddersfield Council has a generally good record on policies for immigrants. The two big points of controversy for most areas are housing and education. Huddersfield does not have a serious housing problem and is making great strides in the rehousing of inadequately housed immigrants. In education, Huddersfield have been pioneers in the provision of special facilities for non-English-speaking children. Though dispersal is practised, it is done with care and primarily to benefit Asian children who have yet to perfect their English rather than merely to keep down the number of black faces in certain schools.

Let us now look at the extent to which, in the other seven areas, there was ground for criticism of local authority policies and the extent to which the community relations committees are aware of this, prepared to put pressure on the local authorities to alter policies, and prepared to make public their views on these matters.

In Bradford, the community relations committee did not even see it as within their scope to engage in any critique of local authority policies and members seemed totally unaware of any grounds for criticism of such policies. This is all the more surprising as a voluntary multiracial body, Campaign for Racial Equality in Bradford and District, published a report on the education of immigrant children[1] which expressed considerable disquiet about the way in which the dispersal policy was being operated and about the indiscriminate and rather clumsy way pre-school medicals were required of 'immigrant' children. The C.A.R.E. report noted that, after considerable pressure, the authorities had ceased submitting British-born coloured children to medicals. There is no evidence that the community relations committee played any part in securing this change.

Some Bradford committee members talked proudly of their committee as so close to the local power structure that inevitably no conflict arises with the local authority. If this is true, then evidence on the educational field does not reflect very well on the committee. In the field of housing, the committee gave no

---

[1] 'Report of Education Sub-Committee 1968', Campaign for Racial Equality in Bradford and District (mimeographed, 1968).

attention to the subject until an opportunity occurred to secure an anonymous donation for a housing project, when the community relations officer entered into consultations with representatives of the local authority. No immigrant members of the committee were involved in these discussions, and the matter was reported to the executive as a *fait accompli*. The local authority certainly received an opportunity to influence community relations committee policies. No one seems to have thought to consider whether the reverse might have been appropriate. Back in 1964, the local authority had been prepared to experiment with special accommodation for single immigrant men. The experiment failed. It might be thought that the community relations committee would have regarded it as one of its first tasks to try to find out why it failed and to recommend new measures that would be successful.

The committee in Wycombe has also done little to scrutinize or question local authority policies, except in one respect. In the field of education, some immigrant members of the committee were gravely dissatisfied with the treatment accorded to coloured children at one of the local schools. The C.R.O. supported them and attempted to draw attention to their grievances. This led to a row between the Divisional Education Officer and the C.R.O., and eventually to an investigation of the situation by the N.C.C.I.'s Education Officer. The Divisional Education Officer claimed that the N.C.C.I.'s officer had found no cause for complaint and had apologized to him. When we asked the latter to confirm this, she refused to comment.

The Wycombe committee, which is dominated by its long-standing white members, did not involve itself in this controversy. Its only formal move on the subject of education has been to set up a panel composed entirely of teachers in the employ of the local authority. This panel, which is chaired by the headmaster of a secondary modern school which contains a special language centre for Asian children, has played a part in securing greater attention to the education problems of immigrants within the Division, and in facilitating communication between the local authority and the community relations committee. But it operates very much as a group of insiders ultimately dependent upon the education system for their jobs or references. The panel has three immigrant members, all Asian teachers who are neither well equipped to speak for working-class immigrants nor really free to attack their employer. There is no provision for ascertaining the points of view of ordinary members of the immigrant community.

In the field of housing, a curious situation has arisen which seems to effectively inhibit the community relations committee from undertaking any examination of housing problems. One of the earliest achievements of Wycombe's committee was the setting up of the Friendship Housing Association in 1962, as a separate body independent of the community relations committee. Several of the long-standing white members of the W.D.I.C. executive are members of the association. This dual membership has led to a situation in which W.D.I.C. executive regards housing matters as the concern of the Housing Association, and not of itself. Scope exists for a valuable alliance in which W.D.I.C. could set up a housing panel to examine local policies, give advice on housing problems, and lobby the local authority on housing matters, working in close touch with the Housing Association. This opportunity has not been exploited. This is all the more unfortunate as the Housing Association, while in effect providing 'interim accommodation' for people on the housing list (a role which most local authorities undertake for themselves), has only been able to develop very very slowly on account of local authority reluctance to provide loans or to adopt a flexible approach to planning regulations. There is perhaps a moral somewhere here for the Housing Association being set up in Bradford.

In general the relationship between W.D.I.C. and Borough Council (who are not, of course, the education authority) is of little significance for either side. No one seems to have established a viable relationship with Borough Council officials. Despite the fact that education and many health and welfare matters are the responsibility of Buckinghamshire County Council, no real contacts have been secured with this body. W.D.I.C. has no county council representatives on its general council, and secures no money from that source. No one seems to have thought such contacts to be necessary.

Two of the community relations committees which are highly sensitive to local authority policy issues find nevertheless that they have to tread very carefully, as their Borough Councils, Hackney and Tower Hamlets, are rather sensitive to criticism. This is perhaps because they are East London authorities with enormous problems on their hands.

In both boroughs the vast majority of rehousing is to meet slum clearance needs. As far as the administration of the housing list is concerned, Hackney's community relations committee is generally satisfied with Borough Council policies. Tower Hamlets' committee is seeking to get the Council's requirement that people must have lived in the borough five years altered to five years in Greater London and one year in Tower Hamlets. This would bring it in line with most other London boroughs. This aspect of Tower Hamlets policy was brought to light in Elizabeth Burney's *Housing on Trial*.[1] She also raised some disturbing points about the Greater London Council housing policy. Neither Tower Hamlets nor Hackney's community relations council seem to have achieved any viable relationship with this enormous authority nor to have made any attempt to study the complexities of its policies.[2] Unfortunately the proposal for a fair housing group, drawn up by a consortium of North and East London community relations committees, was abandoned when it was refused grant aid by the N.C.C.I.

Much the same can be said about attitudes in these two committees to Inner London Education Authority policies. Both committees have established some links with the I.L.E.A., primarily to get the support of educationalists for programmes of education in race relations. This is a particular speciality in Tower Hamlets, building upon initiatives originally taken by the Council of Citizens of East London. Tower Hamlets has also secured I.L.E.A. support for its playgroup.

Neither Tower Hamlets nor Hackney, however, have made a study of I.L.E.A. policies. The authority does not practise dispersal, but provisions for non-English-speaking children leave a lot to be desired. In general the I.L.E.A. faces such overwhelming problems deriving from inadequate provision in the past for education in this part of London that the community relations committees are reduced to making sympathetic noises and backing all efforts to secure the maximum additional help from the

---

[1] Burney, op. cit., pp. 79–109.

[2] For example, the reluctance of outer London boroughs to accept the G.L.C. nomination of black immigrants for rehousing from inner London boroughs under the G.L.C. quota scheme, was not realized by the community relations committees. *Evidence to the Select Committee on Race Relations* (14 January 1971).

government. As with housing, the size of the problem inhibits any detailed criticism.

The only one of the eight committees really well placed to develop effective private consultation with its local authority on matters of policy affecting immigrants is Sheffield. Not only is the local authority well represented on its council and executive, but senior local officials are members of all its subcommittees. This has meant that there has been a tendency for it to restrict its role to securing immigrant acceptance of, and co-operation with, local authority policies to the neglect of ensuring that the local authority adjusts its policies to immigrant needs and points of view. The chairman, as a senior member of Sheffield City Council, has played an important role in ruling out of order any scrutiny of local authority policies and in insisting that allegations of discrimination (made for example by a local headmaster against the housing department) just cannot be true as the City Council follows a policy of 'non-discrimination'.[1] Characteristic of this attitude was an executive committee decision not to submit evidence to the Cullingworth Committee on council house allocation worded as follows: 'In view of the declared policy of the City Council of affording equal treatment to all applicants, the Executive Committee decided not to submit any evidence.'[2]

In general Sheffield City Council is a typical example of the kind of local authority described in *Colour and Citizenship* as providing equality of treatment to immigrants in the narrowly legal sense: 'The difficulties encountered in this sector [local authorities] are not so much of overt discrimination but arise from practices whose intentions may be benevolent but whose results are damaging.'[3] Sheffield's housing policy was criticized in the P.E.P. Report because of the discriminatory impact of emphasis upon time on the waiting list as a key criterion for rehousing.[4] As

[1] This is more or less a direct quote from S.C.C.R. minutes.

[2] The following community relations committees from our sample of eight submitted evidence: Birmingham, Bradford, Ealing, Hackney, and Wycombe. In addition the Tower Hamlets C.R.O. gave evidence on behalf of the Joint Council for the Welfare of Immigrants. Other committees which submitted evidence were Oxford, Wandsworth, Westminster, and Gloucester. *Council Housing Purposes, Procedures and Priorities*, Ninth Report of the Housing Management Sub-Committee of the Central Housing Advisory Committee (London, H.M.S.O., 1969), pp. 165–7.

[3] Rose *et al.*, op. cit., pp. 79–109.

[4] Daniel, op. cit., p. 185. For a general discussion of this issue see *Council Housing Purposes, Procedures and Priorities*, pp. 122–3.

pointed out, local anxieties about the actual impact of housing policies have gone uninvestigated in Sheffield.

A new issue has arisen in Sheffield in the housing sector. The Council is engaged on a substantial slum-clearance exercise in Attercliffe. Substantial numbers of Pakistani households are included in the clearance area, yet many Pakistanis seem to prefer to move to other private houses in the area instead of accepting council houses. Several theories are put forward to explain this:

Pakistanis' preference for home-ownership.

Rejection of local authority housing because the kinds of houses offered and the rules relating to council tenancies make it impossible for Pakistanis to meet obligations towards extended families and friends.

Pakistanis' dislike of 'decanting' to other parts of the town far from either compatriots or places of work.

Lack of awareness of rights, and of the possibility of negotiating to obtain the best possible terms under conditions of compulsory purchase, for example additional payments for 'well-maintained' houses.

The Fair Housing officer of Sheffield C.C.R. is engaged in an intensive study of this issue. His findings may well indicate a need for his committee to urge the local authority to modify some of its policies. In which case it *should* be well placed to turn its relationship with the local authority to some advantage here.

In the field of education, Sheffield C.C.R. has been rather more prepared to use its contacts to press for changes in policy. The problem has been a largely *laissez-faire* approach to the difficulties of non-English-speaking children. The education sub-committee of Sheffield C.C.R. has been continually pressing for some special arrangements to help these children, and at the time of our study special 'centres' were planned for the autumn. These centres are to provide short courses which still sound inadequate, but at least a start has been made.

Birmingham is the only other of the eight committees, besides Ealing, to have made public a document which is deeply critical of local authority housing policies. Many of the Birmingham committee members regard the only justification for their remaining as an 'establishment' committee, appointed by the Mayor, as being that they are theoretically in a position to influence City Council policies. In practice, however, with their puny resources, it has not been possible to get very far even with the study of local policies and their housing report is the only significant report to be prepared so far. Also, the City Council does not seem to be inclined to take much notice of the committee. In fact, the committee is in the invidious position of not being regarded as sufficiently important by the City Council to curb, let alone to consult. John Rex's remarks on the inability of the N.C.C.I. to get the Government to pay any attention to the report of its housing panel are equally applicable to the relationship between Birmingham C.R.C. and Birmingham City Council.[1]

In January 1969 the Birmingham C.R.C. submitted a memorandum on housing policy to the Housing Management Sub-Committee of the Ministry of Housing and Local Government's Central Housing Advisory Committee.[2] The contents of this memorandum were made public and a copy was sent to the Housing Department of the City. The memorandum reflected on the following aspects of city housing policy:

Residential Qualifications
The B.C.R.C. considered that the Housing Department's insistence on five years residence in Birmingham, before housing registration, caused unnecessary hardship. The Committee maintained that this rule discriminated against the coloured community and meant that the criterion of need was obscured. They urged that the period of time be considerably reduced. This point was made by the B.C.R.C. to the Housing Department in October 1967. The Department promised to look into it then, but made no changes in the policy.

Waiting Points
The B.C.R.C. suggested that discrimination in favour of long-term residents was carried further by the heavy imbalance of points for waiting over points for need in the present points system for housing allocation.

---

[1] Rex in T. Burgess (ed.), op. cit., pp. 70–83.
[2] Evidence to the Housing Management Sub-Committee of the Central Housing Advisory Committee (Birmingham Liaison Committee for Commonwealth Immigrants, 14 January 1969). This particular subcommittee is known as the Cullingworth Committee, after its chairman, Professor Barry Cullingworth, a title which we use in subsequent references to it.

Housing Visitors

The B.C.R.C. argued, as Rex and Moore did,[1] that coloured people generally get allocated to inferior council houses, often patched slum houses, because of the scope of bias in the discretion given to largely untrained housing visitors.

Statistics

The B.C.R.C. urged that adequate statistics should be kept to ensure that justice was done to coloured people.

Advice Bureau

The B.C.R.C. recommended that the Housing Management Department should set up a housing advice bureau on the lines recommended in the Seebohm Report.[2]

Integration

The B.C.R.C. opposed compulsory dispersal of coloured council tenants, arguing that 'this would involve treating people as things and would destroy the cultural and social links that exist between people of a similar background. . . . We are convinced that dispersal in the field of housing must be done with great sensitivity with no element of compulsion or direction and can proceed only at the pace of the needs and wishes of the people involved.'

Most of the recommendations from this document have been incorporated in the Cullingworth Committee's report.[3] Yet it was summarily rejected by the chairman of the Birmingham City Housing Committee on the grounds that it favoured immigrants and was discrimination in reverse.

Birmingham C.R.C. were aware of grounds for disquiet about education policy in the city but were still in the process of setting up an education panel. There seems little reason for hope that any recommendations the education panel make will not be treated in much the same way as the housing report. There have been some moves recently by a voluntary committee of educationalists,[4] the Committee for Racial Integration in Schools, to secure

---

[1] Rex and Moore, op. cit., p. 26.

[2] *Report of the Committee on Local Authority and Allied Personal Social Services*, Cmnd. 3387 (London, H.M.S.O., 1968), para. 391.

[3] *Council Housing Purposes, Procedures and Priorities*, Chapter 9.

[4] *Race Today* (Vol. 1, No. 1, May 1969), pp. 24–6.

a review of education policy. This committee have secured the setting up of a local authority working party to examine policies towards immigrants, but there is little optimism about the outcome of this initiative. According to an article in *The Teacher*, 'What all integration groups official and unofficial in Birmingham share is a feeling of isolation from the centre of power. Everywhere complaints are voiced by parents that they have been refused a hearing by the education authority.'[1]

In general, then, optimism about the possibility of the development of a viable relationship between Birmingham City Council and community relations committee, or any other organization prepared to express the immigrant's point of view, is at a very low ebb. It is not surprising therefore that in Birmingham, as in Bradford, militant immigrant organizations, who have no time for the official community relations apparatus, are much in evidence. But whereas in Bradford it is the committee itself that has failed the immigrants, the failure in Birmingham stems from the total weakness of a committee whose leaders, particularly the C.R.O. (who resigned at the time we were doing our field-work to run Bradford's housing project) are as depressed as anyone by their inability to make any impact.

To summarize our findings on the approaches of the eight committees to the examination of local authority policies. Two committees, Birmingham and Ealing, regard it as very much their role to examine and, if necessary, publicly criticize local authority policies. Birmingham does this from a position as an 'establishment' committee. Ealing is very much more a group of outsiders. The end result is much the same in either case, not much attention from the local authority. This is less demoralizing to Ealing's members who are reconciled to an outsider role and do not owe their appointments to the Mayor. In both towns, too, the public commitments of the majority party leaders make it difficult for the community relations committee to establish any effective behind-the-scenes role as advisers on matters affecting immigrants.

In many ways the situation aspired to is one in which the community relations committee or its officers are able to gain access to top local authority decision-makers, and are consulted on decisions affecting immigrants. One C.R.O., the officer of a committee which was not included in our eight, *claimed* that he

[1] *The Teacher* (24 January 1969).

insisted that he should have access to chief officers of the local authority and had warned the authority that he would attack them publicly whenever he disagreed with their decisions *if they failed to* consult him first. These are big demands which it is doubtful whether any one of the eight C.R.O.s we studied would be able to make. There are several reasons why our committees and their officers are generally in rather weak bargaining positions. Their officers are generally of rather low status in relation to local authority hierarchies; few of their members are in any sense in a position to influence the local authority; community relations committees are in no sense essential parts of the local institutional structure; and their positions in relation to the Government do not provide them with any dependable source of support.

The original N.C.C.I. grant to pay the salary of a community relations officer was £1,500. For all the local committees, except those given generous local authority support, this meant that the C.R.O.'s salary could not be in excess of that figure. At the time of writing, four years after this system of grants was set up, the Community Relations Commission is recommending the payment of salaries on the local government scales APT4 and 5, extending exceptionally to the Senior Officer's scale. This means that an inexperienced C.R.O. will start at £1,485 and may expect to move up in due course to a little short of £2,000.

While it may seem invidious to judge status by salary and influence by status, the use here of local authority scales gives us a very clear idea of the place in which local authority officers are likely to put a community relations officer in relation to their own hierarchies. The salary is roughly on a par with that received by a newly-qualified Child Care Officer in London. In other words, it suggests a status for community relations officers a long way below the level of chief officers of a City Council.

The reluctance of many local authorities to grant community relations officers anything more than clerical assistance on a part-time or *ad hoc* basis is another indication of their assessment of the status of C.R.O.s. So, too, are the poor quality premises often occupied by community relations officers. In the vast establishments of the Town Hall of a large county borough or London borough, chief officers, deputy chief officers, and probably a whole host of people of about assistant chief officer status are likely to regard a community relations officer as very small fry.

To overcome this status disadvantage a community relations officer needs either to possess exceptional social and political skills, to enjoy the special favour of key persons in the Borough Council hierarchy, or to have behind him a committee with the power to help him overcome the barriers he will face.

As far as possession of exceptional social and political skills are concerned, one may ask how one finds such people, old enough to have had the experience to enable them to develop these skills, but still not earning £1,500 a year! One source of highly qualified but underemployed people is provided by members of the coloured population held back by discrimination. Naturally many community relations councils have appointed immigrants as C.R.O.s. However, immigrants suffer additional disadvantages in that cultural differences and prejudice will make it difficult for them to establish the 'informal' relationship necessary to offset the low formal position they hold.

On the other hand, some of the more viable links achieved between local committees and departments of local authorities owe a great deal to the particular commitments of certain chief officers. Individuals with such commitments are but rarely found, so it is unlikely that all the key officers of a local authority will be so sympathetic. We found that most C.R.O.s succeed in getting on very well with some but not all the relevant local authority departments in their area. With the increasing centralization of local authority management, in many places the Town Clerk is becoming the individual from whom it is most important for the C.R.O. to have support. Only in Sheffield did we find that there were good links between C.R.O. and the Town Clerk's department.

Councillors who are members of community relations committees may also play an important role in providing high level contacts. We have largely dealt with the evidence on this point already. Our finding has been that although this is sometimes true, notably in Hackney, a large number of councillor members of community relations committees are either entirely passive members or, as in the case with the chairman of the Sheffield committee, interpret their role as one of curbing the committee and ensuring that it keeps its nose out of local authority matters. Even the most valuable councillor members of committees are in some measure ambivalent, since in the last analysis they might have to answer to party groups which are likely to be less sympathetic to the community relations committee than they are.

We may proceed from this point to ask to what extent it is generally true that other members of community relations committees will be able and willing to ensure that their committee commands the attention of the key decision-makers in the local authority. In fact, few committee members are in any position to influence the local authority.

The conception of community relations committees as organizations of organizations, representing all the significant elements in the life of a community, seems to imply that their possession of such support will give them 'influence'. This influence may be based upon either who the members are or upon the power they can wield. The members of committees may have influence because they are members of a local *élite* or because their support is important to the local authority.

In the United States the community relations movement has foundered because of undue emphasis upon bringing together in committees representatives of both black and white *élites*.[1] They have been much too dependent upon the support of their city's Mayor, to operate as effective critics of local authority policies. Killian and Grigg found that the really powerful figures in the Florida town they studied were not involved in the community relations committee. The whites on the committee were 'second-rank' figures highly dependent upon the support of more powerful people.[2] There has been a reaction against this essentially consensual approach in favour of organizing the blacks to form a power block to force concessions from local and national government, and in some cases to reject the whole democratic system and the participation of the Negroes in pluralistic ethnic politics.

It is tempting to apply this sort of analysis to the British scene and to attack community relations committees as similarly doomed to fail because their methods involve what we have called '*élite* strategy' rather than 'power strategy'. We will argue, however, that neither 'strategy' is really applicable to the political structure of an English urban area.

In English cities formal power is highly centralized. Four of

[1] Killian and Grigg, op. cit., and J. Q. Wilson, *Negro Politics* (New York, Free Press, 1960), pp. 88–93.
[2] Killian and Grigg, op. cit., esp. pp. 47–72.

the towns we studied were county boroughs, one-tier local authorities with only the Government to confront at the next level in the system. Three were London boroughs with very wide powers, clearly distinguishable from the powers of the Greater London Council (though two also had their education outside their control, in the hands of the Inner London Education Authority). Only one of the eight towns, Wycombe, was a non-county borough with limited autonomy and a considerable dependence upon a County Council. Yet even in Wycombe, the formal structure of local government and the division of powers between authorities is very clear-cut compared with the situation in American towns and cities. This clear-cut and centralized formal system of government significantly restricts the scope for pressure group activity. Apart from the limitations imposed by central government control, local authorities are in a position to take decisions unhampered by the need to get the consent of other authorities. By contrast, the characteristic of American local government structures which provides particular scope for the activities of pressure groups is the wide dispersal of formal power amongst a number of different institutions.[1]

This situation is reinforced by an absence of any real tradition of public participation in decision-making in British local government. Under normal circumstances, local authorities do not expect the making of decisions to involve anything more than a process in which decisions originating in private consultations within departments, very often not even involving councillors at this stage, are passed with little modification by council committees, which very often meet in private, and then revealed to the public at council meetings, where they normally secure the final seal of approval unaltered.[2] Matters which concern community relations councils like the provision of English teaching facilities, the dispersal of immigrant schoolchildren or the rules for the allocation of council houses are not normally the subject of public debate before crucial decisions are taken.

Furthermore it has been suggested that the clear-cut two-party system characteristic of city government in Britain today

[1] This is shown particularly clearly in E. C. Banfield, *Political Influence* (New York, Free Press, 1961).
[2] Committee on the Management of Local Government, *Local Government Administration in England and Wales* (London, H.M.S.O., 1967), Vol. 5.

involves the aggregation of interests, so that pressure groups need to make themselves effective by adoption by one of the major parties.[1] This aggregation occurs around the class division which is still so salient a characteristic of British politics. The contrast here with the United States is related to the absence in the American scene of such a distinct cleavage and the fragmentation of interests which has provided great opportunities for some kinds of pressure groups. The traditional liberal theory in the United States involved the argument that Negroes should be encouraged to seek advancement through 'ethnic politics'. Recent commentators have shown that as soon as the Negroes tried to do this, the whites, formerly divided on ethnic lines themselves, closed their ranks and dictated *their* terms for Negro participation.[2] Our contrast here is more with American 'liberal' theory than with current social realities.

Our view is that the British situation leaves little scope for pressure group activity at the local level. This leaves us with three alternatives within the existing system: the exercise of influence by individuals who secure access to key decision-makers, pressure group activity through the political parties, and pressure group activity at the national level.

Individuals might be able to achieve something by their ability to get to the ears of senior council officials or the chairmen of committees so that they can influence the decision-making process at a sufficiently early stage to have some impact. Such access will often depend upon social contacts, through golf clubs, Rotary and so on, outside the formal council structure. Are such relationships likely to exist or likely to be relevant in this case?

Let us re-examine the eight areas we studied to ask whether it is likely that any coherent *élite* or power structure can exist in them. Birmingham is both too vast and too much a part of a greater conurbation to be in any way a civic unity. Three members of the community relations committee live outside the county

---

[1] Good discussions of this point are provided in K. Newton, 'City Politics in Britain and the United States', *Political Studies* (Vol. 17, No. 2, 1969), and in an as yet unpublished manuscript by S. L. Elkin on planning and politics under the L.C.C. which he kindly let us see.

[2] Katznelson, op. cit., and S. Carmichael and C. Hamilton, *Black Power* (Harmondsworth, Penguin, 1969).

borough. Probably many of the civic officials live outside too. The chances of rubbing shoulders with key decision-makers in the course of social activities must be very slight indeed.

Two of the London boroughs, Hackney and Tower Hamlets, are almost devoid of middle class. There is little organizational life. For most of the civic officials the borough is merely their place of work. One of the community relations committees, Tower Hamlets, has a number of its own members living some way outside the borough.

Ealing is a more heterogeneous area of London, but it is a new borough created out of three Middlesex boroughs, Ealing, Southall, and Acton, that had little to do with each other in the past. It is an artificial creation, purely for administrative convenience. Much of its middle-class population is highly mobile and employed outside the borough.

Wycombe is similarly a rather meaningless administrative entity but for the opposite reason to Ealing. It is an old borough with a long history, today only part of a larger sprawling suburban area. It is an industrial valley surrounded by an upper middle-class residential area which looks largely to London. This situation has been recognized by the community relations committee which has accordingly called itself Wycombe and District Integration Committee. Several of its active members, including the chairman and the treasurer, live a few miles from Wycombe.

The remaining three committees are based on Yorkshire towns with a strong tradition of civic life, but all three have middle-class suburbs on their fringes. Sheffield[1] and Bradford are rather large to have any really viable civic community structures. This leaves Huddersfield which, perhaps alone of the eight areas, has the sort of urban structure which may make the existence of a local social influence structure a viable possibility. It would be stretching our argument too much to suggest that the absence of controversial issues in Huddersfield is in any way related to this. But the situation in which a Labour alderman is chairman of the community relations committee and chairman of the town's welfare committee despite the Conservative majority on the council, and the community relations officer enjoys good relations with many of the town's leaders and has been active in

[1] W. Hampton, *Democracy and Community, A Study of Politics in Sheffield* (London, Oxford University Press, 1970).

Huddersfield's strong Liberal party, seems to indicate the existence of a fairly close and consensual political *élite*.

There are further difficulties entailed in drawing people of
influence in a community into positive involvement in a community relations committee. First, persons of influence are already
very active in other forms of civic life, and are unlikely to be
ready to spare time for a new cause. Second, influence is a scarce
'commodity', it needs to be conserved. One way in which it can
easily be lost is by going 'overboard' for an unpopular cause.[1] In
one town, not in our group of eight, a university vice-chancellor
refused to involve himself in the activities of a community relations
council whose relations with its local authority were not good
because he was engaged in delicate negotiations with the authority
on some planning matters. One clergyman committee member
we interviewed suggested that senior Anglican clergy are inhibited
in a similar way. Persons of influence support community relations
councils as 'good causes' in a general sense but are unwilling to
push their identification with a minority group to the extent of
working for them on specific issues. As the data on the membership
of committees show, community relations councils find it very
difficult to secure members who can in any real sense have
influence for them in the local corridors of power.

Studies of British civic politics seem to indicate that power is
passing from the hands of a loosely-structured group of semi-
independent councillors highly dependent upon professional
officers, into the control of tightly-structured political groups.[2] It
may be argued that where this situation occurs it provides scope
for a 'power strategy' rather than an '*élite* strategy'. In other
words, cannot immigrants and their supporters secure concessions
from the political parties under threat of the electoral damage
they can do them? Certainly, in all our eight areas, local politics
were structured on party lines. Particularly in Ealing, Birmingham, and Sheffield, this was very important for local decision
making. Only in Ealing have there been significant attempts to
win the immigrant vote. On the other hand, in both Ealing and

[1] R. V. Clements, *Local Notables and the City Council* (London, Macmillan, 1969)
which suggests that influentials largely stand aloof from local affairs, and are prepared
to intervene only when their special, primarily business, interests are at stake.

[2] J. G. Bulpitt, *Party Politics in English Local Government* (London, Longmans, 1967),
J. M. Lee, *Social Leaders and Public Persons* (London, Oxford University Press, 1963),
and Clements, op. cit.

Birmingham, there have been extensive attempts to win the anti-immigrant vote.

Only six local authority areas, all London boroughs, have, according to the 1966 Census, coloured immigrants forming over 5 per cent of their populations.[1] The highest percentage is 7·7 per cent in Brent.[2] Only three of the 700 wards in Greater London have over 20 per cent of their population who were born in India, Pakistan, West Indies or Africa.[3] This shows that there is an absence of areas in England where immigrant voting can be expected to have a sufficiently significant impact upon election results to ensure that attention is paid to their rights.

The Northcote ward in Southall is one of the few in which a significant attempt has been made by the major political parties to bid for immigrant votes. The presence of a large number of relatively well-organized Sikhs in Northcote ward has led to it being regarded as in many respects an Indian ward. Yet a survey of the electors in this ward found that 3,160 (27·8 per cent) were Asian, and 8,218 non-Asian.

In the 1968 Borough Council elections in Ealing, both Labour and Conservative party put up one Indian candidate in Northcote ward. There were also independent anti-immigrant candidates standing in this election. The result of this contest to elect three councillors for the ward, indicated that it is almost as profitable to bid for the anti-immigrant vote in the ward as to bid for the immigrant vote. An Indian Labour candidate topped the poll, but an independent anti-immigrant candidate (a former Labour councillor) came second. The third and fourth candidates were white Labour members, closely followed by an Indian Conservative. Two other anti-immigrant candidates also did well, without having any advantage deriving from being well-known ex-councillors as their colleague was, while two independent Indians secured very low votes.[4]

[1] Rose *et al.*, op. cit., p. 102. The boroughs are Brent, Hackney, Lambeth, Haringey, Islington, and Hammersmith.

[2] J. Doherty, 'Immigrants in London: How Many and Where', *Race Today* (Vol. 1, No. 8, December 1969), pp. 227–31.

[3] *Demographic, Social and Economic Indices for Wards in Greater London* (G.L.C. Research and Intelligence Unit, March 1970). The wards are Northcote (Ealing) with 30·4 per cent, Harrow Road (Westminster), 24·6 per cent, and Kensal Rise (Brent), 23 per cent.

[4] *Middlesex County Times* (17 May 1968). Also G. Thomas, 'The Council Elections in Southall', *Institute of Race Relations Newsletter* (May 1968).

In most areas the wider dispersal of immigrants, their division into different national groups, and their understandable apathy towards local government provide a situation in which any political party is likely to be inhibited in making an unequivocal bid for their support by the very much greater ease with which an anti-immigrant vote can be organized. Consequently political parties are likely to be unimpressed by immigrant and pro-immigrant groups who promise to deliver votes in return for policy concessions.

The above figures on immigrant numbers in various local authority areas are underestimates, because of under-enumeration. The 1966 Census only provides information on the numbers born overseas, none on the British-born descendants.[1] It is clearly possible that the proportions of coloured electors in some wards and constituencies will be substantially larger in the future. However the 1966 figures suggest that such a change in the numbers of black electors would have to be of such a magnitude and would have to be accompanied by such a low dispersal rate that a marked effect upon local politics in the near future cannot be expected.

One further argument against our view is that the very low polls, such as 35 per cent or less, that characterize many local elections, particularly in the London area, might still provide an opportunity for an organized minority to make its presence felt. The case against this view is that there is little evidence at present of immigrants showing a lower rate of non-voting than the white voters in their area. Moreover, if immigrants did organize to try to secure communal political advantages, such a development would transform the whole style of local political conflict in their area. White voters would be shaken out of apathy and a high poll would be achieved.

The multiple elections of Greater London with two, three or four candidates from each party provide an opportunity for immigrant candidates as part of a 'balanced' ticket, as we saw in Northcote ward. This may produce, as in that case, comunally-based cross-voting. But where, as in most elections, competition is only for one seat, we cannot expect to find Conservatives bidding for immigrant votes. To the best of our knowledge there have been

---

[1] For a discussion of these two points see Rose *et al.*, op. cit., Chapter 10.

no coloured immigrant Conservative candidates in single-seat local
or national elections in Britain during the last ten years.

In fact, then, with the exception of the special case of the
multi-seat election involving immigrant Conservative candidates,
it can probably fairly be said that the choice for immigrants is not
between the two major parties, it is between voting Labour and
not voting (or voting for a more minor party, which amounts in
most cases to not voting). Certainly the immigrant community
relations committee members we interviewed conveyed this
impression, and this has been the issue the Indian Workers'
Association in Southall has debated before each general election.

The line taken on race matters by the Conservatives at the
national level largely rules out a local situation in which they will
today bid for immigrant votes in any wholehearted way. As we
suggested when discussing Ealing, though, consideration of the
immigrant vote may marginally inhibit extreme anti-immigrant
actions. On the whole, the major parties are unlikely to compete
for the immigrant vote, so that, at best, organized groups of
immigrants (as did the Indian Workers' Association in 1964 and
1966) can only offer or withhold votes for Labour.[1] If the local
authority is Conservative-dominated, as it was in five of our eight
areas, immigrants are hardly in any position to use potential votes
as a bargaining counter. They may, of course, still try to bargain
with more direct methods, through demonstrations or strikes.

Any attempts to offer votes to the highest bidder in a local
election is likely to be undermined by the fact that for the bulk
of the electorate it is the popularity of the Government that
determines their electoral choice, not any local issues.[2] So any
party whose popularity is high in the country at large can afford
to totally disregard the local electorate when it plans civic
policies, unless the distribution of power on the council is very
finely balanced.

Some committees, largely because of the involvement of
Labour-controlled local authorities in their creation, and because
of the role of the Labour Government's 1965 White Paper in
providing them with funds, succeeded in developing close links
with Labour 'groups', more on an *élite* basis than because of any

[1] John, op. cit., Chapter VI.
[2] R. G. Gregory, 'Local Elections and the "Rule of Anticipated Reactions" ',
Political Studies (Vol. XVII, No. 1, March 1969), pp. 31–47.

vote they could help to deliver. The danger of this kind of closeness to a political party, which may have been tremendously valuable at the outset, has been brought home most clearly in areas where committees of this kind have been objects of extreme suspicion when Conservative groups have come to power. This has been one of the sources of Ealing's difficulties. It is also the danger that the leaders of Hackney committee have worked so hard to avoid, with success so far. Another committee, outside our group of eight, which has suffered in this way is Brent, whose origins lay largely in initiatives taken by leading Labour members in Willesden. All in all, community relations councils can ill-afford to get involved in the political power game. Yet, here is the intolerable nature of the situation, the control of policy-making in large British local authorities is so much a matter of party politics that it is hard to achieve anything by remaining outside politics.

There is one final, and in many ways overriding, reason why a community relations council can have very little hope of achieving significant gains either as a body with connexions with the local *élite* or as a pressure group. The responses they are likely to require of a local authority will be of a positive rather than a negative kind. It seems to us that many community power studies do not make this very important distinction between 'negative' and 'positive' power.[1] They disregard the fact that conservative influentials can much more easily exercise power because they are likely to be primarily interested in preventing things being done rather than in getting things done. By contrast any organization which aims to champion the rights of an underprivileged group has the much more difficult task of securing innovations which upset the *status quo*.[2] They require local authorities to enact new measures, actions which require the support of a majority of councillors, a much more difficult task than that entailed in getting measures dropped. Minority groups may sometimes be

[1] This particularly applies to the work of Dahl and Banfield. R. A. Dahl, *Who Governs* (New Haven, Yale University Press, 1961); Banfield, op. cit. A criticism of their point of view is implicit in Bachrach and Baratz's argument that these writers disregard the possibility that *élites* may restrict actual decision-making to 'safe' issues (P. Bachrach and M. S. Baratz, 'Two Faces of Power', *American Political Science Review* (Vol. LVI, 1962)), pp. 947–52.

[2] Marris and Rein, op. cit., and R. L. Crain, *The Politics of School Desegregation* (Chicago, Aldine, 1968).

successful as 'veto' groups, they cannot hope to secure positive actions on their behalf without a great deal of political ground-work. In the words of Bachrach and Baratz, 'all political systems have inherent "mobilization of bias" and this bias strongly favours those currently defending the *status quo*.'¹ Herman Long has suggested that the achievement of a successful working relationship with an organization like a local authority, wedded to the *status quo*, will involve a rather negative kind of consensus rather than a positive relationship. He argues: 'In a community project geared to involving a balance of different leadership elements in which involving elements of the community power structure has become a strategic goal, the difference in dominant and minority group definitions of the reasons for the existence of inequality of opportunity becomes crucial. There is in these instances the operation of what has been called the "rule of charity" whereby groups recognising their basic differences in interest and orientation refuse to bring to the fore matters which either might embarrass the other or widen the already existing political and socio-psychological distance between them,'² or, in the words of Morris and Rein, their strategy is one of 'co-operative rationality'.

Given that the relationship between the local authorities and community relations committees is a highly unequal one, with the local authority holding almost all the cards, it is not surprising that little happened when Birmingham and Ealing community relations councils sought to challenge local policies.

Hostile local authority groups, as we have seen, may not cancel grants to community relations councils awarded when another party was in control. But even sympathetic local author-ities will not readily alter, for example, housing list qualifications in favour of immigrants. It is for this reason, above all, that we argue that community relations councils, unaided by other powerful bodies, will be unable to make any impact upon local authority policies in their area. If the local authority is willing to make concessions to immigrant needs, it will probably do so

¹ P. Bachrach and M. Baratz, *Power and Poverty* (New York, Oxford University Press, 1970), p. 58. See also M. Lipsky, *Protest in City Politics* (Chicago, Rand McNally & Co., 1970), pp. 197, 201–2.
² H. Long, 'Community Research and Intergroup Adjustment', in J. Masuoka and P. Valien (eds.), *Race Relations—Problems and Theory* (Chapel Hill, University of North Carolina Press, 1961), p. 275.

whether a community relations council exists or not. If it is unwilling, there is little that can be done unaided by such a body.

A good example of failure to get a local authority to take notice of a community relations committee is provided in Katznelson's study of Nottingham. The committee there has made repeated unsuccessful attempts to get the local education authority to provide special language tuition for Asian children.[1]

This leads us to the last two of our reasons why community relations councils are in weak bargaining positions. These reasons are closely related and have to do with the ambiguous position enjoyed by both the Community Relations Commission and local committees in relation to the formal power structure of Britain.

Community relations councils are in no way essential parts of the local institutional structure. Local authorities take notice of government departments in their areas, and of statutory bodies such as National Health Service Executive Councils. The role they play in local communities is quite clear, so too is the backing they enjoy from the Government. Failure to co-operate with such bodies would rapidly bring coercive measures from the Government upon the local authority. In the long run only the local authorities would suffer from their own actions.

Community relations councils enjoy no such special status in the areas in which they operate. In some areas local authorities have ignored ministerial requests to set up such bodies. In three places, Waltham Forest, Warley, and Reading,[2] Borough Councils have refused to give any support to committees set up on voluntary initiative. In fact, in many areas it was only the bait of a matching grant which led to the setting up of community relations councils after 1965. It is one thing to allow the government to persuade one to set up a community relations council, and even to be prepared to support it to the tune of a few hundred pounds a year to exist as 'proof' that the town council is concerned about immigrants. It is quite another thing to accept the right of that council, which owes its very existence to you, to criticize your policies towards immigrants.

[1] Katznelson, 'The Politics of Race in USA, 1900–30 and the United Kingdom, 1948–68', p. 305.
[2] 'No Change from the Council', *Race Today* (Vol. 1, No. 2, June 1969), p. 56.

At a number of points in the preceding argument we have suggested that there is one other alternative approach open to both immigrant groups and to their potential supporters in community relations committees who wish to put pressure to influence policies. This involves paying less attention to trying to influence local authorities directly but instead shifting the locus of pressure group activities to the national level. It is at this level that a great deal of real and ultimate power over local affairs exists. Here we have another fundamental difference between Britain and the United States as even the supposedly independent Government of Northern Ireland can testify, let alone any ordinary English local authority. At this level, the divisive impact of immigrant dispersion can be overcome too.

For the community relations committees the obvious point of contact between themselves and the Government is the Community Relations Commission. Accordingly, in their dealings with local authorities, the local committees have looked to the Commission for support. As a group to put pressure on the Government, the N.C.C.I. largely failed the local committees, as we showed in Chapter 1. The C.R.C. has not yet shown any ability to do any better. There is little reason to expect that it can improve on the N.C.C.I. in this area. But as a central government-backed body, the C.R.C. has also shown itself as unable to get beyond a position in which it can try to influence local authorities informally. It has not been able to force the local authorities which refuse to co-operate with local committees to change their decisions. In this respect the C.R.C. is only as powerful as the Government will allow it to be. It cannot get local authorities to take notice if they know full well that in the last resort the Government will not back it up.

The Commission, despite the statutory basis provided by the 1968 Race Relations Act, has no real autonomy. If it decides to defy its paymaster it can remain as a group of individual protestors, but it, just as much as the local committees, wants to grow in power and influence. It will only do this if the Government is prepared to accept the role it gives itself.

We will now draw together some of the many themes developed in this chapter, and the preceding one, and try to explain the relationship between the goals, structure, and strategies employed by the eight committees in terms of the model outlined in Chapter 3. There we introduced the concepts o. 'co-operative rationality', a strategy based on consensus, with the goal of co-ordination, and 'individual rationality', a strategy which is more change-oriented. We discussed too different types of structure, the 'federated' and the simple. In this chapter we have demonstrated how some community relations committees often lack both the power and the resources to bargain with local authorities on their own terms, yet feel the need to adopt a strategy of co-operation if they are to exert any influence on local authority policies. In the previous chapter we described the vagueness in the goals formulated by some committees. Some committees do not see bargaining and criticism as their role and do not even reach the stage of conflict with local authorities which other community relations committees engage in and lose. In Chapters 5 and 6 we described the membership of the committees, sometimes homogeneous in commitment, sometimes divided within itself. Each of our eight committees can be located at different positions on the integration, change, survival, ritualism model outlined in Chapter 3.

Sheffield community relations committee can be easily identified as the clearest example of the 'integration' agency. Its role has been primarily one of co-ordination. Pursuit of innovation has been sacrificed to the goal of co-operation with the local authority in which it has been very successful.

Bradford C.C.C. exemplifies the position of 'ritualism'. It never aimed to be a change-oriented agency, yet also failed to act in any sense as a co-ordinating agency since it alienated a large number of its immigrant participants and did not develop any links with the city corporation of any significance. Inactivity and paralysis are the most honest words to describe its current behaviour.

Huddersfield gives the appearance of being an 'integration' agency similar to Sheffield in orientation. It has largely developed side by side with the local authority which has not until now given it much reason for complaint. But it has not developed close links with local authority departments. As a result it has preserved slightly more autonomy and has used its own initiative in pursuing areas for research rather than concentrating on the provision of the more traditional casework welfare services provided by S.C.R.C. To a large extent it still retains a rather 'simple structure' in so far as local authority representation on it is minimal and the more conservative elements in Huddersfield institutional life have not been included in the membership. Its true position has yet to be tested.

Wycombe has adopted the role of an integration agency, by trying to embrace within it people of diverse commitments including right-wing attitudes, such as the M.P.'s wife, in the hope that this would give it additional influence. The situation which has resulted is one of ritualism. The immigrant membership is alienated by the emphasis on placation and consensus. The committee has not developed any programme of significance. Links with the local authority are virtually non-existent.

The crisis which we described between the Birmingham committee and its Advisory Council, has been explained in terms of the incompatibilities of all the strategies they were simultaneously pursuing. The resultant deadlock has reduced the role of this committee, too, to ritualism.

Tower Hamlets and Hackney committees both have radical memberships with a strong commitment to change and have been able to preserve comparatively simple structures. Both committees are deeply conscious of their powerless positions relative to their local authorities and have pursued a 'co-operative strategy' in as much as they have avoided doing anything that might totally alienate them. These two committees may therefore be described as close to a situation in which a need for survival has overwhelmed their orientation to change.

Ealing's committee is the only one that has made its commitment to change absolutely clear, with the result that its local authority came close to deploying sanctions against it. It remains to be seen whether the crisis of winter 1968–9 will inhibit the committee in the interests of survival.

The only really clear lesson of the conflict between E.I.F.C. and Ealing Borough Council is that the community relations committee has no real power to harm the local authority so that the latter could apparently act magnanimously and retain this venomless viper in its nest!

There is a danger therefore that, when local authorities ignore rather than coerce them, community relations committees may be in a situation of believing in what has been called by Robert Merton, 'the fallacy of group soliloquies':

Ethnic liberals are busily engaged in talking to themselves. Repeatedly the same groups of like-minded liberals seek each other out, hold periodic meetings in which they engage in mutual exhortation, and thus lend social and psychological support to one another.[1]

The dangers and limitations of such a situation have been described by other authors:

The all weather liberal mistakes discussion in like minded groups for effective action and overestimates the support for his position.[2]

[1] R. Merton in R. McIver (ed.), *Discrimination and National Welfare* (New York, Harper & Row for Institute of Religious and Social Studies, 1949), p. 104, quoted in Killian and Grigg, op. cit., p. 98.

[2] G. E. Simpson and M. Yinger, *Racial and Cultural Minorities* (New York, Harper & Row, 1958), p. 728, quoted in Killian and Grigg, op. cit., p. 98.

CHAPTER 9

Full-time Staff of Community Relations Committees

It is now pertinent to examine two topics which are not central to our theoretical argument but which are nevertheless important in providing a rounded picture of community relations committees. We shall discuss here the full-time staff of community relations committees. In Chapter 10 the relationships between the Community Relations Commission and the local committees will be examined.

The activities of the local committees are largely influenced by the structures which the Commission has expected them to possess. It can equally be said that the roles of the community relations officers are determined by this structure. The N.C.C.I. paid little attention to defining the roles of community relations officers, but the C.R.C. made this one of its first concerns after it was appointed. However the proposals they brought forward stemmed very largely from the requirements of the already-settled structures of the local committees.

Before we examine the arguments which developed over the C.R.C.'s efforts at defining the roles of C.R.O.s, some comments on the general staffing situations in local committees and the kinds of people who have been appointed as C.R.O.s will provide necessary background information.

Comments on the staffing situation in all the community relations committees are as in March 1969, when we were engaged on our study. We know that a number more community relations officers have been appointed since that date, and that, whereas previously assistant C.R.O.s were paid by local authorities, recently the C.R.C. has provided grants to a few committees for such appointments.

The only other community relations committee staff paid out of funds granted by the C.R.C. in March 1969 were the three 'fair housing officers', in Sheffield, Manchester, and Nottingham. Their salaries came from Gulbenkian Foundation grants administered by the Commission.

Thirty-five of the forty-two C.R.O.s are men, and seven women. Five of them are immigrants from India, four from Pakistan, ten from the Caribbean, one from East Africa, sixteen are presumed to have been born in the United Kingdom. We do not know the countries of origin of five.

We secured information on the previous jobs of most of the C.R.O.s. These were very varied indeed. Quite a number came from various forms of social work and possessed social science qualifications. There are also former civil servants, teachers, clergy, personnel managers, clerks, and police officers amongst their ranks. It seems likely that several of the white C.R.O.s will have forsaken more highly-paid jobs or potentially more remunerative careers. Many of the coloured C.R.O.s are highly qualified and may well have been employed below their full abilities prior to entering this work.

The background of the eight C.R.O.s serving the committees we studied are summarized below:

Birmingham: A clergyman who was an assistant to the industrial chaplain to the Bishop of Birmingham. He possesses a social science qualification. Since our study he has left Birmingham to work for a housing association in Bradford.

Bradford: A former police sergeant in Bradford who was a 'juvenile liaison officer' during his last years in the force. An active layman in the Church of England he played a part in lobbying for the setting up of a committee in Bradford.

Ealing: A worker-priest who has lived for many years in Southall, worked on the shop floor in an engineering works, and was involved in trade union affairs.

Hackney: A man who came to England from India in his early teens and completed his education at an English grammar school and the London School of Economics. He has a management qualification. He worked for the London Council of Social Service and was on Camden's committee prior to his appointment.

Huddersfield: The only woman in our group of eight, the wife of a Lithuanian refugee and a local person who was voluntary secretary to the committee before her appointment. She was formerly active in the local Liberal party. She has social work and administrative experience. She resigned from her post just after our study, for personal reasons.

Sheffield: An immigrant from Pakistan who had been secretary of a Pakistani organization in Manchester. He has a Dacca degree and a British social administration qualification.

Tower Hamlets: An immigrant from Trinidad with social administration and community work qualifications from the University of the West Indies. He was employed by the Ministry of Social Security prior to appointment. He is very active in the West Indian Standing Conference.

Wycombe: An immigrant from India who was in social work, having studied social administration at Oxford.

The way in which the community relations movement has developed has meant that all C.R.O.s entered their occupations without particularly clear views of what they had to do or of how secure their jobs would be. Initially people were unprepared to regard community relations committees as anything more than temporary expedients, committed to working themselves out of a job. As time passed, it began to be recognized that rapid improvements in British race relations were unlikely, and that steps should be taken to define more clearly what C.R.O.s were to do, and what kinds of careers they could expect. By 1967 the C.R.O.s had formed their own organization and were beginning to become dissatisfied with the fact that their functions were so ill-defined, that their salaries were limited to £1,500 unless they could persuade their local authorities to provide additional increments, that they could only build up subordinate staff if their local authorities were prepared to help, and that senior posts in the National Committee were being filled from outside the ranks of the C.R.O.s. In other words there was developing that mixture of concern for standards and self-interest which characterizes professional consciousness.[1]

The N.C.C.I. was slow to develop specific training for community relations officers. The officers were assisted in their jobs by brief spells of secondment to observe the work of more experienced officers, by conferences designed not for them alone but also for voluntary committee members and local authority-employed social workers, and by short training seminars.

[1] H. M. Vollmer and D. L. Mills (eds.), *Professionalization* (Englewood Cliffs, N.J., Prentice Hall, 1966).

The most high powered of the training seminars organized by the N.C.C.I. was the one it held at the University of York between 7 and 14 July 1968. The C.R.C. annual report described it as a success.[1] In fact it was considerably marred by the general suspicion of the N.C.C.I. which had developed amongst community relations officers by mid-1968, and by a row over the organization of the course between the N.C.C.I.'s training officer and senior members of the N.C.C.I. staff, as a result of which the training officer was dismissed.

The Community Relations Commission organized a seminar on very similar lines at York in summer 1969. As yet no more sophisticated training programme has been developed. Community relations officers are still recruited from a wide range of backgrounds and with varying kinds of qualifications (even those with social administration qualifications will not necessarily know much about community work). They are still expected to do most of their learning 'on the job'.

The C.R.C. attempts to supplement its positive training efforts by a steady stream of circulars to local committees. It also employs a Senior Development Officer and some development officers for the regions. There were three employed at the time we did our research, responsible for the South, the North, and Greater London, but all based in London. The C.R.C. is believed now to be planning the expansion and the devolution of this team, but at the time of our study, the impact of the development officers upon the C.R.O.s in the field was minimal. It was also a bone of contention with the C.R.O.s that only one of the four 'development' staff had worked as a C.R.O.

In its report published in May 1969 the C.R.C. showed itself to be very conscious of the need to develop a 'professional discipline' for its C.R.O.s. But the vagueness and ambiguity of the approach it recommends can best be illustrated by quoting the report itself.

The second major task confronting the Commission at the present juncture is the development of a new professional discipline and expertise for social workers specialising in the field of community relations. This involves establishing and defining the appropriate professional approach to this form of community service—an approach which requires a nice sense of balance between excessive political

[1] *Report for 1968–9*, para. 72.

involvement on the one hand and over-emphasis on straightforward welfare technique on the other. It also involves the elaboration of appropriate forms of training covering community organization, community development, group work and social administration, all within the context of a specially developed sensitivity to the inter-relation of ethnic minorities with the host community and with one another and to the possibilities of channelling social conflict towards creative and socially beneficial purposes. What is required is the development of a dynamic expertise in changing social attitudes by consent rather than attempting to do so by conflict or dictation—an expertise which will not be pushed off course by the ebb and flow of political events, by the upsurge of irrational emotions or by the impact of local factions and contending personalities. It calls for a strong moral approach, a clear and steadfast sense of purpose and the ability to work effectively and clearsightedly in the midst of unpredictable—and sometimes predictable—political fluctuations. It will be one of the Commission's most difficult but also most rewarding tasks to develop the skills which will transform harmonious community relations from a concept into a positive, practical reality.[1]

The pressure to achieve results which we suggested influenced the development of community relations committees had also had an impact upon the N.C.C.I. This body sought to create an elaborate nation-wide network of committees and C.R.O.s without devoting much attention to the identification of, and planning for, specific lines of development.

We may relate this situation to Rein's conceptualization of the relationship between goals, structures, and strategies in organizations committed to community work. The community relations officers are, in the above quotation, enjoined by the C.R.C. to work for change by means of a strategy that would appear to involve 'co-operative rationality'. The Community Relations Commission prescribes goals and strategies which are incompatible with each other, as we have shown. We revert to this argument here because it seems to us that the development of community relations work without any real attempt to clarify the roles to be played by full-time staff has helped to bring this problem to a head.

What in practice has happened is that community relations officers who have been recruited from a diverse range of social background, have, with few exceptions, one characteristic in

---

[1] *Report for 1968–9*, para. 20.

common, a deep commitment to racial equality. Such training as they have received has further sensitized them to this issue, since the N.C.C.I./C.R.C. has obviously kept them informed of current developments in race relations. Meeting together has further activated consciousness of racial injustices. Hence community relations officers have become more conscious of their goals, at least in generalized terms. But alongside the sensitization on generalized goals, community relations officers have been offered virtually no guidance on strategies.

Latterly, however, the Community Relations Commission has began to make general comments, which suggest that they consider that the reforming zeal of the more militant community relations officers may not be the appropriate approach to community relations work. But since these remarks were made at a time when many C.R.O.s were already involved in the field, and have not been backed by any comprehensive programme of training to teach C.R.O.s appropriate strategies, they at best have fallen on deaf ears or at worst confirmed some people's suspicions about the conservatism of the C.R.C.

Furthermore, the C.R.C.'s efforts at formulating a professional discipline for C.R.O.s commenced, during early 1969, with an attempt to spell out the formal conditions of service for C.R.O.s. This was laying emphasis upon bureaucratization rather than the professionalization, and seems to involve a retreat into what Rein called 'ritualism'. Let us examine this first step towards the definition of the place of the C.R.O. in the system to illustrate what we mean.

During the early months of 1969, the C.R.C. set to work to provide the foundations for this professional discipline by determining conditions of service for C.R.O.s, defining their duties, and providing a statement of professional conduct and standards. Some preliminary papers were circulated to committees on these matters to provide a basis for consultation. After discussions with representatives of committees, these papers were published in summer 1969 and committees were asked to signify that they found them acceptable. We cannot comment on the reactions of our eight committees as these papers were circulated after we completed most of our field-work. We will describe the content of these documents together with comments on their applicability to the situations which obtained in the committees we studied.

The conditions of service for C.R.O.s are closely modelled upon local government rules. They provide for an incremental scale which will enable a C.R.O. to move from the bottom of the local government scale APT 4 at £1,540, through APT 5, and eventually into the Senior Officer's grade which may provide for the C.R.O.'s salary to pass £2,000. We have commented on the definition of the status of C.R.O.s in local authority terms provided by these grades.

The paper on the duties of C.R.O.s maintains the vague approach to the post which has characterized all discussions of it since the 1965 White Paper. C.R.O.s are expected to 'promote and assist in programmes of public education', to be a focal point for inquiries about relations between different groups in the community, to co-operate with local statutory and voluntary bodies, to conciliate disputes lying outside the scope of the Race Relations Board, to assist newcomers to use existing social services, to study the needs of the local area 'in the field of community relations' and to be a source of advice to the local authority on these needs, and 'to stimulate and participate in the widest possible range of activities designed to draw all groups in the community together'.

It is quite clear that the C.R.O.s mandate remains a very vague one. When the proposals were under discussion their woolliness came under fire, notably in a document circulated by the Oxford committee. To its radical critics, the C.R.C. seemed to be advocating a neutral stance for C.R.O.s when in practice there are many situations where a concern for racial equality and for the welfare of immigrants makes such a stance untenable, when being neutral means sustaining the *status quo*. Neither pressure group roles nor the taking of positive steps against discrimination are mentioned amongst the suggested list of duties. The C.R.C. added, though: 'It is hoped that the following suggestions will serve as a general guide but they are not intended to be exclusive'. In fact, many of the items on the list were framed in such general terms that it is quite possible for individual committees to see these other activities as lying within their scope.

We are left, therefore, with the question of whether these bland injunctions are to be taken literally or whether, as with the constitutions of the local committees, they provide a kind of smoke-screen. Ann Dummet clearly took the former view. She wrote: 'The thirteen pages of proposals recently circulated by the Commission to local councils, on the duties, careers and professional standards of local officers, do not include the words race, racialism, prejudice, immigrant, black, white, equality, justice or colour. They refer to "harmonious community relations", "assistance to newcomers" and "cooperation with local and national government". These are not the terms in which we can ever begin to solve our problems, and it is a bitter discouragement to community relations officers to be set such targets.'[1]

In as much as these documents are privately-circulated terms of reference for C.R.O.s and not part of a public relations exercise, Ann Dummett would seem to be right. The C.R.C. were trying to elaborate a co-operative strategy for community relations councils without having thought through the implications of such a strategy for a goal which involves social change.

The third of the papers, on professional conduct and standards, was considerably modified in the course of the discussions with representatives of the local committees. The passages which emphasized the committees' control over their C.R.O.s were softened. Nevertheless, the document made it very clear that the C.R.O. is the servant of his committee, in much the same terms as the councillor/officer relationship in local government. Specific paragraphs emphasize that the C.R.O.'s influence upon committee decision-making should be confined to advice, that he must play no part in the nomination or election of candidates at elections held by his council, that his relations with the Press must be determined by his council, and that he must avoid clashes between his personal interests and his official role.

This is of course the only way a relationship between a democratically-elected voluntary organization and its full-time employees can operate. Nevertheless certain special features of community relations committees lead one to wonder whether this master/servant type of relationship is appropriate at all. An entirely different kind of relationship could be established between a professional official and a voluntary committee, which is by no means foreign to English government. That is a relationship in which C.R.O.s operate as the field officers of the C.R.C., and their committees are merely advisory committees selected by themselves in consultation with the local authority and immigrant

[1] A. Dummett, op. cit., p. 75.

and other local organizations. Such an approach would involve a rejection of 'co-operative rationality' in favour of a positive approach to change. The aim would be 'not to represent community subgroups with different interests but to push for the agency's objectives in relative disregard for these groupings'.[1]

The tendency, which we have shown, for local committees to be unrepresentative, the situation in which C.R.O.s are under pressure to develop activities to justify their committee's existence when a thorough review of the local situation might be more appropriate, and the obvious disparity in expertise between C.R.O. and committee make it regrettable that, in setting up a national network of committees, this alternative form of organization has not been tried. Such an experiment might have been particularly appropriate in areas where local authorities have been unwilling to sponsor community relations committees. We want now to examine how the relationship between C.R.O. and committee has developed in the eight committees we studied. Most of the committee members we interviewed regarded their C.R.O. to be adequate, though there was one officer regarded as unsatisfactory by several of the members of his committee. There seemed to be some substance in the criticisms of this officer, but there are grounds for suggesting that some of his difficulties stem from the poor support he is given by some of these members, most of whom were responsible for selecting him in the first place.

The three C.R.O.s of Asian origin were regarded by some of their members as not altogether successful in establishing *rapport* with West Indians in their areas. There were also some comments from Asian committee members on the problems of communication between the white C.R.O.s, none of whom can speak any Asian language, and the Indians and Pakistanis. There are obviously problems facing C.R.O.s in dealing with people from other ethnic or cultural groups. These cannot be overcome unless community relations committees are able to have a staff sufficiently large to provide a diversity of cultural backgrounds. In fact, however, the one committee which has been in the position to do this, Sheffield, has a C.R.O., an assistant C.R.O., and a part-time caseworker, all from Pakistan. These additional posts have arisen as a consequence of the particular problems of communication

---

[1] Morris and Rein, in Rein, *Social Policy—Issues of Choice and Change*, p. 191.

between local authority social workers and Pakistanis. Nevertheless the absence of a West Indian amongst the staff of the committee excited critical comments from West Indian members. Similarly the fact that Hackney has a C.R.O. of Indian origin, albeit a very anglicized one, serving an area where nearly all the immigrants are from the West Indies, was also criticized by West Indians.

Ealing has appointed a Sikh assistant C.R.O., the committee's second assistant C.R.O., the first having moved to become a C.R.O. in Blackburn. He is likely to enjoy particularly good contacts with the Indians in Southall as he was 'office secretary' for the Indian Workers' Association. Tower Hamlets, too, has been able to employ an Asian woman as an interpreter and assistant to help run the playgroup. One other way to overcome this problem is for the C.R.O. to have a secretary who belongs to one of the minority groups. This is the case in Huddersfield.

It is even more difficult to write freely of C.R.O.'s opinions of their committees than it is of their committees views of them. In addition to the eight C.R.O.s whose work we studied in detail, we also got information through a questionnaire from twenty-two others. Most of them stated that their relationships with their chairman and executive committees were 'satisfactory'. A few complained of a lack of understanding of the nature of their jobs from their committees. It is only to be expected that in a situation in which C.R.O.s are striving to develop effective roles for themselves, some will be held back by committees wedded to the 'immigrants' welfare officer' concept of their role. But most committees were prepared to give their C.R.O. full support in striking out in new directions. In fact one C.R.O. commented unfavourably on the C.R.C. notion of C.R.O.s as servants of their committees and suggested that he saw his role more as that of 'leader' of his committee. A highly-educated white C.R.O., he commented that several committees he knew of with Asian C.R.O.s seemed to maintain rather strict control over their activities.

Another source of complaints from C.R.O.s is the inactivity of many committees. Of the eight committees we studied, only Ealing has developed as a really active voluntary organization. All the other committees lean very heavily on their C.R.O.s. Significantly, five of the committees appointed C.R.O.s as their first positive act after their foundation. Only Ealing (as Southall I.F.C.), Wycombe, and Huddersfield sought to achieve anything as purely voluntary organizations. Wycombe, founded in 1960, had become rather stagnant by the time its C.R.O. was appointed in 1967. Huddersfield's enterprising start was largely due to the industry of the person they subsequently appointed C.R.O.

So, with a very few exceptions, notably the social committee in Hackney, meetings of the committees and subcommittees other than in Ealing tend to be occasions at which members discuss issues and problems and then instruct, often at his suggestion, their C.R.O. to take certain actions. This is another reason for being doubtful about the case for an elaborate voluntary structure.

We were therefore itemizing what are in fact very largely the achievements of the C.R.O.s when we discussed the achievements of their committees. The casework function is almost entirely a C.R.O. function. Similarly, many of the activities involving local authority resources, youth clubs, playgroups, and language classes for example, are a result of close liaison between C.R.O.s and local authority officials. Much of the public speaking is also done by the C.R.O.s. The news-letters, apart from those produced by Ealing and Hackney committees, are also largely written by C.R.O.s.

CHAPTER 10

Local Committees and the C.R.C.

Throughout this book we have made various references to the role played by the Community Relations Commission or National Committee for Commonwealth Immigrants, particularly in relation to the part they have played in recommending specific organizational forms, providing ideas on activities, and exercising some control over C.R.O.s. We will now look at the specific points of contact between the local committees and the C.R.C. and the dissatisfactions which result.

We face extreme difficulties in presenting an objective picture of the relationship between the C.R.C. and the local committees. A great deal has been made in the Press of the efforts of the C.R.C. to dictate to local committees.[1] Accordingly, it has been suggested to us that we should be able to provide evidence on this. Yet, as far as the committees we studied are concerned, there seems to have been very little specific dictation from N.C.C.I. or C.R.C. There are hardly any specific examples of incidents in which local committees or their staff were given unwelcome instructions. Nevertheless some committee members made non-specific allegations that the N.C.C.I. or C.R.C. was autocratic and dictatorial.

There seems to be three possible explanations. The first is that much of the dictation from C.R.C. to local committees is covert. C.R.O.s and others aware of this were unwilling to provide us with evidence on this point. This we regard as improbable. The second explanation, and a more plausible one, is that the autocracy of the N.C.C.I./C.R.C. lies more in its style than in the content of its communications with local committees. A number of people complained of autocratic chairmanship at some

---

[1] 'Why Cousins finds it hard to make brothers of us all', *Sunday Times* (2 November 1969), and reports in the *Guardian* (20 March 1969 and 3 July 1969).

of the conferences called by the N.C.C.I. Frank Cousins admitted to the Press that at times his manner may be a little 'rough'.[1] In some respects, then, it may be true that the C.R.C.'s 'bark is worse than its bite'. Our third suggestion is that a relationship between a Government-backed central body and local voluntary committees partly financially dependent upon it is bound to be a sensitive one. Some people in the local organizations may be expected to take offence at almost anything remotely resembling a directive from the central body. This suspicion has been re-inforced by local doubts as to whether the central body is really either effectively independent of the government or able to influence the government in any way. The Kenya Asians issue reinforced the view that the N.C.C.I. was a tool of government that was impotent when it sought to use its official position to influence policy.

It seems far more significant to point out that the relationship between local committees and the national body is one in which all the national body has been able to provide is £1,500 a year, or recently slightly more (up to £3,500 in exceptional cases), some vague ideas about the functions of local committees many of which sound all right in theory but are difficult to put into practice, and a certain number of meetings, visits, and circulars. Perhaps much of the hostility to the Commission stems more from frustration and a feeling of unrelieved impotence than from the perception of the C.R.C. as a threat, even though it tends to be expressed as if the latter is the case.

We can say very little about the relationship between N.C.C.I./C.R.C. and the local committees because in many respects such a relationship barely exists. Asked about this rela-tionship one committee member said: 'It's all right, they haven't stopped giving us money,' and a C.R.O. said: 'There is no real relationship.'

We asked members of our eight committees whether they regarded the relationship between N.C.C.I./C.R.C. and their committee as satisfactory, and asked those who said 'no' to explain their answers. The same question was put to twenty-two C.R.O.s of other committees.

We need to go through the answers we received from the executive members of the eight committees, committee by

[1] 'Cousins in frail cart on rough road', *The Times* (11 November 1969).

committee. It would be inappropriate to sum the numbers of 'yeses' and 'nos' from all eight committees to try to give some over-all measure of satisfaction with the C.R.C., as replies to this question obviously are a function of the militancy and knowledge-ability of members as well as of the nature of the actual relation-ships. Also, local committees' relations with the N.C.C.I./C.R.C. seem to differ quite markedly from committee to committee. The interviews were spread over about nine months starting from one month before the N.C.C.I. was abolished, so that some changes occurred in the central organization between our first interviews, in Wycombe, and our last interviews, in Birmingham. We will interpret our findings from the individual committees in terms of these factors.

The members of the Wycombe committee were all inter-viewed before the abolition of the N.C.C.I. Six of them expressed dissatisfaction with their organization's relationship with the N.C.C.I. (Five of the six were white members playing key roles in the running of the committee.) Their complaints were largely of administrative inefficiency. The sole dissatisfied immigrant was a Pakistani who complained about the lack of Pakistani appoint-ments to C.R.O. posts. Nine members expressed satisfaction with the relationship between their committee and the C.R.C. Six said they did not know whether it was satisfactory or not.

Wycombe committee had never had any conflict of substance with the N.C.C.I. The complaints were of delays in replying to letters and so on rather than specific disagreements. Only one member expressed a principled objection to the N.C.C.I. over the Kenya Asians issue. Several members said they hoped the C.R.C. would be better. In general, Wycombe committee must be seen as a largely non-militant group dissatisfied with the dying N.C.C.I. because of administrative inefficiency, at a time when everyone hoped that the C.R.C. would be very much better.[1]

The next group interviewed were the Ealing executive. This committee had been very dissatisfied with the N.C.C.I. handling of the Kenya Asians issue, and contains, as we have pointed out, a number of fairly militant people. Yet, only six people expressed dissatisfaction with their committee's relations with N.C.C.I./ C.R.C. Fourteen said they were satisfied. Eight did not know.

---

[1] In point of fact the C.R.C. has continued to come under fire for administrative inefficiency. See p. 273.

However, many of the satisfied qualified their answers. It seems fairly clear that the positive response was largely because the C.R.C. had just been set up, and there was considerable optimism that some of their criticisms of the N.C.C.I. would not be applicable to the new organization. Pleasure was expressed about Cousins' appointment as chairman of the C.R.C.

Several members felt there had been a lack of real help available to the committee from the N.C.C.I., and that insufficient attempts had been made to promote exchange of ideas between local committees. The Ealing committee had supported the moves to try to secure that the C.R.C. was elected by the local committees rather than appointed by the Government. Members were naturally disappointed about the failure of that campaign and apprehensive about the appointments that had been made.

Despite the dissatisfaction of the Ealing committee over the handling of the Kenya Asians issue and the appointment of the C.R.C., they seem to enjoy fairly good relations with the central body. The N.C.C.I. expressed some criticism of E.I.F.C. over the number of individual members allowed by its constitution, but had not interfered in any positive way in its organization or work. During the period we were studying, the committee invited Nadine Peppard to address their council, and gave her a most friendly reception. They have since invited a member of the C.R.C., Professor Titmuss, to address one of their meetings, an occasion on which he launched a widely reported criticism of the 'steady stream of pinpricking' from some sections of the Press over the difficulties of the C.R.C.[1]

The next committee approached was Hackney, in late December 1968 and early January 1969. At this stage it was still true to say that little had been heard from the C.R.C. Early in January the C.R.C. had held a conference for chairmen, a quiet, amicable, and unreported event, which in any case the Hackney chairman was unable to attend. However, the great majority of the Hackney committee, eleven out of sixteen, expressed dissatisfaction with relations between their committee and the central body. One largely alienated member expressed disgust that the committee was so hostile to the C.R.C. but could continue to take its money. Of the remaining five, two thought the relationship satisfactory, and three said they did not know.

[1] *Daily Telegraph* (23 October 1969).

It is difficult to explain the difference on this issue between the Hackney committee and the Ealing committee. In many respects the two committees are equally radical in outlook, and in fact, in its relations with its local authority the Hackney committee has been more conciliatory than the Ealing one. However, Ealing's large committee contains a number of people who have shown little interest in the conflict between N.C.C.I. and local committees over consultation and representation, while Hackney's committee has been right in the middle of the dispute. The Hackney committee contains a number of West Indians close to West Indian political movements in North London, and a white member who resigned from the N.C.C.I.'s housing panel and played a part in the debates over the 'Wood proposals'. Also, Hackney's C.R.O. was, during 1968, actively involved in the national association of C.R.O.s and deeply involved in the arguments over the role of the N.C.C.I.

Hackney's executive condemned the failure of the N.C.C.I. to resign over the 1968 Commonwealth Immigrants Act, but refused to go so far as to support the proposal, put forward at the meeting organized in London by the Rev. Wilfred Wood, to set up a national organization independent of the N.C.C.I. They supported the modified proposals, which became known as the 'Wood proposals'. They added a provision that local authorities should be statutorily required to establish community relations committees in areas of significant immigrant settlement, and that the committees should be given a statutory framework, with respect to their functions and powers, within which to operate.

We should not give the impression, however, that the members of the Hackney committee disagreed with the Ealing and Wycombe members and did not see the setting up of the C.R.C. as providing the hope of a new start in central/local relations. Several made this specific point, but they had been so hostile to the N.C.C.I. that they were less optimistic about a new organization which was employing all the former N.C.C.I. staff.

Hackney members were also critical of the N.C.C.I. for its failure to give much positive help to local committees. Members felt the N.C.C.I. had failed to be sensitive to the views of local committees, and failed to provide enough contact between committees. One member described N.C.C.I. as an 'intellectual club', out of touch with the grass-roots.

All the things we have said about the attitude of the Hackney committee are also true of the attitudes of the Tower Hamlets executive, who were also interviewed in January 1969. Yet ten members of Tower Hamlets' executive said they regarded their relationship with the C.R.C. as satisfactory, five said it was unsatisfactory, and two did not know.

Tower Hamlets' committee were very dissatisfied with the N.C.C.I., had written to it expressing dismay over the sacking of its training officer after the York seminar, and had taken its disapproval over the rejection of the proposal that the C.R.C. should be elected to the point of refusing to nominate anyone for consideration by the Home Office for appointment to that body. Its treasurer had written a short booklet with Wilfred Wood attacking the N.C.C.I. and its concept of local committees. Its C.R.O. had become well known as an outspoken critic of N.C.C.I. and as a leader of the militant West Indian Standing Conference. There can be no doubt about where the leaders of Tower Hamlets committee stood on the N.C.C.I. Once again, we can only explain the difference between their answers and the replies we received from Hackney members by suggesting that some, perhaps less active members, were more ready to be optimistic about the new C.R.C., less ready to write it off before it started.

The next three committees were the three in the West Riding. We visited Huddersfield and Bradford in February and March 1969, and Sheffield in May and early June. During this period a new issue arose to generate conflict between the C.R.C. and the local committees, the publication of the C.R.C.'s ideas on conditions of service, duties, etc., for C.R.O.s.

Despite this we found a very different attitude to the C.R.C. in these three Yorkshire committees. Many of the people we interviewed knew nothing about the C.R.C., many were satisfied with the relationship in a rather indifferent way as typified by the comment quoted earlier, 'they haven't stopped giving us money'. Those who were hostile tended to express their hostility in the forms, 'they are irrelevant', or 'they are totally out of touch with us'.

None of the three committees had passed resolutions condemning the N.C.C.I.'s role over the Kenya Asians, and none of them had joined in the movements to create a new 'democratic' national committee. One or two of the more political members of

these committees spoke of the irrelevance of 'London politics' to
Yorkshire. The chairman of the Sheffield committee has been
noted for his robust determination not to take too much notice
of the N.C.C.I./C.R.C., and his opposition to what he regarded
as unnecessary journeys to conferences and meetings for C.R.O.s
or committee members.

The general satisfaction of the majority of members of the
Bradford and Huddersfield committees with the C.R.C. in fact
reflected their non-involvement with the Commission, as did the
fact that the majority of the Sheffield committee had no view to
express on their relationship with the C.R.C.

The difference is that in Sheffield the chairman has been
outspoken about his view that the C.R.C. is largely irrelevant,
leaving members with a suspicion that all is not well, without any
personal evidence on the point. In Bradford and Huddersfield
there is really no relationship, apart from a quite 'satisfactory'
receipt of a grant. The treasurer and the C.R.O. in Bradford are
the only people in close touch with the C.R.C. They have not
involved other members in discussions on the relationship. The
treasurer is the sole 'dissatisfied' member in Bradford. He
expressed his view on the relationship when, in the midst of a
heated debate on the terms of service of C.R.O.s at a C.R.C.
conference, he said that the argument was unnecessary as they
would all go back to their committees and disregard the C.R.C.'s
views if they wanted to.

In June 1969 we went to Birmingham, a committee that had
considered very seriously its relationship to the C.R.C., as it had
to its local authority. We have commented upon this committee
as the most introspective of the local committees we studied. Its
C.R.O., too, had become well known as one of the most thoughtful
of the local officers, and was secretary of the original National
Association of Community Relations Officers. Four of the members
of this committee were 'satisfied' with the relationship with the
C.R.C., five dissatisfied, and seven did not know. The point that
concerned the members of this committee was the neglect of their
needs.

A particular sore point here was the unwillingness of the
N.C.C.I. to allocate more than the standard £1,500 for the whole
city of Birmingham. As early as February 1968 the Birmingham
committee had appealed to the N.C.C.I. for a grant for an

assistant. This request was refused. At the time of our study the committee had been waiting for three months for a reply to another request for an assistant. Given the Birmingham situation this is one of the most disturbing of the causes for complaint about N.C.C.I./C.R.C. which we heard.[1] Since the original policy of restricting grants to £1,500 per committee was dictated by the Government, one cannot be sure where the responsibility lay for this decision, but steps should have been taken to demonstrate the inapplicability of a policy which put Birmingham in the same category as High Wycombe. As we hunted for the Community Relations Office amongst the large modern buildings of this vast city, the puny nature of community relations efforts in this country was brought most forcibly home to us.

Members of the Birmingham committee were concerned that there is no one from the West Midlands on the C.R.C., despite the fact that they had submitted three nominations, and that the C.R.C. has no regional officer for the West Midlands. Their feelings of neglect were further reinforced by the fact that Frank Cousins had not yet found time to visit Birmingham and had not been able to respond to an invitation from their committee.

Press reports have suggested that relations between the N.C.C.I. and local committees were very bad in 1968,[2] and that relations between the C.R.C. and committees had reverted to a similar state by autumn 1969.[3] Undoubtedly an unhappy situation existed in 1968. Even then, it was only a group of committees, most of which based in London and the South, who were particularly dissatisfied with the N.C.C.I. over the Kenya Asians and who were really committed to the Wood proposals for a reformed structure. We suspect that dissatisfaction ran deeper than this, but there is an absence of concrete evidence on this point.

During 1969 there were a number of disagreements between the Commission and local committees, but the number of incidents reported in the Press has been few. Apart from the arguments about the new terms of service, which were inevitable because the C.R.C. was prepared to consult the local committees (it would

---

[1] Since this was written the Birmingham committee has had a large increase in its grant. This does not, however, dispose of our point about the long period of neglect. Doubtless some of the delay was due to efforts to get Birmingham Corporation to pay more too.

[2] 'Clash in Racial Liaison Work', *The Times* (11 March 1968).

[3] 'Cousins' headache', *New Society*, editorial (20 November 1969).

have been much more sinister if they had been imposed without discussion), three specific conflicts between the C.R.C. and local committees have had Press coverage. One of these reports was concerned with the withdrawal of the C.R.C. grant from the Teesside because of a conflict between Pakistani factions in that area, in which both the C.R.O. and the committee's chairman were involved.

In Newcastle the committee was refused a grant after the appointment of a man whom the C.R.C. deemed unsuitable. According to the Newcastle chairman, the C.R.C. objected to the man because he had been a member of the Campaign Against Racial Discrimination and was regarded as too militant, and because of his youth. After discussions, the C.R.C. decided to base its grounds for objection on his age. He was 24 years old. The story of muddle and eventual deadlock over this matter told by the Newcastle chairman is a disturbing one.

A conflict between Oxford and the C.R.C. came to a head after Ann Dummett's widely publicized resignation from the post of C.R.O. there. The Oxford committee did not wish to be subjected to the control the C.R.C. wished to exercise over its new appointment, and the C.R.C. required the committee to reduce its proportion of individual members (three-quarters at that time). After negotiations the Oxford committee gave in on these points. It is impossible to say whether these incidents represent an unnaturally high level of conflict. The peculiar relationship between C.R.C. and local committee which makes every C.R.O. the servant of two masters does create a tendency for conflicts to arise over both appointments and sackings.

The other issue at stake in the Oxford case is a more difficult one. We have shown that the distinction between the individual and the organization member is in many respects an unrealistic one. Oxford asserted the need to maintain this proportion of individual members so as to ensure full participation by as many immigrants as possible, since many do not belong to formal organizations. In many ways here the C.R.C. is more concerned about the constitutional basis of local committees than about harnessing all available voluntary manpower, and is committed to suppressing diverse approaches to this matter. Chapter 11 will examine this point, since it is our view that the concern for the structure of committees as expressed in the 1965 White Paper has assumed an importance unrelated to the functions of committees.

Of course in the mind of the C.R.C. it is likely that the structure of the Oxford committee is associated with its well-known political militancy. On the basis of our data, there does exist some reason to believe that a more open structure is correlated with militancy. Ealing, Hackney, and Tower Hamlets have admitted individual members quite freely. Birmingham, Sheffield, Huddersfield, and Wycombe are all fairly restrictive on this point. Bradford is theoretically open but in practice has not encouraged individual members. We cannot separate cause and effect here. It may be more correct to say that the more militant committees are more ready to draw in individual members as open voluntary organizations than to suggest that these committees are more militant because of their high individual memberships.

A more general criticism of the C.R.C. which has reached the Press from time to time has been that its administration is inefficient. In November 1969 Sir George Sinclair, M.P., asked a Parliamentary question[1] about these allegations, to which the Home Secretary gave a bland reply.[2] Nevertheless, it was decided that the C.R.C.'s chairman, Frank Cousins, should become full time in order to pay more attention to administrative issues.[3] In December, the C.R.C.'s senior administrative officer resigned, dissatisfied with the administrative framework in which he had to operate.[4]

The evidence from the twenty-two questionnaires completed by C.R.O.s tends to back up the view that the situations and the attitudes found in the eight committees are typical. Eight C.R.O.s stated that the relationship between C.R.C. and their committee is unsatisfactory, thirteen said it is satisfactory, and one refused to comment. The use of a postal questionnaire, which could not at the same time be anonymous, rather than an interview, and the fact that our respondents were C.R.O.s, will both tend to have reduced the extent to which dissatisfaction will have been revealed.

The points the dissatisfied C.R.O.s made were much the same as the members of the eight committees made. They were more inclined to complain about central control, presumably

[1] *Sunday Times* (2 November 1969).   [2] *The Times* (21 November 1969).
[3] *Guardian* (29 November 1969).
[4] J. Reddaway, 'Whatever Happened to the CRC?' *Race Today* (Vol. 2, No. 7, July 1970), pp. 212–15.

because it affects them much more directly. There seemed to be a feeling that the C.R.C. was ready to push them around but was not available, when needed, and was not really aware of the problems faced by officers in the field. This is, of course, a common complaint of people in more typical decentralized bureaucracies.[1]

One specific complaint made by three different C.R.O.s was that the C.R.C. had engaged in dealings with their chairmen behind their backs, which seemed to be aimed at getting rid of them. At worst this is a rather unpleasant divide-and-rule tactic. The fact that the first conference held by the C.R.C. was a meeting for chairmen alone, at which several had an opportunity to give vent to their feelings on the inadequacy of their C.R.O.s, does suggest a certain predilection for this kind of approach. At best this is merely another consequence of the situation in which the C.R.O. is the servant of two masters, which makes it necessary for these two masters to get together when he is deemed inadequate by one of them. Such situations have arisen in the past when thoroughly inadequate C.R.O.s have been asked to resign. In the cases that were revealed to us, however, it is significant that when the points at issue reached the full executive committees, in each case, it was the chairmen who were forced to resign. This suggests that it has been a dangerous policy for the C.R.C. to take chairmen alone into their confidence on such matters. In the last resort the C.R.C.'s problem may be just as much a bad committee as a bad C.R.O. All such situations need to be handled with considerable delicacy. Much of our other evidence suggests that the C.R.C. is not very good at doing this.

We will complete this chapter by describing the main points where N.C.C.I./C.R.C. influence has been or is being exercised on the functioning of local committees.

The most fundamental influence is the role the N.C.C.I. and C.R.C. have played in urging the setting up of committees, in providing most of the original suggestions for their constitutions, and in providing grants to enable them to engage C.R.O.s. In some cases this involved a great deal of work, much of it behind the scenes, in urging recalcitrant local authorities to sponsor or support community relations committees, and in providing advice

[1] M. J. Hill, 'The Exercise of Discretion in the National Assistance Board', *Public Administration* (Vol. 47, Spring 1969), pp. 85–7.

to people who had little idea of the shape they wanted their local committee to take. The fact that the constitutions of most committees are very close to the model constitution circulated by the N.C.C.I. testifies to the high degree of influence exercised by the central organization at this stage. Few committees, in fact mainly only those founded before 1965, can claim to have been really independent of the N.C.C.I. in their early days. In this way the 'parent' role of the N.C.C.I. provides the basis for much of the influence exercised by the C.R.C. today. Most of the committees which are highly suspicious of the C.R.C. are either pre-1965 White Paper foundations, such as Oxford, or had highly independent origins, like Tower Hamlets, or have been set up since suspicion of N.C.C.I. and C.R.C. has become widespread and public, for example Hammersmith.

N.C.C.I./C.R.C. influence is also exerted when a C.R.O. is appointed, a point that was a recent bone of contention between the C.R.C. and the Oxford committee. Obviously as the local committee system has become elaborated the C.R.C. has begun to pay more attention to the selection of C.R.O.s. Ideas have been developed upon the kind of C.R.O.s who are suitable and the C.R.C. has begun to recognize that disastrous appointments (in their terms) can be avoided by care at this stage. One aspect of this increasing attention to selection has been a C.R.C. recommendation that C.R.O.s should be over 30 years of age. To exercise more general influence over the process, the C.R.C. seeks to have its representative included on local selection committees.

The C.R.C. plays some part in the induction and training of C.R.O.s, but, as we have seen, their influence is still very slight. Indeed one might say that it is still remarkably slight.

Once a C.R.O. is appointed, the C.R.C. has, of course, a financial stake in a local committee. Under the N.C.C.I. such stakes were confined to £1,500. Now the C.R.C. has decided, though one understands that the Government dictated this decision, that grants can, in certain circumstances, be up to £3,500.[1] This enables committees, where local authority support is adequate, to ask for small sums for projects and to seek grants to pay for assistant C.R.O.s. Committees inadequately supported by their local authorities can ask for money to make up for this

[1] On this Birmingham is *now* being treated as an exception, needing more than £3,500.

disadvantage. At the time of writing the first assistant C.R.O.s supported in this way are being appointed.

The only other financial support provided by the C.R.C., so far, has been the grants from the Gulbenkian Foundation which they administer, for fair housing groups, playgroups, and a few other special projects, and money provided to pay for local conferences which the C.R.C. sponsors, in conjunction with local committees.

When one contrasts these sums of money with the vast amounts disbursed by the United States federal government to support local organizations set up under the Poverty Programme, they are very puny indeed. The total income of the C.R.C. for 1969–70 is only £300,000, and it and a high proportion of past income have been absorbed by central administrative costs.[1] We set out to study the effectiveness of community relations committees. Any judgement we have made upon the influence of other factors in limiting their effectiveness is inevitably overshadowed by one factor, poverty. While local committees might be thought to have every reason to be grateful to their benefactor, the C.R.C., they are very aware of the fact that the money they receive from that source is extraordinarily little by comparison with many other forms of Government expenditure.

The committees receive a steady stream of correspondence from the C.R.C. Much of this consists of information, from copies and summaries of Government reports to publications like *Race Today* and literature from the Runnymede Trust.

The local committee is also asked to provide information on activities and events in its own area, and evidence for Government committees, such as the Select Committee on Race Relations and the Cullingworth Committee on council house allocation. These provide opportunities for local committees to pass their views on to the C.R.C., something that many committees are glad to do even without prompting.

There is scarcely any evidence, amongst all this correspondence, of dictation from C.R.C. to local committees. Perhaps such

---

[1] *Report of the Community Relations Commission for 1968–9.* The £200,000 received by the N.C.C.I./C.R.C. for 1968–9 was budgeted in the following way:

Central Secretariat	£100,000
Conferences, etc.	25,000
Grants to local committees	60,000
Information services	15,000

dictation comes in verbal forms in visits or telephone calls from C.R.C. staff and at meetings and conferences. But we must re-emphasize that we have found little direct evidence of this. On the contrary many of the people we spoke to suggested that direct contacts with the C.R.C. are all too rare. C.R.O.s find they have no one they can take their problems to.

One particular issue on which there seems to have been very little help from the N.C.C.I./C.R.C. to local committees is housing. Despite the Gulbenkian grants for fair housing groups, despite the enormous importance of this issue, and despite the fact that this is a local problem which committees have found extremely difficult to tackle, the C.R.C. seems to have given this issue little consideration. It does not employ a 'housing officer', and, since the demise of the N.C.C.I.'s housing panel, until very recently even lacked an advisory body on this topic. This inattention is reflected in the very small amount of space given to housing in the first annual report of the C.R.C.

We end, therefore, on a rather negative point about the C.R.C. It emphasizes what has been an underlying theme in this chapter, that, despite the Press attention given to examples of C.R.C. interference with local matters, neglect has been perhaps the main feature of the relationship.

CHAPTER 11

Conclusions

The community relations 'movement' is one facet of what has come to be known as 'community work'. The increase in number, over a short space of time, of community relations officers has its parallel in the increase in number of 'community workers' on housing estates, new towns, and development areas. Community work has been defined as one aspect 'of the far broader issue of how to meet people's needs and give them an effective say in what these are and how they want them met'. This definition goes on: 'It is also part of the whole dilemma of how to reconcile "the revolution of human dissent" with large-scale organisation, and economic and social planning which seems to be inseparably interwoven with the parallel revolution of rising expectations.'[1] The raising of the educational level in the community at large has brought about the emergence of a new generation of voluntary bodies, both middle-class pressure groups and 'client' organizations concerned with the promotion of consumer interest, such as the Child Poverty Action Group, the Confederation of Associations for the Advancement of State Education, the Claimants' Union, the Pre-School Playgroups Association, and many others. Such activities are concerned with the co-operative provision of services not otherwise available and the exertion of corporate pressure for the improvement in the standards of provision made by statutory bodies. The Report continues: 'At the gap between the result of local government action and its purpose, community work should come in to interpret to local authorities how the services appear to the consumer, what is lacking in the services themselves.'[2] We will here re-emphasize the dilemmas inherent in this new vogue for community work especially in community relations work.

Community work has usually been divided into two types,

[1] *Community Work and Social Change*, p. 4.
[2] Ibid., p. 29.

community organization and community development. Community organization doctrine emphasizes working mainly within the existing system of institutions, established organizations, and power relationships, with the aim of eliminating inefficiency and overlap. Community development doctrine challenges that system to some extent by calling for more involvement of the community worker with the 'rank and file' population in order to produce new patterns of involvement and power.[1] Such distinctions have been drawn both in American and British literature on community work.[2] The Skeffington Committee, for example, thought a community forum might be an adequate means of encouraging established voluntary organizations to express their views about local authority plans. It considered that a community development officer was essential to help articulate the views of those (mainly lower income people) who did not participate in voluntary associations yet were likely to be greatly affected (often adversely) by plans of which they were largely unaware before implementation.[3]

Rediscovery (or even re-invention) of the 'community' permeates nearly all recent official documents on the social services. Yet it is hard to disagree with a view recently put forward that:

the uncomfortable feeling persists when reports such as Seebohm and Gulbenkian are read alongside discussions of the ideology of social movements, that the mixture is as before, and only the wrapping is different. Thus the attempt to involve people in decisions occurs at a stage too far removed from the positions where power is actually held and that, once more, the appeal to the community only results in the avoidance of real issues, that in concentrating on social situations a means is found whereby attention can be diverted from social structures. The dilemma into which many social workers have been thrown by the prospect of involvement in political action may not be so real as it appears for, interpreted in this way, community work does not contain the basis for a real confrontation with authority or any major threat to established institutions.[4]

[1] M. Clinard, *Slums and Community Development* (New York, Free Press, 1966).
[2] *Community Work and Social Change*, p. 35.
[3] *People and Planning*, Report of the Skeffington Committee (London, H.M.S.O., 1969).
[4] B. Heraud, *Sociology and Social Work, Problems and Perspectives* (London, Pergamon Press, 1970), p. 94.

The community relations movement is one more manifestation of this type of uncontroversial community work. The community relations movement was not intended by its founders to be anything more revolutionary than an 'institution of the truce'.[1] In fact, a meaningful 'truce' situation never really existed between the white and black population, the black population not having shown itself yet as a sufficiently disruptive threat. In the 1960s governments moved further to the right, denying any real concessions to the immigrant population, which in turn has become more disaffected and alienated by the fiction of the community relations movement. Even to perform a limited role as an institution of the truce, community relations committees would have to have considerable status and power to have ready access to decision-makers and to translate its demands into authoritative terms. We have shown how community relations committees are weak in financial resources, low in status, and lacking in executive power. If they are to be able to perform a co-ordination role effectively, the co-operation of local authorities is vital. We have seen that problems arise because most local authorities are unwilling to conceive of their relationships with the committees as involving any positive commitment on their part. Even if a community relations committee's primary role is a community organization approach, it will involve some attempt at innovation and change as it tries initially to draw all the institutions, public and private, which determine the life chances of people in the locality, within its ambit. We have shown that community relations committees usually fail to involve these crucial institutions in any meaningful way. Sometimes such institutions are not predominantly locally oriented. Mainly these institutions resent interference which might bring about unwanted changes, and the community relations committees lack the power and influence to require their co-operation. If a committee does manage to secure some co-operation, it is usually forced to sacrifice innovation and act as a forum operating on a consensual basis composed of different interests and points of view, rather than as a propagandist pressure group of self-selected, like-minded people committed to trying to effect change. In this situation, community relations committees can become like the earlier local welfare planning

[1] John Rex, *Key Problems in Sociological Theory* (London, Routledge & Kegan Paul, 1961).

councils in the U.S.A. where various subgroups are brought into co-operative participation through representatives, though not all groups in community life are necessarily represented:

This structure serves as an arena in which change is discussed and argued by various sub-groups represented but the federated structure itself remains primarily neutral. The structure is circumscribed by the interests of the groups that have assembled within its fold. . . . Such a structural commitment leads inevitably to an avoidance of conflict whenever possible and the seeking of action in the name of the 'total community' only where overwhelming consensus can be secured from constituent members of the federation.[1]

The limitation in such an approach, as we have emphasized throughout this book, is that it often leads inevitably to the sacrifice of innovation. The same tendency has been commented on with respect to the community action programmes in the American poverty programme. National reformers who made funds available hoped that increase in funds would stimulate change and assumed that the involvement of voluntary and public bureaucracies was a necessary precondition for change:

That the institution might both obtain the funds from established and new sources and resist change was a contingency to which local and national planners seemed to have given little attention.[2]

With regard to the question of co-operating with existing agencies Rein said:

While it is useless to ignore the realities of established institutional power a programme of planned change runs the dire risk of losing its sense of purpose if it relies only on established leadership. Increasingly planners find that the more they work with established institutions the more compromises they have to make, the more difficult it becomes to ensure that funds are spent for innovation rather than for expansion of the status quo.[3]

We have found in the case of community relations committees, the greater the diversity of institutional interest that is embraced by a community relations umbrella, the more easily the existence of a local committee can be legitimated as 'representative' of the 'total community', yet the more likely the C.R.O. will be forced

[1] Morris and Rein, 'Emerging Patterns in Community Planning', in Frieden and Morris (eds.), op. cit., p. 24.
[2] Rein, 'Social Planning and the Search for Legitimacy'.
[3] Ibid.

to sacrifice his prime purpose of bringing about change to the needs of maintaining consensus. Obstacles to good 'community relations' are acknowledged to exist but the approach recommended by the Commission involves the assumption that the 'community' can deal with it by means of a consensus strategy. We have demonstrated the different ideological connotations inherent in usages of the word 'community'. As Warner Bloomberg has put it:

Traditional organisers [i.e., in American communities] have usually portrayed their local social systems in ways distorted by ideology, presenting myths about the settlement's past . . . portraying interest groups as genuine sub-communities and reinforcing beliefs and judgements which effectively read some local inhabitants out of the community.[1]

Which organizations are to be legitimately recognized as members of the 'community' and thereby eligible for affiliation to the committee is decided by the executives of community relations committees. In practice, informal social control is exerted by the executive over elections and 'known' individuals are co-opted into the executive. The Community Relations Commission has recommended that the general council of a community relations committee should comprise 75 per cent organization members and 25 per cent individuals. We have cast doubt earlier on the validity of this distinction. In the last resort the contribution of every member other than the local authority representatives is the contribution of an individual, not a delegate from an organization, since there is virtually no referral back to the sending organizations.

Moreover, most C.R.O.s would consider their general councils to be ineffective, a loose unco-ordinated assortment of people meeting annually, sometimes twice a year, rarely monthly, to hear and echo what has already been decided in the executive.

The fiasco of the Birmingham Advisory Council, the exception to the general rule of 'silent' general councils, is evidence of the difficulties involved in trying to force different organizations with conflicting ambitions and objectives under one artificial umbrella.

[1] Warner Bloomberg, 'Community Organisation', in Howard Becker (ed.), *Social Problems—A Modern Approach* (New York, John Wiley & Sons, 1966), p. 371.

Since all decision-making power is vested in the executive, the C.R.O. is theoretically precluded from using his initiative. Decisions have to be taken by the executive as to whether a certain organization or individual is 'bona fide' or whether a certain role comes within the brief of the C.R.O. Of course, much of the time, matters of this kind are decided by the C.R.O., but it is important to realize that in the last resort, which means when controversy arises, power rests in the hands of the executive. (See for example the important role played by Sheffield's chairman in steering the committee away from controversial matters.)

The structure of a community relations committee also leads to an inevitable emphasis upon working through meetings and discussions, so that much time is spent merely keeping an inactive membership in touch. The constitutionalism and the formality of committee procedure deter participation from people other than the more educated, confident, and urbane. Representation on the committees, as we have shown, is overwhelmingly middle class. The subordination of the C.R.O. to the committee structure as it now exists hampers his initiative without helping him to extend 'roots' into the local community to any great extent.

The activities sponsored by the committees in many cases involve attempts at 'community development' in the sense of direct work in a small neighbourhood: the provision of facilities for children with the intention of eventually involving mothers in their organization; the survey of needs in a redevelopment area; or the formation of multiracial housing associations. These activities, usually located in twilight zones, run on intentionally multiracial lines, and do involve the C.R.O.s in some dialogue with lower income, or more powerless groups. But as discussed in Chapter 7 these activities are usually uncontroversial and are not concerned with fundamental questions of redistribution of power and resources. The projects are not intended to provide separate services for Commonwealth immigrants or compensatory programmes for a multiracial population in deprived areas, on any significant scale. They cannot be equated therefore to the Community Action Programmes in the American War Against Poverty, nor are they necessarily identical to the Urban Programme's Education Priority Area or Community Development Project in this country, where the 'target population' has been more clearly identified according to specific quantified criteria of deprivation.[1] The community relations committees' areas and programmes are more diffuse in coverage and objectives.

There is and always has been, some confusion as to what objectives the movement should pursue, and as to whether the programmes recommended are relevant to the achievement of the over-all declared aims. Community relations work is not just community work. Community work itself has been criticized for its facile theoretical assumptions but community relations practical work seems to be even more confounded by its lack of theoretical grounding. Any attempt to formulate a programme for the amelioration of race relations must involve consideration of the psychological, social, cultural, and structural dimensions of prejudice and discrimination. The difficulty in evaluating the Community Relations Commission on its own terms is that it does not make it clear what its terms are. If one gives the Commission the benefit of the doubt, despite its disappointing behaviour in the past, and accepts that it does really want to see the rights of Commonwealth immigrants protected and community 'harmony' maintained, one still cannot escape from the fact that these two goals may be incompatible and that one may need to be subordinated to the requirements of the other. The particularly important point to be made about 'harmony' is that this may appear to exist in a caste or class-ridden society and even in a racialist society. Harmony itself does not indicate the existence of equality.[2] One of the quietest periods in American racial history, 1895–1915, witnessed the construction of the massive system of institutional racialism as it is known today, and has been called the nadir of Negro American history.[3]

There is an obvious need for an agency to press for the rights of Commonwealth immigrants and their dependants, and for an agency to stimulate the mutual education of citizens of a multi-racial society. The Community Relations Commission seems to have failed to achieve the effective performance of either of these functions.

[1] For a critical appraisal of these, see R. Holman, *Socially Deprived Families in Britain* (London, National Council of Social Service, 1970), pp. 174–86.

[2] R. Bastide and P. Van den Berghe, 'Stereotypes, Norms and Interracial Behaviour in Sao Paolo, Brazil', in *American Sociological Review* (Vol. 22, 1957), showed that Brazil was by no means a racially equal society even though it was apparently harmonious.

[3] Rayford Logan, *The Negro in the U.S.—a Brief History* (Princeton, Van Nostrand, 1957).

As far as the first of these two functions is concerned, the role of defending the rights of entry of Commonwealth immigrants, which have been increasingly encroached on since 1965, has been abnegated by the Commission. Their failure to make an effective protest against the Commonwealth Immigrants Act of 1968, and against the more recent exclusion of fiancées and some categories of dependants of immigrants, means that the local committees have received little guidance or encouragement from them to take up individual cases of hardship. Constant watch on the decisions of immigration officers is kept not by the C.R.C. but by the Joint Council for the Welfare of Immigrants, who make attempts to persuade the Home Office to reconsider particular cases.[1]

When the Home Office announced that dependants would henceforth need entry permits, it was the J.C.W.I. which negotiated with the Government for the establishment of information centres in the Commonwealth countries, and was prepared to go ahead on this on its own initiative when a committee of inquiry under Sir Derek Hilton advised only the enlargement of British High Commission's facilities.[2]

Local community relations committees have dealt with some cases but these have been comparatively few in number. This is not surprising given the limited knowledge of the existence of the committees amongst many immigrant communities. Moreover, in some cases, committees have followed the lead of the C.R.C. in being unwilling to tackle issues of this kind to any extent. We have quoted evidence on this with regard to the Birmingham committee, where the committee's limitation of the activity of the C.R.O. in this field can be contrasted with the fact that the last chairman of the ill-fated Advisory Council had done some good work of this nature.[3]

Protesting against the inhumanity and arbitrariness of immigration control procedures and helping people deal with the immigration authorities will inevitably be very largely a short-term and small-scale function, given that the majority of the dependants of Commonwealth immigrants have arrived or will have to do so very soon if they are not to forfeit their eligibility,

---

[1] First and Second Annual Reports, Joint Council for the Welfare of Immigrants.
[2] J. McNeal, 'Immigration and the Advisory Services', *Race Today* (September 1969), and J. McNeal, 'The Hilton Report', *Race Today* (November 1969).
[3] *Race Today* (February 1970).

and the number of new entrants from Commonwealth countries is falling every year. However there are far larger areas of rights which coloured immigrants are entitled to as British citizens, in the public spheres of education, housing, and social welfare, and the various private spheres of provision. Community relations committees should have a vital role to play in relation to the assertion of these rights.

The Race Relations Board exists to take positive measures against discrimination. The existence of the C.R.C. and the local committees may be justified if they are seen as agencies working to prevent discrimination from occurring. As far as influencing the operation of public agencies such as local authorities are concerned, it is vital for the C.R.O. to have sufficient status and power to be able to criticize local authorities effectively. Because the C.R.O. is often partially financially dependent on the local authority, and because it is important to maintain good relations since the C.R.O. has no coercive powers to deploy in the event of the local authority deciding he is too troublesome and deserves to be discouraged, the C.R.O. is often in a role similar to that of a community worker paid by a local authority. The dilemma for community workers generally was recognized by the Seebohm Committee but no solution was proferred. Talking about citizen participation they say:

The participants may wish to pursue policies directly at variance with the ideas of local authorities and there is certainly a difficult link to be forged between the concepts of popular participation and traditional representative democracy. The role of the social worker in this context is likely to give rise to problems of conflicting loyalties.[1]

The community relations committee has the worst of all possible situations. It is a voluntary organization, yet cannot use all the pressure group tactics of public exposure and criticism because it is a quasi-statutory body dependent on the support of a Government-created national agency. At the same time, it has no statutory powers of its own and cannot compel a local authority to co-operate or even, in some cases, acknowledge its existence.

The second of the two functions suggested for local committees involved mutual education. The C.R.C. seems more ready to acknowledge this one. Discrimination is to be prevented according

---

[1] *Committee on Local Authority. . . .* para. 494.

to the C.R.C.'s programme by a general policy of 'education' of the British community. It is beyond the scope of this book to examine exhaustively the sociological and psychological literature on prejudice, or to suggest and test any hypotheses of our own on this subject. Suffice it to say that despite the quantity that has been written on the subject of attitude change, the evidence remains inconclusive. The recent attempt to gauge the extent of tolerance and prejudice in British white society towards coloured immigrants[1] has been seriously questioned on methodological grounds.[2] The extent of the problem is not yet known, for example the number of those inclined to intolerance, or the origins and generators of various kinds of attitudes. It may well be necessary to have a general programme of education to disabuse people of their misconceptions.[3] There is no guarantee that people will prefer to listen to or retain the 'truth' or that correct information will change attitudes and behaviour, especially when the government's restrictive policy on the entry of coloured immigrants and the exploitation of race for party political advantage have helped to create a climate of opinion in which Commonwealth immigration is seen as a source of 'social problems'.

Contact does not of itself lead to greater tolerance.[4] What some experiments in attitude change have shown is that participation by individuals of equal status with common interest in a common activity can lead to modification in attitudes. Allport concluded that four characteristics of the contact situation are of the utmost importance. Prejudice is lessened when the two groups:

possess equal status in the situation;
seek common goals;
are co-operatively dependent on each other;
interact with the positive support of authorities, laws, or custom.[5]

[1] Rose *et al.*, op. cit., Chapter 28.
[2] D. Lawrence, 'The Incidence of Racial Prejudice in Britain', a paper presented to Race Relations Group of the British Sociological Association (3 January 1970). See also C. Bagley, *Social Structure and Prejudice in Five English Boroughs* (I.R.R. Special Series, 1970).
[3] For example 24 per cent of Dr. Abrams' sample thought that there were more than 5 million coloured people in Britain. Rose *et al.*, op. cit., p. 570.
[4] Bettleheim and Janowitz, op. cit., pp. 71-2, and P. H. Mussen, 'Some Personality and Social Tactics Related to Change in Children's Attitudes towards Negroes', *Journal of Abnormal and Social Psychology* (XLV, July 1950).
[5] G. Allport, *The Nature of Prejudice* (Cambridge, Mass., Addison-Wesley, 1954).

However hard the C.R.O. tries to get out beyond the committee structure to communicate with the operators and clients of other local institutions, it is obvious that, for example, one C.R.O. lecturing schoolchildren or police cadets for a 45-minute session tacked on to their normal courses cannot do much to change attitudes. He is operating in the face of cultural preconceptions so deeply entrenched that they influence behaviour often quite unwittingly. The C.R.C. seems to place great faith in conferences, lectures, news-letters, and pamphlets with little evidence that these overt media reach the right people and with no idea whether they will have any real impact.

The fact that any government-sponsored educational programme on racial equality will fail if the government itself does not ensure that it, and other public and private organizations which it has the power to influence, provide equality of treatment, brings us back inevitably to the first of the two functions we listed.

We have shown that the Commission in *theory* considers that it has two goals: to secure the civil rights of coloured immigrants, and to reduce prejudice and encourage racial harmony. We have however also shown that programmes for the reduction of prejudice demand certain prerequisites, such as prior equality of status (and a positive commitment on the part of authorities), if they are to be successful. The location within the social structure of the individual is an important factor in creating and perpetuating attitudes.[1] The P.E.P. Report and other studies have shown that discrimination is more likely to be experienced by well-educated coloured job applicants, implying that coloured people are perceived as suitable only for low status jobs.[2] Attitude change on the part of the white population demands the prerequisite of accompanying structural change in the socio-economic situation of coloured immigrants and the maximization of the 'choices' available to them. The Race Relations Act exists to prevent obstacles in the way of social mobility of coloured people. Its approach is based upon the traditional civil rights 'equality of opportunity' philosophy. As such, even if it is effective (which has not altogether been the case up till now), the legislation will help

---

[1] F. R. Westie, 'Negro White Status Differentials and Social Distance', *American Sociological Review* (1952).
[2] Daniel, op. cit., p. 81, and R. Jowell and P. Prescott-Clark, 'Racial Discrimination and White Collar Workers in Britain', *Race* (Vol. 11, No. 4, April 1970).

only those who have the initial wherewithal to improve on their situation.

Accordingly the Commission, which is assumed to have a more total commitment to the betterment of the whole immigrant community than the Board, since the latter is inevitably concerned with individual cases, may be expected to come up against another dilemma. It can interpret its role in terms of assisting the Board in the removal of barriers to the upward mobility of the few. It has also to face up to the fact that such an approach evades the problems posed by the continuing presence of large numbers of coloured people amongst the ranks of the least privileged in our society. This means that not only does it have to face up to the question of what should be the distribution of coloured people throughout our social structure, but ultimately what should be the shape of our social structure. This is a new complication to the traditional socialist or radical problem of distinguishing between, and choosing between, equality of opportunity and real equality as an objective for policies. An organization committed to the betterment of an underprivileged group, albeit one currently lacking equality of opportunity, cannot evade the issue even if it is prepared to set the removal of this kind of inequality as its goal, if only because the competitive disadvantages of underprivileged groups prevent them from availing themselves of the formal, legally protected, opportunities presented to them. These disadvantages include in particular the deficient resources of our decaying urban areas. Many writers have pointed to the presence of Commonwealth immigrants as acting as a 'barium meal' in serving to highlight the deficiencies in the decaying inner cores of our urban system.[1] Territorial justice is a prerequisite for social justice. The barrenness of the older doctrine of equality of opportunity for the individual has been recognized in the case of working-class children in our educational system.[2] The overwhelming majority of Commonwealth immigrants in this country are working in manual jobs. Proportionately more coloured than white people live in furnished accommodation or in overcrowded conditions. Their children are being taught more often than not in what are now designated educational priority areas. They,

[1] Burney, op. cit.
[2] *Children and their Primary Schools*, A Report of the Central Advisory Council for Education (Plowden Report, London, H.M.S.O., 1967).

20

together with the white children of manual workers in their areas, will leave school to go on to manual and low grade jobs. They will be discouraged from having 'unrealistic aspirations'.[1] Discrimination cannot be proved in the case of under-achievement. Yet any agency with a mandate to prevent racial inequality is not beginning to touch its field of responsibility if it does not consider issues such as these. The N.C.C.I./C.R.C. has not shown itself to be ready to face them. There are doubts whether it has the will to do so, but what is quite clear is that the government has not really given it the power for this function. On one of the rare occasions where the N.C.C.I. took the initiative in emphasizing the need for 'positive discrimination', when it produced a pamphlet on areas of housing need in 1967, the government took little notice of it.[2]

It would seem that it is in this context, the situation of low-income white and black populations, in the twilight areas of the conurbations, that the community relations committees' community development activities could in theory fulfil some purpose. However, a greater emphasis on community development, in the sense of organizing a neighbourhood to articulate its needs, also has its limitations. Chapter 3 illustrated how conflicting interests can exist at a neighbourhood level.

Even radically intentioned attempts at organizing a neighbourhood have come to grief through the lack of an adequate philosophical and ideological framework to guide the course of action.[3] Our analysis of political power would suggest that only some of the problems of underprivileged groups can be solved through neighbourhood level changes.

S. M. Miller and P. Roby have pointed out that in the twentieth century, the notion of class must be widened not only to focus on property and the market, but to include control of and access to public services.[4] In the welfare state many important elements of the command over resources become available as public services and the distribution and quality of these public

---

[1] D. Nandy, 'Unrealistic Aspirations', *Race Today* (Vol. 1, No. 1, May 1969), p. 9.
[2] Rex, op. cit., p. 78. The pamphlet was *The Housing of Commonwealth Immigrants* (London, N.C.C.I., April 1967).
[3] S. Aronowitz, 'Poverty Politics and Community Organisation', *Studies on the Left* (Vol. 4, No. 3, summer 1964), for a criticism of Alinsky's approach.
[4] S. M. Miller and P. Roby, *The Future of Inequality* (New York, Basic Books, 1970), p. 10.

services affect the absolute and relative well-beings of all individuals.[1] An attempt to challenge the prevailing stratification system constitutes what Bachrach and Baratz have called a 'key issue':

A key issue is one that involves a genuine challenge to the resources of power or authority of those who currently dominate the process by which policy outputs in the system are determined. . . . A key issue is one that involves a demand for enduring transformation in both the manner in which values are allocated in the polity in question and the value-allocation itself.[2]

The same authors have stressed how advocates of change must win, at all stages of the political process, issue recognition, decision, and implementation of policy, whereas defenders of existing policy need only win at one stage of the process.[3]

Organization on immediate neighbourhood issues is obviously needed but the additional strategy that is necessary is the tying up of local issues to broader questions of national policy. Even the more radical attempts to stimulate participation by the under-privileged on a wider than local scale have not yet resolved how to make the transition from negative protest to positive action. Michael Lipsky has portrayed the obstacles encountered in protest activity by essentially powerless pressure groups, attempting to work broadly within the system.[4] He suggests that protest activity is a problem of bargaining in which the basic difficulty for the powerless is the lack of political resources to exchange. The problem of the powerless in protest activity is to activate third parties to enter the implicit or explicit bargaining arena in ways favourable to the protestors. Lipsky points out that the particular dilemma of protest leaders is that they must appeal to many constituencies at the same time. They must simultaneously sustain and nurture the protest organization, maximize the impact of third parties in the political conflict, and maximize the chances of success amongst those capable of granting the desired goals. He concludes after demonstrating how these activities often conflict:

Alinsky is probably on the soundest ground when he prescribes protest for the purpose of building an organisation. Ultimately powerless

---

[1] Ibid.   [2] Bachrach and Baratz, op. cit., pp. 47–8.   [3] Ibid., p. 58.
[4] M. Lipsky, 'Protest as a Political Resource', *American Political Science Review* (Vol. LXII, December 1968).

groups in most instances cannot depend upon activating other actors in the political process. Long run success will depend upon the acquisition of stable political resources which do not rely for their use on third parties.[1]

There are limitations on the efficacy of protest activity at a local level, but even if there were not we do not think that the C.R.O. could conceivably act directly as a radical community mobilizer. The community relations movement is a government-sponsored exercise. It would be unrealistic to expect a subsidized revolution. The C.R.O. is in a role similar to that of any community worker paid by a local authority. S. Miller and F. Riessman have pointed out that a conflict model may not only be unuseable in certain situations, it may be only minimally usable by some groups.[2] They suggest that many official poverty agencies in the American War of Poverty brought unproductive trouble upon themselves by acting as though they could ignore the constraint of being a government-supported agency and could compete with non-governmental groups free to organize protest. They suggest that in certain cities Community Action Programmes might be more effective if they adopt what the authors term a 'third party strategy', and try to mediate between the organized poor and the bureaucracies. They stress that this strategy depends on pressure from more militant 'second force' groups, functioning *outside* the system. The 'third party' orientation is essentially an 'inside' strategy working within the system to be changed.[3] The authors conclude that the two forces, though they should articulate each other, have separate functions and goals. Radical community workers can organize their constituency. Functioning within the system on government money, C.A.P.s do not have this freedom. Yet without grass-roots and civil rights pressures, C.A.P.s might be unable to make the vital connexions in the social service system.

We have spelt this argument out because we see it as in some ways expressing the dilemmas experienced by community relations committees. If one is to be realistic one can only expect the government to sponsor an agency performing the 'third party

[1] Ibid.
[2] S. M. Miller and F. Riessman, *Social Class and Social Policy* (New York, Basic Books, 1968), p. 229.   [3] Ibid., p. 239.

role'. But community relations committees fail to perform even this function effectively because of lack of resources, low status in the eyes of the local authority, and lack of central government backing.

There is, however, one way in which pressure can be put very effectively upon local government, and that is through the central government machine. If the government really wanted to ensure the success of the community relations movement, it could put pressure on local authorities, if necessary through its control of grants. Both the special provisions for help to local authorities with immigrants in their areas under section 11 of the 1966 Local Government Act and the help entailed in the 'urban programme' provide opportunities to ensure that community relations are taken seriously. Similarly, loan sanctions and subsidies for council house building could be made conditional upon the adoption of equitable house allocation policies. The £25 million allocated for the whole of the Government's 'urban programme' over a three-year period, 1968–71, cannot be expected to effect very much change. Still, it is a pity that the role of C.R.O.s in local decision-making in the expenditure of this money depends entirely upon them taking the initiative and succeeding in getting local authorities to pay attention to them. They have no power to require local authorities to consult them on this matter.

The C.R.O.'s power in the public and private spheres depends upon the support of central government. Their support from local authorities is rarely an asset and often a liability, and their support from the non-official members of their committees largely irrelevant. They could therefore be expected to operate much more effectively without the constraints imposed by the existing local committee structure. The local immigrant and pro-immigrant organizations would equally operate better as independent pressure groups outside the structure imposed by a consensual committee.

It would have been better if C.R.O.s had been in a position to create two kinds of organizations to work with: federal committees of representatives and experts to act in an advisory capacity rather than as controllers, and local grass-roots organizations to operate as autonomous bodies with, as far as possible, C.R.O.-backing. Voluntary organizations at present are not democratic or representative in any true sense. It seems spurious to justify the control of community relations committees over professional staff in terms of 'democracy' or 'community control'.

In fact we feel that activities are necessary on a variety of fronts and under the aegis of a wide range of organizations. In particular there is a need for the various immigrant groups to organize themselves politically and certainly not to regard the community relations committees as substitutes for such organizations. In this connexion we can only quote words spoken over a hundred years ago by a black American, Frederick Douglass, which appear to have inspired Stokely Carmichael among others:

Those who profess to favour freedom yet deprecate agitation are men who want crops without plowing up the ground; they want rain without thunder and lightning. . . . Power concedes nothing without demand. It never did and it never will. Find out just what any people will quietly submit to and you have found out the exact measure of injustice and wrong which will be imposed on them and these will continue till they are resisted with either words or blows or with both. The limits of tyrants are prescribed by the endurance of those whom they oppress.[1]

There could be much to be gained at the national level by immigrants organizing but, as we showed in Chapter 8, the lack of geographic concentrations of immigrants of any considerable size militates against their being able to act as power groups on local levels. Yet certain decisions which are often crucial for the life chances of the individual are taken at the local level, e.g. in the field of education or the allocation of housing. For this reason an effective pressure group which will constantly examine local authority's and other agencies' policies is essential, with strong 'vertical' support both from a vigilant Commission and from national immigrant organizations. In this, the C.R.C. and its staff *could* play a vital role.

Miller and Reissman have pointed out how militant protest groups can move the centre of gravity further to the 'left' by raising the saliency of issues and may therefore provide inside 'third party' agencies with more leverage in mediating the demands of minorities with traditional agencies and power structures.[2]

---

[1] West India Emancipation Speech, August 1857, quoted by Carmichael and Hamilton, op. cit., p. 14.
[2] Miller and Reissman, op. cit., p. 231.

We conclude by reiterating that the community relations movement has suffered, ever since the 1965 White Paper, from an obsession with the structure of local committees to the detriment of clear thinking about objectives and policies. This tendency, which has been exacerbated by the C.R.C.'s commitment to spelling out job specifications for C.R.O.s which make them clearly the servants of the local committees, may to some extent be the result of a desire to avoid some of the more fundamental political questions associated with the role definition problem. The difficulty now is that a bureaucratization process has been initiated which threatens to carry the movement along in its path so that structures will become too rigid to be easily altered.

This potentially impotent condition could have been avoided if the local organization of this work had been left longer in a more flexible form, with centrally employed C.R.O.s charged with the task of formulating strategies appropriate to their areas, and prepared to regard volunteers as people to work with rather than under.

Above all, the community relations movement has not been able to emerge as an effective force because of the unwillingness of the government to back it effectively, either with sufficient funds, sufficient power, or with other policies compatible with the doctrine of racial equality for which it is supposed to stand. Even in the very best of circumstances its task would have been difficult, and would have been dependent upon a really effective national political assault upon not only racial inequality but also upon social inequality.

Index

Immigrant organizations (U.K.), 19;
and Kenya Asians crisis, 26; and
V.L.C.s, 29; factors encouraging, 125;
linguistic-based, 126; native
characteristics, 128; and multiracial
committees, 131–2; and C.R.
committees, 133–7, 139, 140, 141,
148, 152–4; definition of, 137, 138;
ethnic orientation, 139; classification,
139, 141; religious and socio-
economic needs, 141–2; membership,
142

Immigrant pupils, exclusion of Indians
from Southall schools, 39–40, 41;
dispersal policy, 39–40, 41, 45, 137,
139, 227; percentage in various
schools (1968), 45, 49, 53; banding
system, 137; school provisions,
197–8, 198, note 1; in E.S.N. schools,
199, and note 2; school leavers, 199;
language teaching, 248; in
educational priority areas, 289–90

Immigrants, response to interview
request, xii; welfare-orientated
treatment, 1, 5, 20, 29; and
V.L.C.s, 2, 5–7, 29; responsibility for,
4–5; obsession with their
improvement, 30; D.E.S. definition,
39; and work, 52, and note 4;
pressure to conform, 61;
percentage in towns, 62; and
'twilight areas', 73; cultural and
religious heritages, 73–4; in C.R.
committees, 85, 87–8; non-
participating groups, 159; impact on
receiving country, 165–6; and their
behaviour patterns, 167; needs of
non-English-speaking, 173–4;
influence on party politics, 242–4;
alienated by community relations
movement, 280; need for group
organizations, 294; education—
social class disequilibrium, 295, *see also*
Coloured immigrants

Immigrants Advisory Bureaux, 138, 139
Immigrants Advisory Committee, 7, 107
Immigration control, 11; Government
concern, 13; White Paper (1965) and,
15, 16, 31; M.P.s and, 117; legal
advice to immigrants, 174, 175; effect
on Commonwealth immigration, 287

Indian Association, 126, 142
Indian Communist parties, 129

Indian Social Clubs, 141–2, 151
Indian Society of Great Britain, 126
Indian Workers' Association (I.W.A.),
local branches, 7, 132–4, 136;
Southall membership, 39, 75, 136,
142, 218, 222, 245, 262; and anti-
immigrant agitation, 40; meetings,
86; Punjabi membership, 126;
competition for office, 128, 131–2;
kinship and activist groups, 128; on
executive committees, 142

Indians, in selected areas (1966), 38,
44, 45, 48, 53, 54, 55, 56; Census
underenumeration, 53, note 1;
percentage in towns, 62; on C.R.
committees, 102, 116, 140, 142–3;
areas of residence, 125; sending
regions, 125; education, 145;
Southall concentration, 216, 218;
election candidates, 221, 243; as
C.R.O.s, 254

Industrial Society, 181
Industry and industrialization, and
community autonomy, 63; and
community power structure, 63;
insufficiently localized, 64;
accelerates social disintegration, 66;
immigrant response to its demands,
70; and discrimination, 181, 182,
183; unrepresented on subcommittees,
182

Inner London Education Authority,
239; rejects dispersal policy, 45;
allocates West Indian children to
E.S.N. schools, 192, note 2; links
with C.C.T.H. and H.C.R.C., 230–1

Institute of Personal Management,
181

Institute of Race Relations, 1968
Conference, 30, 31, note 1; study of
employment, 199

Integration, work of voluntary
organizations, 1, 9; Government
concern, 13, 19; linked with
limitation, 16; White Paper (1965)
and, 16, 60; illusory competence,
29–30; Jenkins' concept, 30, 164;
pre-condition of community, 60;
produces divisive factors, 131;
goal of C.R. committees, 164;
interpretations of its meaning,
164–5; disruptive impact, 166;
community relations approach, 166–7